YOUR MONEY
OR
YOUR LIFE

Also by Alvin Hall

Spend Less, Live More

Plan Now, Retire Happy

Money Magic

Winning with Shares

Money for Life

What Not to Spend

The Stock Market Explained

YOUR MONEY
OR
YOUR LIFE

A Practical Guide to Solving
Your Financial Problems and
Affording a Life You'll Love

Alvin Hall
with Karl Weber

HODDER &
STOUGHTON

First published in Great Britain in 2002 by
Hodder & Stoughton

An Hachette UK company
This edition first published in 2014

1

A CIP catalogue record for this title is available from the British Library

Trade Paperback ISBN 978 1 444 72417 2
eBook ISBN 978 1 444 71667 2

Typeset by Palimpsest Book Production Ltd, Falkirk, Stirlingshire
Printed and bound by Clays Ltd, St Ives plc

Hodder & Stoughton policy is to use papers that are natural,
renewable and recyclable products and made from wood grown
in sustainable forests. The logging and manufacturing processes
are expected to conform to the environmental regulations
of the country of origin.

Hodder & Stoughton Ltd
338 Euston Road
London NW1 3BH

www.hodder.co.uk

To the many generous people who have shared their financial problems, frustrations, dreams, and accomplishments with me. Our conversations, whether brief or long, continue to inspire me.

Acknowledgements

I thank the following friends and colleagues for generously using part of their precious personal and professional time to help me keep the information and guidance in this revised edition "on the money:" Sara Cameron, Ciara Foley, Mike Hall, Paul Kavanaugh, Paul Killik, Emma Knight, Sarah Lord, Vicki McIvor (my agent), Van Keith Morrow (of TypeRight, Inc.), Robert Willson-Pemberton, Sarah Pennells, Claire Ramus, Eric Raphael, Emily Robertson, Mauro Romano, Warren Shute, and Rowena Webb.

CONTENTS

INTRODUCTION

You *can* do it yourself.

This revised and updated edition of **Your Money or Your Life** has the same objectives as the first: to give you the tools and insights you need to take, and keep, control of your finances – which involves understanding both the numbers and yourself; to enable you to reach your financial goals and establish the financial security you want in your life; and to help you make your money work smarter for you. Also I want this book to equip you with strategies that will help you avoid financial pitfalls and, perhaps more importantly, with the tried and true steps that really work when you are putting yourself back on the right financial track following a mistake or setback.

In the ten-plus years since I wrote the first edition, the economic environment has changed significantly – involving everything from interest rates to job security and prospects to the property market. New products, schemes and regulations have been created. Organisations have changed their names. And many individuals and families have experienced financial distress and hardships that they could not have imagined and perhaps did not plan for.

During this time I've continued to do money make-overs, talk about personal finance on radio and television programmes, and write articles about the subject for magazines and websites. I've also talked to people on high streets, on trains and planes, in restaurants, and at all types of events who asked me many interesting questions about their finances. I've incorporated all of these additional insights and wisdom I've gained from these experiences into this new edition.

I still want you to think of this book as your personal DIY guide for your money: a step-by-step, user-friendly and practical guide to handling your money properly. It will help you develop plans that are most appropriate and beneficial for your specific needs and goals; strategies that suit your means as well as your personality; and common sense perspectives that assist you in avoiding the pitfalls and preparing for unexpected events that can happen in your and anyone else's life.

Of course, there's more than one way of managing your money wisely. Throughout this book, alternative methods are explained and you're encouraged to use the information presented and discussed as a basis for developing strategies that are comfortable for *you*. In short, I want to help you learn how to help yourself.

Many years ago, when I was a student at Bowdoin College in Brunswick, Maine, I met a wonderful and wise woman named Bitsa Wood. A strong, nurturing, earth-mother type, Bitsa once said to me, 'The greatest gift parents can give their children is the ability to cope with life – to think through problems and solve them on their own. This is a gift of strength that stays with them a lifetime.' I have kept Bitsa's words in mind as I developed the strategies in this book.

I have tried to make all of the information as clear and accessible as possible. You don't have to understand economics or advanced mathematics to take control of your personal finances. You need only a few basic facts and some uncomplicated procedures that anyone can easily master. If any of the ideas I present seem unfamiliar or original, that may be simply because no one has ever mentioned them to you before – or because you weren't ready to listen when they did.

Experience, Not Genetics

'Have you *always* been good with money?' Virtually every interviewer asks me this question. And when I answer 'No,' they seem surprised. Many people want to believe that we are all fundamentally unchangeable – that it's basically impossible to really change and improve. That's why people make comments like, 'I've never had a head for finances,' 'I take after my parents – they were bad with money and so am I,' or 'We never learned about personal finances in school.' All these statements may be true but the underlying mindset is wrong. There's no need to remain trapped in our limitations, endlessly repeating the mistakes and frustrations of the past. Life is about maturing, growing and learning, and this applies as much to your personal finances as to any other area of life.

Everything I've said here applies to me – in spades. It's no secret that I've made mistakes with money. In my youth, shortly after I graduated from college, I got too many credit cards and I was spending thoughtlessly, eating out with friends, buying concert and theatre tickets, books, too many clothes and a lot of other stuff I can no longer recall. I was sinking deeper and deeper into debt, making payments late, incurring penalty fees, and almost defaulting. I still remember what it was like to lie awake at night wondering whether I was going to pay my rent or the minimum payments on all of my credit cards (I paid the rent so I would have a roof over my head), and trying to figure out how I was going to get myself out of the financial riptide I had gotten myself in.

Eventually, I vowed to myself that I would find a way out of my stressful, depressing situation with credit cards, store cards, car loans, overspending, etc. and never, ever let it happen again. I then analysed, with brutal frankness, what I'd done wrong. For anyone in debt this is often the first and worst step: looking back on your spending with regret and maybe even disgust, as you go through your statements. What I saw made me recognise and start accepting that the problem was me, not the proverbial 'they' on whom it's so easy and tempting to blame our problems.

The key was gaining control of myself and *my* emotional financial demons. Easy? No way. Let me tell you, it was a struggle then and the same old struggle can pop up out of nowhere even today. I still have to check myself when I see the aphrodisiac-like word 'sale' in an advertisement of a shop whose products I love. Even as I write about it now, I can still feel a knot forming in the pit of my stomach. I have to use a lot of willpower to resist temptation and not set foot in the store or visit its website.

The first exercise in this book – keeping a financial diary – is designed to help you understand your own financial weaknesses and demons, those unexamined emotional stimuli that often underlie how you sometimes

Alvin says . . .

Most people can learn and want to learn from other people's experiences in order to avoid financial mistakes and traps. However, there are a small number of people who must go through the fire and rain themselves, not just once but maybe several times, before they learn the important lessons. As hard as it may be to watch and endure, it is best to let this person go through financial hardship without your financial help. Be emotionally supportive but not financially supportive. Some people only learn from their direct experience – no matter how unfortunate it is.

spend money. Once you recognise the situations and emotions that cause you to overspend or use money in ways that undermines your financial security, you can avoid them or develop ways to mitigate them when you know they are coming on.

Magical Thinking About Money

Money is magical in many people's minds. As a result, they believe that there's no need to apply common sense and control to money. For some people this causes them to have a lackadaisical attitude about knowing bank balances, saving for the future, keeping track of important financial papers and planning for the emergencies. For others, this magical thinking results in a sense of entitlement: 'Why should I have to worry about money?' They believe they should somehow be exempted from all thinking and decision-making about money. Instead of having to make hard choices, that person should simply be able to get anything and everything he or she wants when he or she wants it – as if it's their birthright. A key component of magical thinking about money is the belief that money will somehow always be there.

Deep inside, we all know that this is a dream or, more accurately, a delusion. Sometimes (far too often I fear) it takes an unexpected change or emergency for the person to see the need to be practical and prudent. For nearly all of us, money is limited and the hard choices about how to use and preserve it can't be evaded forever. However, this needn't prevent anyone from creating and enjoying a comfortable, satisfying and economically sound life. Several art advisers and dealers I know have said to me that the most interesting and satisfying art collections they have seen and continue to see are those of people who have limited funds and therefore have to think carefully about the money they are spending, the importance of the work to them and to their collection, and the long-term pleasure or satisfaction they will get from the work. In short, because these collectors have financial limitation they must prioritise what they spend their money on.

There is a universal lesson here. If you make the right choices for your financial situation and your goals, you can be happy spending more thoughtfully and carefully. You'll stop saying 'I don't know where my money goes' because you will know; you will feel the money-related stresses in your life slowly but surely dissipate; and you'll see your own path to a balanced, contented day-to-day relationship with money while at the same time building long-term financial security. And most importantly, you will know that you have the ability to achieve it for yourself.

Master the Basics: The Key to Financial Literacy

When you first get your hands on a little money, knowledge of how to use that money wisely doesn't automatically follow. We've all heard about sports, film and music stars or celebrities who made fortunes and then quickly squandered them. This has also happened with people who won the lottery. It takes knowledge, self-discipline and a bit of work to manage money intelligently. Ask any rich family who has managed to hold on to its wealth across several generations.

You may protest, saying 'But the rich have professionals to advise them.' True – but anyone who turns his money over to an adviser without controls is likely to find it gone in a shockingly short time. History shows that people who don't know how money works don't manage to hold on to it for very long.

Everyone – those just starting out and those who already have money – need to be financially literate. The basic building blocks to becoming financial literate are already taught in the basic mathematics that everyone learns at school. The examples used in these classes may not always involve pounds and pence but the underlying concepts are the same ones involved in managing money properly. As you go through life you build on the basics, gaining more and more knowledge, typically on an 'as needed' basis – i.e., when you need to know about mortgages, then you learn about them. This book will help you increase your overall financial literacy through a series of hands-on activities. Make no mistake: these exercises will benefit you only if you really work through them yourself and understand them. That's how you become more literate about money and finances. Put pencil to paper or fingers on a keyboard. Make sure you understand the logic behind what you're doing. I want you to develop your own financial plan or refine the one you already have using the guidance I'll provide in these pages. I promise that you'll emerge a more knowledgeable, wiser person – and potentially a more financially secure one as a result.

Give Yourself Choices

Perhaps the most tragic thing about bad money management is this: *It takes away your choices in life.*

Here is a sad – and all-too-typical – example. I interviewed a young woman who had just given birth to a beautiful baby daughter. Understandably, she wanted to stay at home with her child. But through the entire pregnancy, she and her husband had continued to manage their finances as if they were two single people with no responsibilities other than themselves. They enjoyed luxury holidays, lived very nicely (although not quite as nicely as they wished), racked up a growing pile of credit card debts and didn't save a penny.

Even after the baby was born, this young mother did not want to reduce her spending. 'I don't think it's right for me to have to do that,' she defiantly told me. The result? Mother had no choice but to keep working. By saving nothing and spending to the maximum of the family income (and beyond), she had destroyed the possibility that she could stay at home and raise her own daughter. She was miserable – but it was all her own doing.

Please don't let a similar misfortune happen to you

– whether as a result of a life-changing event like the birth of a child or from an emergency like the sudden, unexpected death of a spouse or partner. By accepting the fact that the priorities in your life will need to change at different stages, by making a few small sacrifices today, by saving and investing a certain percentage of your earnings, and by remaining knowledgeable about the specific financial details of your life, you can guarantee that tomorrow you'll be able to make the choices that you need to. That's what matters the most. This book will help you to think about your priorities and goals for the present and into the future as your life goes through different phases. Most importantly, it will help you create a plan that will bring about the end results you aim for.

I've met and still meet with people who've lost their financial way. In many cases, their future choices have become severely limited as a result. Sometimes it's too late to do much other than recommend a totally new start; other times I'm able to help them re-open doors to choices or solutions that appeared to be closed forever.

My fondest dream would be for this book to eliminate the need for money makeover shows like *Your Money or Your Life*. While I know this is overly optimistic, I also know – because I've seen it happen again and again – that if someone really wants to change his or her financial life for the better, they can and they will. Handling your personal finances properly requires three things: being honest with yourself, establishing a plan that suits you and being diligent and tenacious in executing that plan.

If you are having financial difficulties, use this book to conquer your personal financial demons and set yourself on a better path. If you're good with money, use this book to accomplish two objectives: to avoid the money troubles that haunt so many individuals and families and to make your money grow in the way that is most suitable for you. You can do it by yourself or with the help of a financial professional. If you want to become more financially literate, then read sections of this book that interest you so that you get the learning process started. Regardless of your initial motivation for picking up this book, I want the end result to be your personal financial self-empowerment.

1

YOUR MONEY AND YOUR EMOTIONS

Understanding and Taking Charge of the Ways You Spend

The Secret Meanings of Money

The key to making better choices about your money begins with understanding your own approach to earning, spending, saving and investing. To do this, you need to uncover the secret meanings that money, risk and reward have for you. Once you've done this, you can begin developing a more positive and enriching style of financial management that you can realistically live with and that enables you to accomplish the goals you set for yourself.

A crucial step to understanding your own attitudes towards money is to recognise how you *really* handle money and what makes you handle it the way you do. Some of the most useful insights are gained from the unexamined emotions that underlie your actions. The bad news is that too many people delude themselves about their spending habits. They simply don't want to know the truth and its real consequences. The good news is that there's a simple process you can use to recognise, understand and gain control of your money delusions or weaknesses, whatever they are. (This same process will also help you to see any strengths you have in handling money.) All that's required is a little effort – and the willingness to face reality, even if it's a bit humbling.

Your Daily Spending Diary

The process begins with keeping a daily diary of income and expenses for a month.

Why a diary? Why not just sit down and list everything you usually spend money on, without the effort of keeping a diary? The answer is simple. No one – and I mean *no one* – is really capable of remembering accurately everything he or she spends money on from one day to the next, let alone from one week to the next. I often recall how the American poet Robert Frost – who had serious money quarrels with his in-laws – once put it:

> Nobody was ever meant
> To remember or invent
> What he did with every cent.

So if you try to write down your money habits from memory, I promise you that the picture you paint will be inaccurate and probably flattering – deceptively so.

And why an entire month? Because anything shorter doesn't represent a serious commitment to change. A spending diary for a week or two, for example, isn't long enough to provide a real sample of what you're spending your money on.

There's no way around it – the daily diary for a full month is the only way to go. Use a page for each day.

In addition to listing *everything* you spend money on, write down your related thoughts and feelings when you're spending and a brief summary of what you did that day. Use the form found on page 15 as your template. Feel free to make 30 photocopies to use for an entire month or set up a similar template on your handheld device (such as your phone, iPad, tablet, or similar product) that you can use throughout the day. See the sample form on page 16 for an example of what a filled-in diary page might look like.

Record credit card spending on the day you make the purchase, not the day you pay the bill. Don't overlook online, telephone or catalogue purchases. Record bills (mortgage, utilities, insurance premiums and so on) on the day you pay them.

What if you're married or have a financial partnership with a partner, housemate or family member? (In this book, I'll refer to all these arrangements as 'partnerships'.) In that situation, it's best if you and your partner can do the diary exercise at the same time. Make up two diaries and work through the process together. When it comes to creating the One-Month Spending Summary (as described later in this chapter), combine the information from both diaries into a single form.

Of course, if your partner refuses to take part in the process, so be it. Don't let that become an excuse for your own shirking! Go ahead and create your own diary. You may well find that later, when your partner sees how much more organised (and prosperous) you've become, he or she will be eager to jump on the bandwagon and join you.

If your diary is to be accurate and complete, you'll need to bring it with you wherever you go and record the expense immediately – otherwise you're apt to forget about it. If toting the diary around feels awkward, try using the Notes feature on your mobile or Smartphone to record the information. You could also use a 3 × 5 inch note card, which fits easily in your pocket or bag. Then, at the end of the day, fill out your diary from the notes you've kept. Does this sound like 'a pain' or 'too much trouble'? That feeling is your first psychological checkpoint; if you believe you don't have 15–30 minutes available to write down and add up your daily expenses, you're building up excuses for remaining disorganised and out of control.

YOUR DAILY SPENDING DIARY

Date: _____

What you did: _____

_____

_____

How you felt or what you thought: _____

_____

_____

What you spent:	**What it cost:**

TOTAL SPENDING FOR THE DAY: £ _____

YOUR DAILY SPENDING DIARY

Date: 1 April 2014

What you did: Bus to work. Lunch with Kate. After work had a bite at the pub with Geoff. Home at 8. Watched telly and went to bed.

How you felt or what you thought: Had a little row with boss at work – what a pain!

But felt better after seeing Kate. Great movie on the telly.

Looking forward to date with Nick tomorrow. Life's not so bad after all, although it's clear I need to lower some of my expenses.

What you spent:	What it cost:
Bus fare to work	2.40
Coffee	2.75
Petrol fill-up – half tank	40.00
Lunch – salad and green tea	5.95
Dinner at pub – curry and a pint	16.50
Magazine	2.95
Bus fare home	2.40
Jacket from dry cleaners	6.50

TOTAL SPENDING FOR THE DAY:	£ 79.45

What Your Daily Spending Diary Will Teach You

The diary exercise will show you the reality of where your money is spent – which is likely to provide a number of surprises, some perhaps unpleasant. It will make you keenly aware of the money you're spending daily that tends to 'disappear' with little fanfare. For example, when I went through the exercise, I was a little amazed to realise how much I spent to support the technology I use and travel with – everything from earphones (which I always seem to forget to pack) and music on iTunes that I want to listen to during my trip, to apps and adapters. It was ridiculous and added up to more than I would have thought, especially because I bought most of the items as I packed for my trip or while waiting in airports and train stations, with the added cost for 'convenience'. It was cheaper for me to buy two of every support device I needed and keep them packed in a small pouch, ready to toss in my luggage. So that's exactly what I did. I also gave myself a budget for iTunes purchases; thus, this amount of spending dropped substantially.

Eating out or ordering takeaway is another costly habit that easily gets out of control. The once-a-week dinner out easily escalates in price. One glass of wine becomes two glasses or perhaps a bottle; the occasional dessert becomes routine. Soon the thirty-pound treat costs forty-five pounds – a 50% increase. And it doesn't stop with a weekly dinner. You're so busy that you find yourself grabbing takeaway meals from the nearest shop rather than cooking at home – first one day a week, then two, then three. The same happens with lunch. And then there are the quick snacks, the tea breaks with pastries, the weekend brunch . . . the damage to your bank account and to the often delicate balance of your overall finances can be enormous. (And it doesn't help your waistline, either.)

Three Responses

I've found that most people who really pursue the diary exercise react in one of three ways.

(1) *Sudden surrender.* Some are so shocked or disturbed about what they learn that they throw up their hands. Often they abandon the diary after just a few days. This reaction amounts to a refusal to take control and responsibility over your own behaviour. In fact, it sometimes goes along with an attempt to blame others for your money woes: 'Oh, I'd do better if it weren't for my wife – she's the one who really overspends with the credit cards.' 'It wouldn't matter how much I spend at the hairdresser if only my husband made a decent salary – he's the real problem.' 'The trouble starts with the kids – they never stop begging for the latest toys they see on the telly or that their friends have. How am I supposed to say no?' If you fall into this category, don't expect sympathy from anyone. Whatever the causes of your money woes, they are *your* problems and only *you* have the power to fix them. The key question is whether you have the will to do something to help yourself or want to remain a victim.

(2) *Rapid turnaround.* Others quickly see their money habits and problem patterns and begin to take control of them even during the diary exercise itself. Simply *paying attention* to where the money goes seems to make a measurable difference. By the end of a month, with a seemingly small amount of effort, they discover that they've cut back on needless or wasteful spending, that

they can pay their bills more easily, that they can feel the stress and anxiety lessening and that – if they apply more effort and discipline – they can turn their entire situation around. Importantly, they start looking forward to creating a financial future that is more comfortable and secure. These people were probably psychologically strong and well-disciplined to begin with and simply temporarily forgot the positive ways of relating to money. They sincerely want to make a change and the knowledge they gain from doing the diary is their key to success.

(3) *Thoughtful analysis.* People in this group work through the entire diary exercise without analysing their behaviour or making any changes until the end of the month. For them, the diary process is a purely mechanical one: they jot down their spending each day without reflecting on it. Then they forget about it until it's time to make the next entry. Only two or three times during the month do they sit down to add up the totals and compare their impressions with reality. By the end of the month, having seen how bad their spending habits really are (whether in one or two selected areas, or across the board), they make a plan for improvement. For this group, change is a matter of reflection and deliberation.

Whichever group you fall into, your reaction to the diary exercise will give you an indication of how you tend to deal with money issues. It's an issue we'll be returning to over and over again in this book.

Your One-Month Financial Record

After you've faithfully recorded your spending for a month, it's time to take the next step – to create your

One-Month Financial Record. This is a record and analysis of how you're actually spending your money, based on the diary entries. This record will become the basis for a budget that you will create to improve your money habits, reduce the associated anxieties and increase your financial security over the next year and afterwards.

To perform this analysis, you can use the forms on pages 26–30. Again, feel free to make a photocopy of the book pages for this purpose or create your own spreadsheets on your computer. Another option is to use personal financial management software (such as Quicken®) or an app. These will typically walk you through the budget-making process and let you create customised reports and charts. Of course, if you use a personal finance software or App, the details of your budget may look different from those we'll examine in the next few pages of this book. Regardless, it will be quite easy for you to find the right numbers from your spending diary to use in analysing where your money is going – for better and for worse.

If you use the forms I provide, you'll see that the first page is for listing your sources of income and the amounts. Most people just have a few income items each month. They're usually easy to remember and keep track of. Enter income items for the same month as your spending diary on page 16. Only enter cheques, automatic deposits or transfers and cash you actually received during the month. Use actual take-home amounts rather than 'gross' or 'pre-tax' amounts. (If you're self-employed, estimate the amount you'll owe in taxes and deduct that. Enter the remainder as your income.)

▱Alvin says . . .

Never count cash advances from credit cards, bank overdrafts, home equity loans or unused balances on credit cards as 'income' or as real money that belongs to you. These are *not* forms of income. Instead, they are forms of debt as we'll discuss in more detail in Chapter Two. You'll seriously distort your financial picture if you think of any of these as 'income'.

Next, fill in the expenses pages. Do this by going through your monthly diary entries line by line. Sort your expenses into categories as shown in the form on pages 26–30. Read through the whole form before you get started. Notice that the various expense categories are numbered 1 through 66. (Don't be frightened. Not all these categories will apply to your situation.) This is designed to make it easier for you to match up your diary entries with budget categories. You can flip through the pages of your diary and label each entry with a number for the corresponding budget category. For example, when you find a diary entry for mortgage payment or rent, label that with the number 1. Then add up the amounts you spent in each category. (If you do this using a spreadsheet, then totalling the expense in each group will be easy and will eliminate the chances of you making an error.)

Filling in the spending record form will be a fair amount of work. But most people will get it done in an hour or less, depending on how orderly your diary has been kept. Once the form is complete, you'll be ready to study it to get a better handle on your real money habits.

Tweaking the Numbers . . . But with Care

If you know that this month is not typical in some way, you should adjust your figures in particular categories. For example, if you stayed at home ill for a week and therefore ate at home, spent nothing on entertainment and made none of your usual expenditures during that time, take that into account: increase your spending in those categories to represent a typical month. By the same token, if this month's spending includes a few hundred pounds on home repairs or on car repairs (something that only happens once a year or so), reduce your spending accordingly. But beware! Don't fall into the trap of convincing yourself that the bad habits uncovered by your diary are just a one-month aberration. We all tend to do this – like the golfer who's convinced that the round of 85 he shoots once a year is his 'real' game, while the 100 he shoots every other Saturday is due to bad luck. If you fool yourself in this way you'll miss the chance to really learn something from your diary exercise.

Analysing Your Spending

Your end-of-the-month analysis should focus on these questions:

- What per cent of your total income are you spending on housing, food, transport, clothing, entertainment and each of the other categories?
- What percentage of your total income do you spend on essential things? What percentage do you spend on discretionary or impulse items?
- How much consumer debt are you carrying and what percentage of your total annual income does it represent?

What percentage of your monthly income must you use to make payments on your outstanding debt?

- How much money are you depositing into savings each month? How often do you make withdrawals from that account and for what purpose?
- How does the analysis of how you currently use your money represent your personal priorities?
- Can you make the changes that will enable you to get out of debt and/or save for both your short-term and long-term goals?

Naturally, if you're spending *more* in a month than you take in, you must take action to stop the 'red ink' immediately. But there may be other signs of trouble as well:

- If your total consumer debt and the payments you make on it are a significant percentage of your annual pay.
- If you're spending more than you ever realised on categories like entertainment, drinks, toys and hobbies.
- If your spending on unnecessary or luxury items is making it hard for you to find the money for necessities.
- If unplanned spending (those notorious 'impulse purchases') takes up a significant portion of your monthly income.

These and other warning signs mean it's time to take better command of your money. As it is, you are facilitating your own cycle of money woes, your own entrapment and your own mess – which this exercise should help you see in black-and-white, or glaring red! It should be clear to you that your long-term needs and goals will suffer.

Day-to-Day Patterns

Look for time-related patterns to your spending, earning and saving. On Fridays, do you have a habit of buying something (a piece of clothing or some cosmetics, an electronic gadget, some new songs from iTunes) or spending money at the pub just to treat yourself? When you shop for groceries, do you buy a lot of food that looks delicious but that ends up sitting in the refrigerator until it goes bad and must be chucked? Do you routinely buy 'a little something' several times throughout the week because you feel you deserve it (although in truth you've done nothing special during the week)? Do you take your kids shopping or buy them presents the Saturday after payday to compensate for your being away at work? How does your spending coincide with your moods? Do you spend when you want to feel good about yourself? Are you more reckless in the middle of week, at the end of the week, or during the weekend? What situations make you most vulnerable to spending, especially overspending? Can you sense when you're about to give in to the urge?

Emotional Patterns

Also look for emotional or psychological patterns to your spending, especially careless, excessive spending in particular categories. When do you lose control? Perhaps it's when you get paid and there's money in your pocket or bank account. Perhaps it's when you have an argument with your spouse, your partner, your parents, or your kids. Perhaps it's when you have 'a bad day' at work or home (and so feel you 'deserve' a treat). Perhaps it's when you've accomplished something – finished a project at work, for example, or passed a course at university – and want to 'celebrate' by spending. Identifying these patterns or *spending instigators* (as I like to call them) is the first step towards gaining control of them, instead of letting them control you.

YOUR ONE-MONTH FINANCIAL RECORD

For the month of: **in the year:**

Income

1. Salary (take home)   £
2. Government benefits
3. Child support
4. Investment income
5. Rental income
6. Other (specify)

TOTAL INCOME: £

Spending

A. Fixed costs

HOME

1. Mortgage or rent   £
2. Electricity
3. Gas
4. Water rates
5. Telephone (fixed line)
6. Telephone (mobile)
7. Internet service
8. Television subscription service

9. Council tax payments

10. Buildings insurance

11. Home contents insurance

    HOME TOTAL (items 1–11):   £

TRANSPORT

12. Car loan payments   £

13. Petrol

14. Car insurance

15. Commuting costs (monthly transport card, etc.)

16. Other transport (e.g., car or bike rentals)

    TRANSPORT TOTAL (items 12–16):   £

DEBT (LOANS, CREDIT CARDS, STORE CARDS, ETC.)

17. Credit card payments (list each separately)   £

18. Store card payments (list each separately)

19. Personal loans (list each separately)

20. Catalogues (list each separately)

21. Other (specify)

    DEBT PAYMENT TOTAL (items 17–21):   £

OTHER MONTHLY BILLS

22. Child care   £

23. Child support

24. Student loan repayment

25. Life insurance

26. Private health insurance

27. Other (specify)

    OTHER MONTHLY BILLS TOTAL (items 22–27):   £

LESS-THAN-MONTHLY EXPENSES

(Estimate your spending for one year in each category. Then divide that figure by twelve. Enter the result in the column on the right.)

28. Television licensing fee   £

29. Tax (not covered by PAYE)

30. Home repairs

31. Appliances

32. Car purchase

33. Car repairs

34. Other (specify)

    LESS-THAN-MONTHLY EXPENSES TOTAL (items 28–34): £

OTHER EXPENSES

35. Food (at home)   £

36. Cleaning supplies and toiletries

37. Laundry, dry cleaning, ironing

38. Medicines and medical costs

39. Other (specify)

    OTHER EXPENSES TOTAL (items 35–39):   £

FIXED COSTS TOTAL (items 1–39):   £

B. Discretionary spending

FOOD AND DRINK

40. Meals at restaurants   £

41. Pub/off licence

42. Takeaways

    FOOD AND DRINK TOTAL (items 40–42):   £

ENTERTAINMENT

43. Movie rentals and other premium TV services   £

44. Magazines, newspapers, books

45. Music (downloads, CDs and others)

46. Tickets for cinemas, concerts, sports, etc.

47. Other outings

48. Hobbies

49. Kids' activities

50. Gambling

51. Other (specify)

    ENTERTAINMENT TOTAL (items 43–51):   £

AROUND-THE-HOME

52. Home decorating   £

53. Gardening

54. Antiques and collectibles

55. Pets (including vet)

56. Other (specify)

    AROUND-THE-HOME TOTAL (items 52–56):   £

LESS-THAN-MONTHLY DISCRETIONARY EXPENSES

(Estimate your spending for one year in each category. Then divide that figure by twelve. Enter the result in the column on the right.)

57. Holiday travel and lodging	£
58. Christmas and other seasonal gifts	
59. Birthday and other non-seasonal gifts	
60. Other (specify)	
LESS-THAN-MONTHLY EXPENSES TOTAL (items 57–60):	£

OTHER EXPENSES

61. Clothing	£
62. Toys (for children)	
63. Gadgets (for grown-ups)	
64. Hairdresser or barber	
65. Other beauty (manicures, spa, etc.)	
66. Other (specify)	
OTHER EXPENSES TOTAL (items 61–66):	£
DISCRETIONARY SPENDING TOTAL (items 40–66):	£
TOTAL SPENDING (FIXED + DISCRETIONARY)	£

Your One-Month Spending Summary

Next, use the form on page 36 to create a One-Month Spending Summary. (A filled-in sample is shown on page 37.) You'll calculate:

- The percentage of your total after-tax income spent on fixed costs vs. discretionary costs
- The percentage spent on each expense category

To calculate percentages, divide the amount spent on a particular category by your *total* monthly spending. Multiply the result by 100 to convert it into a percentage. For example, in the sample Summary on page 37, the amount spent on 'Home' is £1,050, while the total monthly spending is £3,480. Using a calculator, you'll find that 1,050 ÷ 3,480 = 0.3017. (Actually, the result is a very long decimal, but only the first few decimal places really matter.) Multiply this by 100 and round it off to the nearest number, and you get 30.17%.

Naturally, no two people will have spending percentages that are exactly the same in every category – nor should they. After all, each of our lives has different priorities. There are no absolute 'right' or 'wrong' percentages. But you might spot numbers that are clearly out of line and spending patterns reflecting disordered priorities that are hurting you.

By way of comparison, the UK Office for National Statistics regularly compiles data concerning what they call 'Components of household expenditure', which go towards making up the 'Family Spending Report'. The most recent report reflects typical family spending for the previous year. Therefore, the 2013 Report would reflect spending data collected in 2012. To read current and past editions of the Family Spending Report, visit the UK National Statistics website:

www.statistics.gov.uk
[Note: Look under the heading 'Economy', then under 'Personal Finances' for the subcategory of 'Consumers and Customers'.]

Like many statistics, these are subject to their own biases and should only be used as guidelines. Nonetheless, it is interesting to see what the average UK household spends in particular areas. You may find that spending that seems 'normal' to you and your friends differs substantially from what the typical person in the UK actually spends.

I strongly encourage you to visit the website and compare your spending in the areas that I often find to be 'danger zones' for many individuals and families. How many of these stand out in your analysis of your spending?

- *Clothing.* Since clothes vary so much in style and cost, from the very basic to high-end designer fashion, spending on clothes varies a lot too. (We all know people who could easily spend half their income on shoes alone!) 4–5% of your annual income appears to be a good benchmark for spending in this area. How does your percentage of spending compare with the number shown in this year's Family Spending Report? If your spending is much greater than the percentage reported, you may have a problem.
- *Food and non-alcoholic drinks.* This is one of the easiest categories to lose control of, whether buying too much

in a supermarket that then gets thrown away or by overspending on takeaways, in restaurants and in pubs. The Family Spending Report pegs the average spending in the category of food and non-alcoholic drinks at around 11%. Note that this does not include the cost of alcohol, which is included in a separate category. Were it included, this number would probably be closer to 13%. If your spending on food and drink is noticeably higher, why not consider always shopping with a list of what you will buy and cook at home more often? The combination reduces waste, is cheaper and is usually more nutritious.

- *Entertainment.* Called 'Recreation and Culture' in the Family Spending Report, it is the second highest category of spending. In truth, spending here can vary wildly. One night of 'painting the town red' for a young, single person can cost as much as many families spend on entertainment in a month. What is your percentage of spending in this area? Is it far out of line? If so, look for ways to scale back.

- *Toys for children.* Naturally, how much you spend in this area will depend on whether or not you have children, how many you have and their ages. But it will also depend on the attitudes you want to instil in them. In families where the parents behave as if toys are symbols of acceptance and love, or as if having the latest plaything is the only sure way of having fun, the demand for toys tends to become an ever-growing pressure. Beware. As a parent, the fun can quickly vanish when the bills can't be paid and the anxiety starts to mount. Children can often sense this change even when parents are trying to hide it from them.

- *Christmas and other gifts.* Here, too, the attitude and spirit that prevails within the family is crucial. Don't fall into the familiar traps of regarding gifts as evidence of love, of using gifts as a way of competing for attention and favour, or of trying to make up for eleven months of indifference with one month of lavish generosity. Ironically, I often hear stories where many family relationships have been deeply fractured by overspending on Christmas gifts in a misguided attempt to 'buy' family happiness and harmony.

- *Personal beauty, including cosmetics and other beauty supplies, as well as trips to the salon or spa.* The Family Spending Report says that average spending in this category runs about 1% but I've met individuals who have a powerful and costly weakness for the latest and most lavish lipsticks, nail varnishes, face creams (available only in France or the US, of course) and other beauty treatments. Believe me, a daily walk in the fresh air (or even a weekly tumble in bed) will do far more to put the roses back in your cheeks!

- *DIY, especially kitchen makeovers, remodelling lounges, adding a conservatory or redoing a garden.* Home projects are classic 'money pits' that can suck up cash with no apparent limit. (We'll talk more about this in a later chapter devoted to finance and your home.)

- *Mobile phone bills and roaming charges.* It's shocking how quickly the cost of a few 'chit-chats and smiles' (paraphrasing Aretha Franklin) can mount up, especially when the phones, particularly Smartphones, are used indiscriminately. Watch out, especially when you are travelling abroad! Checking your emails too often and downloading data is usually quite costly.

As I've said, these are some of the most prominent money trouble spots I've encountered while analysing people's finances and spending habits. But your trouble spots may be different from any or all of these. Now is the time to look for them and begin dealing with them.

By the way, I *do* practise what I preach. I keep a one-month financial diary periodically just to see how my spending habits have changed over time. Several years ago, the one-month diary revealed that I spent too much money on magazines and newspapers. I got that under control. A few years later, when I did the exercise again, I found I was spending too much on music downloads, apps and devices to support the technology I use at home and in my work. Then I gave myself a budget that I've diligently held to and have made choices that are better thought out. During a recent stay in London, my diary revealed that I'd fallen into the habit of spending an alarming amount on taxis. How did it happen? Without realising it, I wasn't allowing enough time to use the tube or walk to my meetings. It was just too easy to pop into a cab even for what I thought would be short, inexpensive rides. The problem, of course, is that fares of 8, 12 and 15 pounds quickly add up, especially on a busy weekday when I have several stops to make.

Thanks to the diary, I recognised the problem before it got out of control. I'm planning more time between appointments, allowing me to use public transport or walk. If I liked biking more, I would do that. Why not? The extra exercise benefits both my wallet and my waistline.

YOUR ONE-MONTH SPENDING SUMMARY

For the month of:	in the year:	
TOTAL INCOME:	£	

A. Fixed costs

	Amount (£)	% of total
HOME	£	
TRANSPORT		
OTHER MONTHLY BILLS		
LESS-THAN-MONTHLY EXPENSES		
OTHER EXPENSES		
TOTAL FIXED COSTS:	£	

B. Discretionary spending

FOOD AND DRINK	£	
ENTERTAINMENT		
AROUND THE HOME		
LESS-THAN-MONTHLY EXPENSES		
OTHER EXPENSES		
TOTAL DISCRETIONARY SPENDING:	£	
GRAND TOTAL OF SPENDING	£	**100%**

YOUR ONE-MONTH SPENDING SUMMARY

For the month of: *April*   **in the year:** *2014*

TOTAL INCOME: £3,500

A. Fixed costs	Amount (£)	% of total
HOME	£1,050	30
TRANSPORT	372	11
OTHER MONTHLY BILLS	320	9
LESS-THAN-MONTHLY EXPENSES	190	5
OTHER EXPENSES	419	12
TOTAL FIXED COSTS:	**£2,351**	67

B. Discretionary spending		
FOOD AND DRINK	£279	8
ENTERTAINMENT	310	9
AROUND THE HOME	100	3
LESS-THAN-MONTHLY EXPENSES	90	3
OTHER EXPENSES	350	10
TOTAL DISCRETIONARY SPENDING:	**£1,129**	32
GRAND TOTAL OF SPENDING	**£3,480**	**99%**

Financial Fitness

As you study your One-Month Spending Summary, look for psychological 'hot spots' – things that make you feel anxious, tense, guilty, angry or even vengeful about money. For many people, dealing with financial issues feels a lot like struggling with their weight. In fact, I've talked to many people who worked successfully on their finances and also ended up getting their figures under control at the same time – with very little effort.

I think this is because both of these areas are fraught with emotional baggage. Many of the same anxieties, needs, wishes, fears, tensions, disappointments and dreams we associate with food are also associated with money.

Money is apt to be a distraction from the real emotional issues that drive your behaviour. You may discover that you've been spending to make yourself feel better, to attract others, to get revenge, to show off your status or to buy love. Circle the items on the Summary that you find yourself feeling strongly about and think about what they mean. If you share your financial (and personal) life with a spouse or other partner, talk about those hot spots with him or her. Simply becoming *aware* of the psychological weight that you attach to financial and material things can often help you begin to master that burden.

Taking Control: Creating Your Spending Plan

So far, you've been studying your past and present financial behaviour – how you currently make and spend money. In the process, you've learned quite a bit about what makes you tick and about the personal and financial weaknesses that have got you into trouble in the past. Now it's time to use what you've learned to create a spending plan – a budget – that will help to take control of your financial behaviour in the future. What you want is a budget that is realistic, liveable and responsible; a plan you can really carry out that will give you a chance of reaching *all* your personal goals, both day by day and over your entire lifetime.

You may have tried to create and live by a budget in the past, only to give up in despair. That's a common experience. It happens for many reasons. Sometimes people create budgets that are too rigid, too austere or too complicated. Sometimes they fail to adjust their budgets as their needs, priorities and abilities change or they try to follow plans that have no connection to their own psychological realities. And sometimes they are simply 'undisciplined' – which is usually another way of saying that they are too lazy to stick to a budget, or they let instant gratification easily and repeatedly blind them to their need to be more financially disciplined.

I don't want you to repeat past patterns of failure. Instead, I want you to develop a spending plan that makes sense *for you*. And I want you to review it, think about it, adjust it, revise it and improve it as often as necessary so that you feel comfortable with it. Your budget must be a *living* document – one that you can not only follow but *enjoy* following.

Making adjustments to changing conditions is a continual challenge. As I write, most of the world economies are still trying to recover from a worldwide recession. The first thing I did when the recession began was to trim my spending and review all of my expenses. For example, with interest rates at an all-time low, I remortgaged my flat and lowered my monthly payment substantially. I restricted myself to eating out no more than two nights a week and set a maximum amount I could spend each time. A long-time friend and his wife decided to get rid of one of their two cars for much the same reason.

Adjusting like this before you are forced to gives you a wonderful feeling of being in control of your own destiny rather than helpless. I've noticed that feeling out of control often makes people angry, which leads to bad decisions.

Sometimes, a degree of self-denial is essential. If you've developed bad spending habits, there will be a period of adjustment as you break those habits and develop better ones – and that means pain. But the pain should be offset by an increasing sense of pleasure: pleasure that comes from having more money in your pocket or purse, more savings in the bank, smaller balances on your credit cards and fewer burdens on your conscience. And through it all, you should be able to allow yourself an occasional reward – a special treat, an evening out, a purchase 'just for fun' – without wrecking your budget or undermining your growing sense of control.

Alvin says . . .

If you still have trouble controlling your spending, try what I call the Ten Pound Trick. When you have an irresistible urge to go shopping, put just ten pounds in your wallet and head to your favourite high street or shopping centre. Your challenge is to find something that satisfies your urge to spend, costing ten pounds or less. Most likely you will find that you come home with some of the money left over – which you should save.

Secrets of Making and Keeping a Realistic Budget

Start with your One-Month Spending Summary. Use this as the basis for a new monthly budget. Your budget will be a spending plan that lays out guidelines you'll follow for how much to spend in each basic category in the months to come.

From all the self-analysis you've already done, you may have some excellent ideas on how to alter your past spending practices. If so, now is the time to turn those ideas into concrete plans. Here are some specific recommendations that can help you.

- *Plan for saving.* As we'll discuss in more detail in Chapter 3, your budget ought to make it possible for you to save about ten per cent of your monthly take-home pay. For most people, this is an amount they won't even miss. As you look through your spending diary, I'm sure you'll be able to find places where you can save this per centage or even more. (It's easy to calculate ten per cent of any number: simply move the decimal point one place to the left. For example, ten per cent of £2,900.00 is £290.00.) So *start* your budget with a line labelled 'Savings', in which you pencil in ten per cent of your monthly income. Now work on filling in the rest of your budget so as to keep that line intact! (We'll talk about what do with your savings in a later chapter.)
- *Trim your fixed costs.* List these costs as tracked on your Spending Summary. You may not be able to change many of these but you can still look for opportunities to save. To take one example, is it possible to reduce your spending on transport? Transport costs

are steadily increasing, especially in contrast to what people earn. So depending on how you get to work, you may not have much control of this rising cost. However, rather than just complaining about the increase, look for ways to lessen the impact of the increase in your budget or to keep your costs relatively flat. Perhaps you can walk to the train station instead of driving. Maybe you can get by with one car rather than two. Or perhaps you can cut down the amount you spend on petrol by combining two or more chores into a single trip, by walking short distances rather than driving or even by trading in your old car for a more efficient model. Scrutinise each line in the same way.

- *Get control of your discretionary spending.* Here is where the greatest opportunities for reductions are likely. Study each spending category carefully. Look for instances where you are spending money without receiving much physical, psychological or emotional benefit in return. Do you accumulate magazines with little chance to read them? Cancel the subscriptions and save a few pounds a month. Do you own shirts or blouses you've scarcely worn? Only buy clothes when you really need them and save a few more pounds. Are three nights out at the pub per week getting a little stale? Cut back to one night and you may enjoy it more – while saving even more too. And as for that smoking habit – try adding up all the pounds you'll save if you can break it once and for all.

After jotting down preliminary spending figures for each category, add them up. Have you managed to arrive at a total at or below your monthly take-home salary?

If so, congratulations – you have a spending plan that should work, at least on paper. If not, study the numbers again, looking for the additional cutbacks needed to balance the budget.

Being Real

I just used the word 'balance' and indeed that's the key word. If your budget isn't truly balanced – not only fiscally but also psychologically and emotionally – it probably won't work. Your budget should reflect your personality, your priorities, your interests and your dreams. When spending cuts are needed, trim the things that don't matter to you while preserving as much as possible from the things you really care about.

You may have a consuming passion few people share. If so, your budget ought to accommodate it. I know a woman named Nancy who collects 'snow domes', those glass bubble-shaped souvenir items that make a little snowstorm when you shake them. She finds them at jumble sales, auctions, curiosity shops – you name it. Nancy could never really live with a family budget that didn't allow her to buy a snow dome or two from time to time. Of course, it would also be irresponsible for her to budget £100 a month for her hobby – she and her husband have relatively modest incomes and two strapping children outgrowing their clothes almost monthly – but £20 a month is affordable and, however trivial this all sounds, it is essential for Nancy's mental health.

In the same vein, don't try to live by a budget that allows you no room for self-indulgence. Sometimes a little 'luxury' makes all the difference between happiness and depression. It can even save a relationship. My co-author on the first edition of this book Karl and his wife Mary-Jo lived through a number of financially painful years when their three children were small and their jobs weren't very lucrative. But they made a special point of finding the money to go out for dinner alone together once a week. Some weeks it was all they could do to pay a local teenager to sit with their kids for an hour while they went out for a hamburger or a pizza. Yet having the opportunity to treat themselves in this small way – and, more important, to have a little private time for a relaxing chat – made a crucial difference in their marriage and family life.

So, the art of improving your spending habits is very much a balancing act. You need to balance:

- Consistency . . . with flexibility
- Self-discipline . . . with realism
- A sense of control . . . with occasional self-indulgence

One step that will do a lot to help you trim needless spending is to reduce the amount of credit card interest you have to pay every month. That means cutting the burden of debt that may well be dragging you down financially. In the next chapter, we'll look at how you can accomplish that goal.

2

CONSUMER DEBT

*How You (Probably) Got Into It
and How to Get Out*

The Awful Truth about Credit Cards

Credit is simply another word for the right to borrow money. The word *credit* comes from the Latin for 'I believe', which makes sense: when a bank or other lender gives you credit it is saying, in effect, 'I believe you'll repay me.' To this day, the way a person handles credit is considered a mark of his or her personal integrity. What's equally important to remember is that the way you manage credit can have a profound positive or negative effect on your financial future. That's why I've chosen to speak about it so early in this book: it's one of the most crucial keys to getting your money life in order.

In the UK, credit is rather widely and easily available, especially in comparison to the old tight-money days of a generation ago. For this change you can thank the late Prime Minister Margaret Thatcher. A staunch believer in free markets, the Iron Lady pushed British banks to ease up on credit and make loans, especially home mortgages, available to more people. However, this change had some unintended consequences, creating the temptation that comes with easy access to credit cards and, with it, the danger of excessive debt. Statistics released every year about consumer debt show that it has steadily increased and has damaged the financial situations of thousands of people in the UK. A recession or an economic slowdown only increases the negative impact in the lives of people who carry too much debt.

We all know people who have maxed out on their credit cards . . . and have applied for a couple more to pay the next month's expenses or the big influx of bills!

But if you think I'm about to launch into a tirade about the evils of credit and the bad faith of the credit card companies, think again. The awful truth about most credit cards is that in themselves they're neither bad nor good. In fact, they're a very convenient way to make purchases and manage one's monthly expenses. And for a few things (like shopping online, making an airline or hotel reservation, or renting a car), they're practically impossible to do without. So it would be unfair to totally demonise credit cards. If too many people have gotten themselves too deeply into debt – and they have – a substantial portion of the blame must be placed squarely where it belongs: on the people themselves, or at least on those who succumb to temptation and therefore misuse and abuse credit.

If it makes you feel any better, the truth is that I've been guilty of credit abuse myself. In this chapter, I'll explain how I climbed out of the deep hole I dug for myself, one purchase and cash advance at a time. Saving myself from debt didn't require magic, just a bit of determination and hard work and, above all, the adoption of a new attitude towards money and debt.

The 'False Validation' Syndrome: the Psychology of the Credit Card Offer

A major part of our debt problem is the psychology that often surrounds getting a credit card. Many people who receive solicitations from credit card companies in the post misunderstand what they mean. They think of them, consciously or unconsciously, as validating their worthiness: 'If the bank sent me the offer, then it must think I can handle credit.'

Perhaps it is flattering to receive a credit card offer in the mail – and the direct-mail experts who write the letters and design the brochures are clever enough to make them sound personally appealing. But remember that these are solicitations and they are only sent out to benefit the banks, stores and credit card companies. They want to give you a credit card not as a service to you or as a validation of your worth as a hard-working citizen but because they view you as someone from whom they can make a lot of money – either through interest that accumulates on your outstanding balance or through the small fee merchants pay each time you use the credit card in their stores or online.

Of course, modern marketing methods are designed to capitalise on our credit card psychology. Once you receive the solicitation in the mail, it's temptingly easy to sign your name and return the prepaid form. It's even easier on the internet where all you have to do is fill out the form and click send. Many people try to justify their debt-laden finances by explaining, 'I got into debt because they offered me the card.' The innocence and naïveté of this statement would be touching if it weren't so horrifying. It assumes that the burden of responsibility lies with the credit card company. It's true that the credit card marketers deserve some blame for their indiscriminate blanketing of the population with credit but the real responsibility for controlling your debt lies with you. After all, when the bills are due, *you* will have to find the money to pay them – no one else!

How the Debt Mountain Grows

Of course, the problem only begins with the credit card solicitation. Once you get the card, it's all too easy to use it and to do so without keeping track of how much you are spending or what your are spending on. The card company logos seem to be displayed in every shop window, inviting you in to acquire the enticing wares, whether or not you have any cash in your pocket or purse. And because there's a lag of up to four weeks between the time when you do your shopping and the moment the bill arrives in the mail, it's easy to be absent-minded about the debt or pretend that it isn't 'real'. After all, who knows what may happen between now and when the bill comes? 'Maybe a rich uncle (of whom I've never heard) will die and leave me his diamond mine in South Africa or his oil wells in Dallas! Or maybe I'll win the lottery. It could happen!'

Of course, it *doesn't* happen. (I know it doesn't – I've been waiting in vain for the same phone call myself!) But the credit card bill arrives without fail (have you ever noticed how very punctually your bills arrive every month, while payments due to you seem to take forever to show up? How irksome!) and the bill always seems to be half again as large as you expected. You scan the list of purchases and discover all kinds of items you'd forgotten about: the fancy lunch with a friend that you splurged on, the blouse or pair of shoes you plumped for because they were on sale, the weekend getaway you took at the last moment. You realise, with an uncomfortable feeling in your stomach, that there is just no way to pay the full bill – at least not this month.

That's when the real debt crisis begins to build. Once they get into debt, many people make only the minimum required payment each month. I'm told that around 50 per cent of all credit card holders in the UK fall into this pattern and the figure is even higher in the US. They may even feel virtuous about it: 'I paid the requested amount, right on time. Doesn't that make me a responsible credit card holder?' Indeed it does – from the point of view of the credit card company. They *love* customers who pay only the minimum amount each month. Why? Because the balance that is carried over to the next month accrues interest. Making the minimum payment will keep your debt alive virtually *forever*.

You may ask, how is that possible? Most cards set the minimum payment at ten per cent of your balance; however the interest charge is often higher than ten per cent. This means that, at least in theory, even if you make the minimum payment on time, there'll *always* be a small additional amount being added to your unpaid balance, even if you *never* make another purchase.

For every month you carry a credit card balance, you are paying a little more interest on the money due. In reality, that increases the price of what you've purchased. Think about that: if you splurge at a store during your lunch break today, you may still be paying for that handbag or that camera attachment two to three years from now. And when the interest payments are added in, a £20 item may end up costing £40 or more. Some bargain!

A simple example illustrates how an item charged on a credit card can cost you much more than the actual purchase price. Let's imagine you use a credit card to buy a £100 Christmas gift for your beloved. The card's annual percentage interest rate is 18 per cent, or 1.5 per cent per month, on the outstanding balance. Let's assume that you leave the £100 balance outstanding for a full year. As the chart below shows, by the end of 12 months the interest added to your balance would *not* be just £18 (even though this represents 18 per cent of £100). The actual interest would be higher because each month the interest is calculated on the original charge *plus* the accumulated interest.

Month	Starting balance	Monthly interest rate	End-of-month balance
January	£100	1.5%	£101.50
February	£101.50	1.5%	£103.02
March	£103.02	1.5%	£104.57
April	£104.57	1.5%	£106.14
May	£106.14	1.5%	£107.73
June	£107.73	1.5%	£109.35
July	£109.35	1.5%	£110.99
August	£110.99	1.5%	£112.65
September	£112.65	1.5%	£114.34
October	£114.34	1.5%	£116.06
November	£116.06	1.5%	£117.80
December	£117.80	1.5%	£119.57

By leaving the balance outstanding, you are in effect adding almost 20 per cent to the purchase price.

Reflect for a moment. Have you ever bought something – for example, a television that cost £600 – on a credit card and let the balance remain outstanding for a few years, making only the minimum payments before you paid it off? How much did that television *really* cost you when you add in the interest? When you finally take off those blinders, what you see won't be pretty.

The ultimate danger, of course, is that, as the months pass, your balance due continues to grow. (Do you really believe that you'll stop making credit card purchases altogether?) Eventually, the bill becomes so great that you begin having difficulty making even the minimum payments each month and you get the overwhelming feeling that you will never be able to get out from under the growing pile of debt. The result can be a complete financial collapse: a ruined credit rating, bankruptcy and at its worst, a shattered life.

The Secret Workings of Credit and Store Cards

I'm telling you all of this not to frighten you. No, I take that back. I *do* want to frighten you. But that's simply to get your attention. Now that you see how very serious credit card debt can be it's time to get a grip on it.

To begin, let's review how credit and store cards work, since this has a major impact on your financial well-being. Their interest rate rules are not actually 'secret' but so few people take the trouble to understand them that they might just as well be secret.

Stalking the Elusive APR
Every time you use a credit card or store card, there is the potential that interest will be charged. Interest, of course, is a fee for borrowing money – and when you

don't pay a credit or store card bill in full immediately you are in fact taking out a loan for the amount owed. The amount of interest you are charged is called the *annual percentage rate* (APR) and is usually charged on your average daily balance during the billing period. The APR varies from one card to another. When you apply for and get a card, you receive a 'Terms and Conditions' sheet, generally covered in fine print, which spells out the rules of the card in excruciating detail. One of these provisions is the APR.

If you've never done so, look up the APR on each of your credit and store cards right now. Finding it may take some doing. You'll notice that several rates may be offered, depending on the precise kind of card you hold. This is a widespread practice in the credit card industry, as the figure below illustrates. Those people who qualify for premium cards (for example, labelled *platinum* or *gold*) are typically charged lower APRs than one pays on regular, non-premium cards. The premium cardholders usually pay a higher annual fee for the privilege.

	Purchases		Cash	
	Monthly Interest Rate	Standard Balance	Monthly Interest Rate	Cash Advance Balance (the APR includes the handling fee)
Platinum	1.240%	15.9% APR	1.349%	19.2% APR
Gold	1.456%	18.9% APR	1.492%	21.3% APR
Classic	1.456%	18.9% APR	1.492%	21.3% APR
First Classic	1.667%	21.9% APR	1.667%	23.8% APR
initial Visa	1.873%	24.9% APR	1.873%	28.1% APR

You'll see that the APR is listed both as an annual rate and as a monthly rate. The monthly interest rate listed is *less* than one-twelfth of the APR. This is so because compounding – the charging of interest on interest – multiplies the cost of credit over time. Finally, you'll notice that the interest charged on cash advances is *higher* (sometimes substantially so) than on purchases. The rate on cash advances also differs depending on the type of card (premium or non-premium) you have.

You may be a bit shocked at the interest rates charged on your credit card purchases. These rates are higher than most people realise. It may be that when you signed up for the card originally you were charged a much lower 'teaser' rate. Of course, this was simply a marketing ploy by the card company to make the card really attractive to you. The credit card issuers gave you fair warning that the teaser rate would give way to their usual higher rates after a number of months – the longest being around 30 months. But many people forget about this and fail to notice when the higher cost kicks in.

Interest rates on store card purchases are even higher than on credit cards, ranging up to 31 per cent. The other main difference between store cards and credit cards is that store cards don't offer cash advances. Otherwise, the two kinds of cards work almost the same.

How Timing Affects Your Charges

Other factors affect how much interest you'll have to pay. One factor is timing. For cash advances, interest charges generally kick in immediately, the moment you walk away from the ATM or the bank teller with the cash in hand. This means that even if you pay your bill in full the week it arrives, you'll have paid some interest for the privilege of using the company's money. In addition, you may be charged a fee of up to 1.5 per cent of the amount of the cash advance. Although this isn't called 'interest' it has the same effect: it increases the cost of borrowing.

The system is a little different when it comes to

purchases. Here, the interest charges begin after a so-called *grace period*, which ends when your next month's credit card payment is due. Thus, if you buy a pair of shoes on 15 September, for example, get the bill for them on 1 October and pay the bill in full by the due date of 7 October, then you'll pay no interest on the purchase. But if you pay your October bill only in part and carry over the rest until November (and perhaps beyond), interest on the shoes (as well as other purchases you make) will be tacked on to the bills and will continue to mount, month by month.

Unexpected Fees

It may get worse. You will also be charged a late payment fee, in addition to the interest, if your payment is not received on time. In effect, this increases your interest charges beyond the official APR. Another fee may be assessed if you carelessly go over your credit limit. This could easily happen if you are close to your limit and you incur fees and interest charges that increase your outstanding balance beyond your limit. And, of course, if you continue to carry a balance from month to month after the fees are added to your account, you will end up paying interest on these fees as well!

Rethinking Credit Card Debt

Fortunately, many people today realise these facts about the high cost of carrying debt from month to month. They are written about frequently in newspapers, magazines and websites. Nonetheless, some people continue to use credit incorrectly and it costs them countless thousands of pounds in interest payments, enriching the banks needlessly.

When evaluating their use of credit, people tend to

look at the 'credit available' line rather than the 'debt outstanding' line on their monthly bills. They seem to feel comforted by the fact that there is still money available to them, as if it represents some sort of gift motivated by the generosity of the bank or credit card company. Others regard it as a kind of safety net, like a bank balance, that they can draw upon without consequences in their time of need.

Of course, this is not so. Your credit available line simply indicates the amount of money you can borrow (and pay interest on). To think of it as a gift or an asset of any kind reflects an unfortunately deluded sense of entitlement. It's one of the greatest causes of financial problems among people I've met over the years.

Fighting Back Against the Menace of Debt

Here are some tips for keeping your credit card debt under control.

Overcome Your Credit Card Dependency

Limit the cards you have. First, consider how many credit cards you actually need. My answer is: one or two, maybe three if you travel extensively for business. I *do* recommend having a card. They're useful in various situations, such as international travel. A major credit card makes it easier and faster to rent a car or buy a plane ticket. In an emergency, you wouldn't want to be stranded in Istanbul or Buenos Aires without a credit card. But one or two cards will suffice; there's no need to sport the array of five or ten cards I see many people carrying. Having fewer cards makes it much easier to track the amounts you owe, the payment due dates and other details of your debt.

Avoid store cards. I urge you *not* to use store cards at all unless you pay the full balance every month on time. As I've noted, they charge the highest interest rates of any credit cards. In fact, the Credit Department is often the most profitable business segment in many retailing companies! This means that the stores are making profits not so much from selling coats or lamps or television sets but from charging their customers interest on their debts. Why contribute to that?

Actually, there is one useful benefit to holding a store credit card. It often entitles you to receive special sale announcements and offers for 'preferred customers'. I like getting those myself – in fact, I got a card for Bergdorf Goodman's, a posh US department store, specifically for the announcements. But when I shop at Bergdorf's, I only use their card during special promotions when substantial additional discounts are offered on store card purchases. Bergdorf's happens to be my favourite store and this is the one and only store card I have. But, as you can see, I rarely use it.

When you do use any credit card, pay off the full balance every month. This means spending each month only what you can afford to pay for that month. If necessary, postpone purchases. If you're in doubt as to how much your outstanding balance is, you can call the customer service phone number provided on your card to get the amount. More conveniently, you can set up access to your credit account using the Internet so that you can check it easily or have alerts pushed to you periodically during the month. (I remain surprised at how many people don't take advantage of this useful service.)

Cut your own limit. Another way of curbing your spending is to call the credit or store card company and ask them to reduce your credit limit to an amount you can afford to pay off in full each month. For some people, this will be a very difficult call to make. In essence, it's an admission that you can't control yourself. You may even feel that you are rejecting the sense of approval or validation that the company gave you by extending credit to you. Don't let these misgivings dissuade you. Be strong about it; lower the limit to what you can afford.

If you are not willing to take these kinds of steps to reduce your credit card dependency, then perhaps you really don't want to be in control of your finances.

⊳⊲*Alvin says . . .*

- Keep one or two credit cards – maybe three if you travel extensively for business . . . but no more!
- Avoid using store cards. But if you do, use only one and take maximum advantage of discounts and perks without spending more than you can afford to pay off in full each month.
- Pay off your credit card bill in full every month.

Minimise the Interest You Pay

Take advantage of your credit card's interest-free grace period. This period exists only on purchases, not cash advances. The grace period may range in length from zero to fifty-five days, depending on when your next month's bill comes due. At the end of the grace period, interest charges kick in. So the best money-saving strategy is to buy at the beginning of the grace period and pay off your purchase in full just before the end of the grace period. Payment can be made directly via the Internet. The payment usually shows in your account on the day it is made. If you're paying by post, then the payment must be received at the credit card company's offices by the end of the grace period and it usually takes two to three days for the money to be credited to your account. Jot down in your paper or electronic diary or calendar the date on which you must mail your payment to the company to take full advantage of the grace period.

This is one of the advantages of cutting back on the number of cards you hold. It's easy to keep track of the grace periods on one or two cards. When you have several cards, this strategy is likely to become too complicated to follow.

I've used this technique myself for years. I always knew in advance when the big seasonal sales were scheduled. I would buy a few items with my credit card and keep the money to pay the bill in the bank, where it would be earning interest for me. Then just before the end of the grace period I would send in a cheque or use online banking to pay for the full purchase amount.

There *are* times when you may have to use your credit card for purchases you can't pay off in full immediately. If the roof develops a leak or the cooker goes, you may need to overspend. For some people, Christmas is also such a time. If this happens to you, minimise the damage to your finances by giving yourself a fixed deadline to pay off the larger-than-normal bill – no more than six months. If necessary, cut your other spending to make this possible. Your main objective must be to pay off the debt as quickly as you can.

Some people practise what I call 'serial monogamy' with their credit cards. This means that they use just one credit card at a time but they switch from one card to another frequently. Often they switch in order to take advantage of low or nought per cent teaser rates. They jump from one card to another, moving their debt balances as they go. Use this technique *only* if you've established – and are adhering to – a clear limit as to when you're going to pay off the debt. It's *not* wise to use this method as an excuse for letting your debt hang on indefinitely. And if you do jump from one card to another, don't forget to cancel the old card! Having too many outstanding lines of credit will generally hurt your credit rating, even if you've paid off the money you owed.

In any case, you should realise that the serial monogamy game can only go on for so long. In time, the credit card companies will catch on and stop offering you cards with great teaser rates.

⌬ *Alvin says . . .*

- Use your card's grace period to save interest expenses.
- Make and stick to a payback deadline if you are carrying an outstanding balance.
- If you play 'serial monogamy' with your credit cards, be careful. Use the period of the nought per cent or lower per cent offer to pay off your debt, instead of moving it from one credit card to the next.

Practise Tough Self-Love

Some people find it really hard to follow the kinds of credit card rules I've laid out in the last couple of pages.

They feel financially empowered and secure opening up a wallet full of cards, knowing they can buy whatever they want wherever they want. The idea of cutting back to one or two cards, of paying off their bills in full, of strictly limiting the times they shop – these ideas are almost unbearably frustrating and seemingly impossible to follow.

If this psychology applies to you, go further than I've suggested so far: *get rid of your credit cards completely.* Yes, cut them up! Torch them! If the thought makes you anxious, causes you to nearly panic, or reduces you to tears, think about how sad it is that a piece of plastic and the indebtedness it enables dominates your daily financial life, dominates your thoughts day and night. Shred those cards – for your own happiness' sake. Believe me, you'll be glad you did.

I wouldn't feel right about giving this advice if I hadn't lived through the experience myself. Growing up poor in the 'panhandle' area of northern Florida, I was raised in the Southern Baptist tradition of discipline, self-denial and shame. In reaction, when I moved to Miami as a young man, launched a successful career and began to earn a little money, I went a bit mad. No matter what or how much I bought there were always more beautiful things worth acquiring, from cashmere coats to decorative objects to fancy dinners and nights out.

Unfortunately, I was not earning enough money to really afford all the things I was enjoying. But I thought I was being clever – getting what I wanted today and figuring out how to pay for it tomorrow. I made only the minimum payments each month when the bills came due and I continued to buy things using my stash of credit cards. So my debt kept getting larger and larger month to month. But as long as I could afford the minimum payments, I felt all was fine with my finances. When new credit card offers came through the mail, I viewed them in a quite self-serving way. I thought, 'The credit card companies like me – they really like me!' And I returned their affection by using the card proudly when shopping at the stores and then paying the minimum each month. When you consider that I had no fewer than *twenty-nine* cards, you can see the trouble I was in!

In the end, only a course of tough self-love saved me from a real financial crack-up. I took the shears to all but one of my credit cards. (Today I limit myself to three, largely because I travel so much.) I paid off my debt by taking a second job selling 'men's furnishings' in a department store in the evenings, on weekends and as a substitute when a co-worker could not make it. Every single penny I earned from this job was allocated to paying off my debt. It took nearly two years, but I did it! And I promised myself that I would never, ever do this to myself again.

As my income gradually grew over the course of my career, I managed *not* to revert to my old, deluded free-spending ways. Instead, I learned to control my behaviour using what I'd learned about my own money psychology. I figured out how to save first and then reward myself for a period of frugality with a single small, but perfect, treat: an art book I'd coveted, a chilled martini (shaken not stirred) at the King Cole Bar at the St Regis Hotel or a half-price ticket for a play I wanted to see. And I learned to enjoy the fun of tending my growing bank balance – and eventually my stock portfolio.

> ### ⌦ *Alvin says* . . .
>
> Remember how (in Chapter 1) I urged you to set aside ten per cent of your income for savings off the top every month? If you can't do that and pay off your credit card debts in full every month at the same time, then you are spending too much.

Beyond the Credit Card

Credit card debt is the biggest bugbear haunting most people in the UK. But there are other kinds of debt that need managing as well. Let's take a moment to consider them.

- *Mortgages* are loans used for buying property. We'll save our discussion of mortgages for Chapter 4, which is devoted to property ownership.
- *Unsecured loans* are bank loans given without security – that is, against which property or other assets are *not* pledged. They are very expensive and should generally be avoided, although they are relatively easy to get. I'd steer clear of such loans unless they are the only way to manage or cover the cost of some unexpected, unavoidable problem.
- *Bank overdrafts* are actually a kind of unsecured loan. Sometimes the interest rates charged on overdrafts are relatively attractive compared to other types of

borrowing – namely credit cards. However, the over-draft limits are generally low and a fee is charged whenever you exceed the limit. And since interest is charged from day one, using your overdraft privilege is *not* a smart way of managing your monthly expenses.

- *Second secured loans* (or *second mortgages*) are bank loans against which your home is pledged as security. These are popularly used as a means of getting access to the equity that has built up in property due to price appreciation and using cash to pay off credit card and other debts (in which case they are sometimes referred to as 'consolidation loans'). Because the interest charged on second secured loans is lower than credit card interest, such a loan is preferable to carrying a huge credit card balance. But be careful: if you fall behind on your loan payments you could lose your home! So be very conservative about this form of borrowing.
- *Car loans* are secured loans for the purpose of buying an automobile. They're quite common and, since the monthly payments are usually manageable, most people don't run into problems with them. But do shop around among various lenders; the interest rates on car loans vary greatly and you shouldn't assume that the arrangement your dealer offers is the best available.
- *Hire purchase* (also called *rent-to-buy*). People with low or transient incomes are often enticed to use this type of credit as a means of buying appliances, furniture and other expensive items. If you can possibly avoid hire purchase plans, do so because you can get trapped. Interest rates are high and pre-payment is

generally forbidden. So even if you receive a windfall and want to pay off your debt early, you won't be able to get out from under the steep interest costs. And if, for some reason, you're unable to make the sixtieth payment, for example, you may lose your furniture and all the money you've sunk into it, even though you were never a day late with any of the first fifty-nine payments. If you must go this route, reading the fine print is essential. Never rely on the salesperson's description of the deal: read every word with your own eyes before signing anything.

- *Pay-day loans* are easy-to-get, short-term loans (usually 30 days or less) made to people who have run out of money before they receive their next pay cheque or their pay is deposited into their accounts. The interest rates charged on pay-day loans are beyond excessive, with many companies charging 2,000 per cent per year. The loans define the word usury! And as you would expect, the lender tries to keep the borrower from focusing on the annual interest rate; instead the lender keeps the borrower focused on the seemingly small amount of money it will cost for the 30-day pay loan. People who are already in financial trouble or who can't get loans elsewhere are the targets of pay-day lenders. But taking the money makes the person's financial problems substantially worse, not better. The lender's terms typically require that the loan be repaid by continuous payment authorisation (CPA) or direct debit from your bank account. This means that if, for example, you don't have enough money in your account to meet the required payment, the lender can adjust the debit amount and take all of the money you do have in the account, leaving you with little to live on. There have also been cases where pay-day lenders have taken too much money out of a borrower's account. Pay-day loans should always be avoided because the cost – real and emotional – can be nothing short of astronomical. [NOTE: In April 2014, regulating pay-day loans and all forms of consumer lending became the responsibility of the Financial Conduct Authority (FCA) when it took over the responsibility from the Office of Fair Trading (OFT). See the upcoming section on Regulation of Consumer Lending.]

Another type of consumer debt is those tempting nought per cent financing offers for furniture and appliances in the newspapers, magazines and on television. 'Buy your dreams now and pay no interest for six months or a year!' At least, that is what the ads want you to infer. But is it really that easy or that cheap? Not quite.

In most of the 'nought per cent' financing deals, the payment schedule you receive is calculated on a longer period than the period of no interest. For example, suppose you sign a contract to buy a set of furniture with no interest for the first six months. Your payments are calculated on a 12-month repayment schedule instead of the six-month nought per cent interest period. When the six months are up, if you pay the outstanding balance immediately then you indeed will pay no interest. But if you do not, the interest on your remaining payments will be exceedingly high.

The trouble doesn't stop there. Some contracts allow the interest on your balance to be recalculated over the entire time of the contract, not just the period of the remaining balance. In other cases, pre-payment is forbidden. If you must go down this route, reading and understanding the fine print in your contract is essential. I can't emphasise this enough.

Regulation of Consumer Lending

April 2014 began a new, stronger era of consumer credit regulation in the UK. The Financial Conduct Authority (FCA) took over the responsibilities of the Office of Fair Trading (OFT) and therefore became responsible for all consumer lending. In its press release, published in March 2013, the FCA says its 'regulation will apply to any firm or individual offering credit cards and personal loans, selling goods or services on credit, offering goods for hire, or providing debt counselling or debt adjusting services to consumers.' The FCA wants to make sure that the consumer has the accurate and clear information he or she needs to make an informed decision when using any type of credit. This requirement includes any and all advertising by the lender. Misleading or deceptive ads are prohibited. Additionally the lender will be required to determine if the borrower can afford the loan.

The FCA has proposed much tighter regulation of all aspects of pay-day lending, for example, capping the cost (fees and interest rates) of the loan, requiring lenders to qualify the borrower as someone who can afford the loan, requiring greater clarity in the lenders' advertisements and more. The FCA's goal is straightforward but also involves a delicate balance: to stop pay-day lenders from abusing and exploiting consumers, while at the same time permitting the industry to remain a functioning business sector.

Check the FCA's website for up-to-date regulations of pay-day loans and other forms of consumer lending.

Borrowing from Friends and Family

Finally, a word about borrowing from friends and family: *Don't!* Sorry to be a bit flippant but I want to emphasise the risks involved in mixing affection with business. It takes a very strong relationship to survive when money changes hands. There are just too many opportunities for awkwardness, resentment, guilt and anger. What happens if you need to make a late payment? Will your mum or cousin Sheila charge you a late fee, as the bank would, or will she simply smile and say, 'Never mind,' all the while seething with annoyance whenever the subject comes to mind? What if there's a disagreement about the borrowing terms? It's very easy for two honest, well-intentioned people to remember the same conversation in radically different ways. Who can arbitrate such a dispute without being bloodied in the emotional crossfire?

Yes, it's tempting to take advantage of the generosity of loved ones. A loan between relatives or friends involves no application forms or credit checks. And there *are* some rare relationships in which all involved are honest, secure and forthright enough to deal with the inevitable stresses of finance without suffering hurt feelings or embarrassment. But please avoid becoming indebted to friends and family if you possibly can. It's bad enough having money difficulties – why screw up your personal life in the bargain?

▷◁ *Alvin says* . . .

If you must borrow from a friend or relation, handle it as a business transaction. Write a note that mentions the amount borrowed, the payment scheme, the interest to be charged and what happens if you fail to repay. Then live up to those terms – religiously – if you ever want to have a happy Christmas dinner or a civil family holiday again.

Getting Out from Under: a Step-by-Step Approach

If you're deeply in debt, first step back from the problem and get a handle on it. Here's a three-step guide to organising your debts properly and developing a get-out-of-debt plan. Use it in conjunction with the form entitled, 'Your Credit Card Debt Reduction Plan' on pages 73–74.

Step 1

List your cards. Gather the most recent bills for all your outstanding credit or store cards. Don't forget any! Check with your spouse or partner – he or she may have a card you rarely or never use. And don't forget the card you may have left in your other wallet or purse or in a desk drawer. List the cards on the form provided. (It is probably easier to create a version of the form using spreadsheet software.) In the second column, list the annual interest rate on each one. You should find this figure on your monthly bill. If not, look on the

Terms and Conditions sheet you received when you first accepted the card. (Call the company for a copy if necessary.)

Step 2
Sort your debt. Now reorganise the list of credit cards from Step 1, arranging them in order from the *highest* to the *lowest* annual interest rate. (If two cards happen to have the same interest rate, list the one with the larger outstanding balance first.) Fill in the other information requested on the form: your total outstanding balance on each card and the minimum monthly payment required.

Step 3
Create your pay-off plan. Start by deciding how much of your debt you can afford to pay off each month. Push yourself a bit! If you're in serious debt, you won't be able to get out unless the amount you repay each month *hurts* a little. So if you think (for example) that you'd be comfortable repaying £200 every month, try for £250, £300, or when possible, you could stretch to even more. The philosophy is the same as with physical training: no pain, no gain. Write in the amount you decide at the top and bottom of the form as shown in the example on page 76.

Now it gets just a little complicated. Copy the list of credit cards from Step 2 in the form provided into Step 3. (If you find it tricky to fill out the form, see the sample we've provided, all filled in. It appears on pages 75–76.) Then allocate your monthly repayment amount as follows:

- Starting with the second card on the list, write in the minimum payment required. Then do the same with the third card, the fourth card and so on, to the bottom of your list.
- Add these minimum payment amounts together. Then subtract this sum from the total monthly repayment you've committed to.
- Allocate the remaining balance to the first card on the list. (If this amount is more than you owe on the first card, then allocate the difference to the second card.)

Do you see what we're doing? We're setting up a plan so that you'll pay off the *maximum* possible amount on the card with the *highest* interest *first*. This is the card that is costing you the most in needless interest expense every month. The sooner you get that monkey off your back, the more you'll benefit. Yes, it's important to pay off all your debts and you shouldn't be satisfied until every card has been paid off in full. But you have to start somewhere – and the best place to start is with the card that hurts you the most.

Follow the monthly repayment plan we've just created until the first card on your list is completely paid off. When that happens, celebrate by cutting up that card and closing the account. Then make a new plan, with the next worst-offending card at the top of your list. Continue the process for as many months as it takes to clear out your list altogether, from top to bottom. It's important to remember that other types of consumer debt, not just credit card debt, can be included in this debt-reduction plan.

YOUR CREDIT CARD DEBT REDUCTION PLAN

Date _____

STEP 1. LIST YOUR CARDS. On the form below, list all your outstanding credit cards. In the second column, list the annual percentage rate (APR) on each one.

Credit card   Interest rate (%)

_____

_____

_____

_____

_____

_____

_____

STEP 2. SORT YOUR DEBT. Reorganise the list, arranging your credit cards in order from the _highest_ to the _lowest_ annual interest rate. If two or more cards have the same interest rate, then arrange them beginning with the largest outstanding balance. Fill in the other columns indicated.

Credit card	Balance due (£)	Minimum payment required (£)	Interest rate (%)

STEP 3. YOUR PAY-OFF PLAN. Decide how much of your debt you can afford to pay off each month. Write that figure here: £   . Also write it at the bottom of the second column in the form below under Total Monthly Payment.

Copy the list of credit cards from Step 2 in the form below. Then allocate your monthly repayment amount as follows:

- For the second, third and later cards on the list, write in the minimum payment required (as shown in Step 2).

- Add these figures, and subtract that amount from the total monthly repayment.

- Write the balance next to the first card on the list. (If this amount is more than you owe on the first card, then allocate the difference to the second card.)

Credit card   Monthly payment (£)

                                      TOTAL

YOUR CREDIT CARD DEBT REDUCTION PLAN

Date 1 May 2014

STEP 1. LIST YOUR CARDS. On the form below, list all your outstanding credit cards. In the second column, list the annual percentage rate (APR) on each one.

Credit card	Interest rate (%)
ABC Bank	17.5
Northern Bank	15
XYZ Company	23.5
Jones Store	27
Harringtons	20.5

STEP 2. SORT YOUR DEBT. Reorganise the list, arranging your credit cards in order from the *highest* to the *lowest* annual interest rate. If two or more cards have the same interest rate, then arrange them beginning with the largest outstanding balance. Fill in the other columns indicated.

Credit card	Balance due (£)	Minimum payment required (£)	Interest rate (%)
Jones Store	790	16.49	27
XYZ Company	240	6.67	23.5
Harringtons	1,720	35.83	20.5
ABC Bank	4,350	72.50	17.5
Northern Bank	2,175	60.42	15

STEP 3. YOUR PAY-OFF PLAN. Decide how much of your debt you can afford to pay off each month. Write that figure here: £450.00. Also write it at the bottom of the second column in the form below.

Copy the list of credit cards from Step 2 in the form below. Then allocate your monthly repayment amount as follows:

- For the second, third and later cards on the list, write in the minimum payment required (as shown in Step 2).

- Add these figures, and subtract that amount from the total monthly repayment.

- Write the balance next to the first card on the list. (If this amount is more than you owe on the first card, then allocate the difference to the second card.)

Credit card	Monthly payment (£)
Jones Store	274.58
XYZ Company	6.67
Harringtons	35.83
ABC Bank	72.50
Northern Bank	60.42
TOTAL	450.00

Now the Good News

As you move down the list, you will actually begin paying off your debts at a faster rate. Your new total payment on the next debt down the list will now include the minimum payments you were making before. Also, because interest rates are lower on the later cards, more of the money will be going to pay off the principal (as opposed to interest, and interest on interest). In short, the longer you stick with the plan, the easier it works and the faster your progress. But remember: *don't* add any more debts during this period. As you pay down each item, be sure to cancel the credit or store card so that, as we said in the first section, the weapon is no longer in your hands.

What about Borrowing to Pay Off Your Debts?

If your debts are large, it could take years – and a lot of discipline – to get out of debt. With this long, winding and narrow road stretching out in front of you, you might be tempted to get some relief by borrowing enough money (perhaps secured by your house) to pay off all your credit and store cards at one time. You would then have a single repayment cheque to write each month that would, most likely, be for a smaller amount than the total you are currently paying by making only the minimum payments on all of the cards. Of course, it usually takes longer to pay off the consolidation loan. The result is that you can end up still paying quite a substantial amount of interest.

But the interest isn't the most significant problem with consolidating your debts into a single loan. The biggest danger comes from the sense of relief that you feel when your monthly payment decreases. All too often this leads to further spending (which I call 'relief retail therapy') and a spiral into an even worse debt problem. So, consider consolidating your debt *only* if you're very self-disciplined and if you've made a strong personal commitment to steering clear of the shopping centres, the high streets, the discount shops, the online sites and the travel agencies until you have paid off the loan.

What about Help from a Third Party?

No, I am not referring to your parents and their bank account! While having a martini at one of my favourite hotel bars in London, I began chatting with the young couple sitting at a table next to mine. The lady confessed that she had had a huge amount of credit and store card debt but her father had paid all of it off. She had promised him that she would not get another credit card. But guess what? She had gotten one anyway and was keeping it a secret from her father. When I gently questioned her further, she said she was sure if she got into trouble with the new credit card, she would confess and he would bail her out again. As for repaying the money he had used to pay off her past debts, she responded only with a beguiling smile and fluttering eyelashes. I wondered how she would respond if I said, 'You got yourself into this mess of debt and it is your responsibility to get yourself out.'

For those who are truly overwhelmed by debt, third-party help is available from two quite different sources: 1) charitable or government-funded organisations, 2) debt management companies (also called *debt consolidation companies*). The most widely known of the charitable organisations that help people with debt problems are: Citizens Advice (www.citizensadvice.org.uk), Debt Advice Foundation (www.debtadvicefoundation.org), National Debt Line (www.nationaldebtline.co.uk) and StepChange Debt Charity (www.stepchange.org) which used to be called CCCS. The services of all these organisations are free and each will help you – be it in person, by phone, or online – work with your creditors to get debt under control. For example, the people at StepChange may be able to help you negotiate a gradual repayment plan with your creditors. Thus, you can reduce your debt while keeping your home and avoiding bankruptcy. Importantly, with each of the debt counselling charities, you have to take charge of your finances rather than hand them over to someone else. In order for you to benefit most from their services, you must be honest with yourself and them about the extent of your debt problem.

Debt management companies, in contrast, are for-profit companies that advertise enticingly about relieving the burden and stress of too much debt. Can you watch TV without seeing their ads? To me, this is as much a sign of their marketing savvy as it is of the increasing problem of personal indebtedness in the UK. These companies work in two ways. First, debt management companies put you on a budget that requires you to make one payment to the company each month. It then allocates this money to your creditors according to a plan it has worked out with them. Second, the debt consolidators arrange a long-term loan that you use to consolidate your debts. You must then make prompt, monthly payments to the company.

Sounds easy? For many people who want a low-sacrifice and somewhat parental-like solution to their financial and psychological debt problems (i.e., let someone else handle this for me), the debt management companies can be a somewhat Faustian pact. These for-profit organisa-tions have a less-than-stellar reputation. Some of their clients have complained of excessively high fees, poor administration and sometimes high-handed attitudes. I recommend you avoid this type of 'helper' altogether and arrange to pay off the debts yourself.

◄►Alvin says . . .

Being deeply in debt is likely to cause serious psychological and emotional stress. Don't let this stress lead you to make hasty decisions that may worsen your plight. Think through your dilemma carefully and deliberately, and invest the time and hard work needed to resolve it honourably. If you do, you'll emerge from the ordeal a stronger and wiser person, as well as solvent.

Understanding Your Credit Status

You've probably heard about *credit reference agencies*. If you've ever been turned down for a credit card or a loan, you may have blamed 'the agencies' for putting a 'black mark' on your credit report. If so, you may have a backlog of resentment against these organisations without really understanding their role.

Contrary to what many people believe, credit reference agencies are not 'credit police'. The agency does not give you black marks on your credit rating or offer any evaluation of your credit. It simply reports information it receives from credit card companies, stores and banks as to your history of borrowing and repaying debts. Those who are considering offering you future credit use this information in making their own, independent decisions as to whether they want to lend to you.

CallCredit, Equifax and Experian are the three leading UK consumer credit reference agencies. The chances are excellent that each of these companies already has a credit reference file (also called a *credit report*) about you. Most of the information they have on record is undoubtedly correct – but some of it may be wrong or dated and here is where trouble lurks.

Errors in an individual's credit reference files are unfortunately fairly common. Since there are no national ID numbers in the UK (unlike in the US, where Social Security numbers are used for this purpose), your identity is tracked based on your name and address. And, of course, it's quite common for two people – or several people – to have the same name or names that are confusingly similar. As a result, cases of mistaken identity are not uncommon. Correcting such errors can be very time-consuming but it's very important.

Therefore, don't assume your credit rating is correct even though you may be regularly receiving credit offers in the mail. It's quite possible that your history, as tracked by CallCredit, Equifax and Experian, may contain one or more errors that will affect you when you apply for a mortgage, credit card or other loan. Negative data about you – an indication that you missed a payment or defaulted on a past loan, for example – may cause you to be rejected by a bank or, perhaps, accepted but charged a higher-than-normal interest rate.

To start the process of checking or cleaning up your credit record, order a copy of your report from each of the three agencies. You can request your report online at the websites below or by writing to addresses provided on the websites:

CallCredit Ltd: www.callcredit.co.uk

Equifax Ltd: www.equifax.co.uk

Experian Plc: www.experian.co.uk

With each request, you'll need to indicate your full name, your date of birth, your current address and any addresses you've lived at during the past six years. Each site tells you the specific information needed. For each report, there's a fee set by statute at £2.

Once you've received your reports, study them carefully. If you find any mistakes, contact both the credit reference agency and the company involved in the error: for example, the bank that has mistakenly claimed you never repaid a loan. I strongly suggest you communicate in writing (rather than by phone) and keep copies of your correspondence.

Remember, CallCredit, Equifax and Experian cannot 'fix' your credit rating, settle a dispute with a lender or approve your application for credit. The most they can do is make certain that their reports reflect your credit history accurately. Anything more that's needed to make you an attractive credit risk is your responsibility.

The Information Commissioner's Office (ICO) provides detailed information explaining credit, credit reference agencies, how to get and correct your credit reference files, as well as answers to frequently asked questions.

This independent authority's information on credit can be accessed at the website:

www.ico.org.uk/for_the_public/topic_specific_guides/ credit

The ICO provides a helpline (the phone number is available on the website) where you can receive guidance about how to approach solving your problem. Additionally, they also instruct you how to file a complaint if you cannot resolve the problem. Your filing may give the ICO the information it needs to help you resolve the problem. At the website it clearly states that the ICO cannot award compensation. It can only help you correct the information in your credit report.

What a 'Good Credit Rating' Means – and How to Get One

Being a 'good credit risk' means that you're considered responsible and likely to repay any debt you incur. (Remember what *credit* means: it's the lender saying, 'I believe in you.') That's a good thing – but it's not without dangers.

For example, what does it mean if you get a lot of credit solicitations in the mail? It's both good and bad. On the good side, it means that the credit card companies know that you pay your bills on time. However, it may also mean that you make the minimum payment each month! That means you pay a lot of interest and the credit card companies enjoy a lot of profits off you. To be blunt about it, they see SUCKER written on your forehead. No wonder they seem to gather around you like sharks around a wounded dolphin.

No Credit History?

On the other hand, if you've always paid all your bills in cash you may get turned down when you apply for a loan or a credit card. The reason is simple: never having used credit before, you have no credit history, no credit reference file and therefore no credit rating. This may seem unfair: 'Why should I be penalised for managing my money so efficiently that I never have to borrow?' Nonetheless, in the eyes of lenders, paying in cash doesn't make you a good credit risk – it puts you in the same category as money launderers!

The same problem sometimes afflicts people who've only recently stepped out on their own financially: recent college graduates, for example, or newly divorced people.

Fortunately, there's a simple solution. Get a credit card or store card (only at a store you frequent), use it a few times a month and pay your bills promptly and in full. After six months or so, you'll have established a credit history which should help you in borrowing. So if you know, for example, that you're interested in buying a home and therefore will need a mortgage in the next year or two, take steps necessary to create a good credit history for yourself.

Too Many Self-Inflicted Black Marks?

On the other hand, if you've got a bad credit record that you fully deserve, the solution is more difficult. Cleaning up a poor credit rating may take some time and patience.

If past late payments are a problem, then three to six months of consistently on-time payments should begin to improve your credit rating. However, if your credit history is blotted by a county court judgement (CCJ) against you or a legal bankruptcy, expect to wait six years to be able to borrow again.

Obviously, the moral here is: If you've never been in credit trouble, vow to keep it that way. It's much easier to maintain a clean record than to clean one you've previously smudged.

Alvin says . . .

Borrowing money is a little like riding a tiger: it will get you where you want to go a lot faster than walking, but if the tiger gets the chance he'll turn on you! Don't let that happen. Stay in the saddle and make sure debt knows who is in control.

3

THE IMPORTANCE AND JOY OF SAVING

It's Easier Than You Think

'I just can't save'

Why do so many people believe they can't save? Some think that, given the costs of simply living day to day, they will never have enough money left over to save. Some even appear to take a perverse pleasure in it. They boast, 'Oh, I'm terrible at saving! Money just slips through my fingers and half the time I have no idea where it's gone!' This includes some people you'd never expect to hear talk this way, such as people who manage budgets on their jobs. Sometimes they explain, 'After working on budgets and financial projections at work all day, I can't bear to think about money when I get home.' I suppose it's the old story: the house a builder lives in is never finished.

Oddly enough, the people who boast about their financial ineptitude rarely seem to be apprehensive about their futures. They seem to assume that somehow, someone or some event will save them from their own wasteful ways with money.

How do they expect this to happen? Perhaps they are hoping to inherit money. But depending on the sudden death of people you love isn't the happiest route to financial success – even if it were reliable. You never know whether one of the *other* nieces or nephews will turn out to have been Aunt Mildred's *real* favourite. And getting on one of those television game shows that pays lots of prize money to the winner offers no guarantees either. Haven't you noticed how tricky those last few questions or challenges tend to be?

Happily, it's not necessary to rely on a stroke of good fortune for your future financial well-being. In reality, saving is one of the easiest things to do . . .

Why Save?

Learning to save is the first essential step towards guaranteeing a better future life for yourself and your family. Unless you are capable of saving, you'll have little chance of ever enjoying real prosperity, let alone wealth. And unless you have a cushion of savings behind you at *all* times you run the risk of becoming truly desperate, even destitute, more quickly than you might think is possible – shocking as that idea may be.

As I write this last statement, I think of my own financial situation. If I did not have savings, what would have happened to me financially following the horrific terrorist attacks on New York's World Trade Center and following the Lehman Brothers bankruptcy filing? In both cases my livelihood was significantly affected.

Many of the financial firms I consulted with and taught for were located in or around the World Trade Center buildings. In the wake of the tragedy, they halted most employee training and other functions that once provided a major source of my income. So, even as I grieved, along with millions of others, over the terrible loss of lives, I was also scrambling to deal with the personal impact of a huge loss of income.

When Lehman Brothers declared bankruptcy, the company still owed me for some unpaid invoices. Not only was it likely that I would never be paid that money (and we are not talking about a small amount) but all of the work that I had been scheduled to do for the remainder of the year was also g-o-n-e. This was a double whammy! And to make the already bad news even worse, I would not be able to replace the work I did for Lehman with a new client because the financial services sector and banks were in a crisis that was expected to last for years. Cost-cutting, not continuing business as usual, was their primary focus. Frankly, the situation was unnerving and depressing. The financial injury became a financial insult when in early 2014 the bankruptcy judge handling the Lehman case rejected my compensation claim, even with proof that the work had been completed. So all the income owed to me was lost.

Luckily, I have followed my own advice about saving. Because I'm self-employed, I've always been very conscious of the need to maintain an emergency fund. That fund kept me solvent through both of those unexpected situations and, should something else happen, it will help to keep me solvent then too.

If You are Self-Employed

Self-employed people should be diligent in setting aside money for taxes. This will help them avoid the common, self-inflicted horror of having to scramble to come up with the full amount of the tax bill all at one time. Follow these steps:

1. Work out your own potential tax liability. HM Revenue & Customs (HMRC) has a section on its website that will help you to do this. It's called, 'Find out how much Income Tax you need to pay and the allowances you can claim' and can be accessed at:
www.hmrc.gov.uk/incometax
2. Deduct the correct percentage from each cheque you receive and deposit that amount into a separate savings account dedicated to taxes. Remember you have to pay taxes twice a year!
3. Recalculate your income and tax liability periodically (at least once per quarter) to make sure the money you are saving will be sufficient to cover the amount you will owe HM Revenue & Customs.

Above all, don't put your head in the sand about your potential tax liability. Inevitably, HM Revenue & Customs will bite the parts left sticking out.

It Can Happen to You
You may be thinking, 'But I'm not a freelancer. I have a steady, reliable job with a regular pay cheque. Why do I need an emergency fund?' The truth is that *everyone* is subject to financial emergencies. In fact, statistics show that most people will suffer a significant loss of income at some point in their lives; a loss that can plunge them into a desperate crisis, even poverty, if there's no financial cushion to fall back on.

The emergency you face could take many forms, including:

- A business slowdown or plant closing that causes you to be made redundant

- A severe economic downturn that affects all business sectors
- A personal injury that prevents you from working
- A devastating illness
- An accident that destroys your car
- A mental, emotional, or social problem that afflicts a family member
- A fire that destroys your home and property
- An acrimonious, financially debilitating divorce
- An unexpected legal calamity, such as an arrest or a lawsuit

I will never forget a lady I worked with on my television series who could have been the poster girl for the importance of having savings. A year before I met her, she and her partner had joint earnings of £60,000. They enjoyed that income to the fullest, enjoying luxury holidays and buying presents for their small child. They even spent £13,000 on a cruise to Jamaica in order to fulfil their dream of being married by a ship's captain.

Within a few months, everything changed. First, her husband's business began to go very badly and the debts started to mount. Then he left her. Weeks later, she was made redundant from her job. Because she had no savings, her parents ended up paying her mortgage. Now, as an unemployed single mum, she became dependent on state benefits to get through each month.

Please don't say, 'It could never happen to me.' Deep inside, you know it could. You owe it to yourself and your family to be prepared for such emergencies.

The goal of saving three to six months of your living expenses strikes some people as very ambitious. It's certainly more than most people have on hand. But I'm convinced it represents a realistic emergency fund, one that will probably allow you to find ways to navigate safely through many of the financial storms you're likely to encounter. Anything less is all too likely to be quickly depleted in the face of a true emergency or a time when it is difficult to find work.

Accumulating four to six months' income won't happen overnight. For most people who embark on a serious saving programme, it will take several years – maybe four to five – to reach this target. That's all right. Many of life's worthwhile achievements take that much time: graduating from college or university, getting a career off the ground, raising a child to school age. The key is to set your sights on reaching the goal and be persistent in pursuing it. Once you've built up the emergency fund, it must remain in savings untouched, ready to spring into action when the need arises.

▷◁ Alvin says . . .

Begin saving now with the goal of having four to six months of either *after-tax income* or *living expenses* in a liquid savings account. *Liquid* means easily accessible at full value. Money invested in property is not liquid, since property may be difficult to sell at a moment's notice and if you *must* sell it quickly you may not be able to get the full value. Your emergency savings should also be in a safe account – one with virtually no risk of loss. Shares, bonds, unit trusts and other investments carry significant risk and therefore don't qualify on this score. I recommend using a bank or building society account for your four to six months' savings since such an account is both liquid (you can withdraw the money at any time) and very safe (the value of your funds is insured up to a statutory limit).

Put Saving First

The problem many people have with saving is that it is the last thing they think of doing or want to do with their money. Most spend their income mentally before they receive it. You need to reverse that 'spend first, save last' impulse. Here's how.

Begin by deciding how much you want to save. A good target is 10 per cent of your take-home pay. (Ten per cent will allow you to build a four-month emergency fund in about six years.) But if that amount seems like a daunting goal, don't make that into an excuse to do nothing. Many people can't start at the 10 per cent level. I certainly could not when I first started working. If necessary, begin by saving whatever you can afford – even if it's no more than £20 or £30 or £50 a month – and gradually increase the amount when you're able.

Whatever amount you decide to target, take this money out of your pay cheque *up front* before you spend a penny on anything else. Better still, arrange for direct debit from your current account into a savings account.

Deposit this 'top 10 per cent' into a *limited access* bank account. This is a special account from which only a limited number of withdrawals are permitted each year. Ask your bank manager about such an account; they will gladly help you set one up. You can also set it up yourself online. Then – and this is critical – think of the account as being sacrosanct, too valuable and important to be violated with any withdrawal. Don't get a cash card for this account. If the bank sends you one anyway, cut it up. Most importantly, when you make your spending plans, don't factor this money into your income. You know the old saying, 'Out of sight, out of mind.' Keep your savings account out of the sight of your spending impulses. Think about the account only when you deposit money into it and when you look up your balance, to congratulate yourself on how nicely it's growing.

Saving Secrets

Here are some other tricks that can help make saving easy (or at least easier):

- *Maintain your savings account in a different bank from your current account,* preferably one that's a few minutes' walk out of your way rather than just a step or two from your office door or your home. This helps to create a psychological barrier that discourages you from withdrawing money. Incidentally, searching for a new bank account gives you a chance to investigate opportunities for earning a better interest rate on your money – a second benefit that's not to be overlooked, especially during a time when interest rates are low and banks are competing for your deposits.
- After launching your savings programme, *look for opportunities to increase the amount you set aside each payday.* For example, earmark half or all of your next salary rise for savings. This is surprisingly easy to do; after all, you've been living on the lower amount all along. Just pretend you got half the rise you did, or none at all, and enjoy watching how the rate at which your savings grow suddenly increases. Do the same with end-of-year bonuses, cash gifts or inheritances from relatives and other windfalls.
- Finally, *change your debt habit into a savings habit.* Here's what I mean: suppose you've been setting aside an amount each month to pay off your credit cards

– £200, let's say. Once you get all your debt paid off, start banking the same £200. You won't miss the money, since you haven't been spending it anyway. Use the same technique when you've finished paying off any loan or your mortgage.

Matching Saving with Fun

Does all this sound rather self-denying and harsh? Perhaps you want to protest, the way small children do, 'I never get to have any fun!' If so, consider building some fun into your savings programme by tying it to giving yourself something you want. Decide in advance what categories of spending are most gratifying and enjoyable for you then link that kind of spending to saving.

For example, if clothes are your weakness, then every time you spend money on a piece of clothing deposit the exact same amount into your savings account. Do this with whatever is your weakness – splurging on cosmetics or fancy electronics, going to the cinema, buying books and music, or whatever. Thus, the pleasure of treating yourself will be associated with (and increased by) the happiness of building up your cash reserve.

The Magical Payoff: Compound Interest

Once you begin your savings programme, a magical reward will start to appear automatically. This reward is *compound interest*. Not only do you earn interest on the money you save but through compounding you earn interest on the interest. The result is that your money grows much faster than you might anticipate. See the tables on page 94 for a simple example of how this works, based on the assumption that you save £100 per month.

As you see, the long-term benefits of compound interest

can be truly startling. If you want to get *really* excited, project how much money you can accumulate if you set aside more than £100 per month. It's a simple matter of multiplying the figures in the chart to reflect the amount you are saving. For example, suppose you save £300 per month, a figure that's within easy reach for many people. Multiply the figures in the chart by three. If you earn an average annual rate of six per cent interest on your money over 30 years, you'll have over £300,000 when you retire. Not a bad nest egg. It's important to keep in mind that interest rates do change over the time you save. During the time I've been saving they have been as high as 12 per cent and below one per cent. It's important to try to get a good, safe yield on your savings regardless of what the current interest rate is.

▷◁ Alvin says . . .

People tend to believe that the current interest rates they are experiencing will last their entire lifetime. This is especially true during times when interest rates are low. It becomes an excuse not to save because your money isn't earning a lot. The truth is that interest rates can, and mostly will, vary substantially over one's lifetime. By continuing to save during times when interest rates are low, you'll have the money ready to benefit more from compounding when interest rates rise, as they inevitably will.

The Brilliance of Compounding

Suppose you saved £100 per month for a period of thirty years – say, from the age of thirty-five to sixty-five. How much money would you accumulate without earning interest? How much would you accumulate if compound interest were paid? The charts below show the answers.

THE BRILLIANCE OF COMPOUNDING

Suppose you saved £100 per month for a period of thirty years – say from age thirty-five to sixty-five. How much money would you accumulate without earning interest? How much would you accumulate if compound interest were paid? The charts below show the answers.

I. WITHOUT INTEREST

Time elapsed	0% interest (£)
1 year	1,200
5 years	6,000
10 years	12,000
15 years	18,000
20 years	24,000
25 years	30,000
30 years	36,000
INTEREST EARNED	0

II. WITH INTEREST (COMPOUNDED MONTHLY)

Time elapsed	4% interest (£)	6% interest (£)	8% interest (£)	10% interest (£)
1 year	1,222	1,234	1,245	1,256
5 years	6,623	6,977	7,355	7,736
10 years	14,694	16,388	18,335	20,438
15 years	24,529	29,082	34,727	41,295
20 years	36,513	46,204	59,196	75,544
25 years	51,117	69,299	95,723	131,783
30 years	68,912	100,452	150,252	224,129
INTEREST EARNED	**32,912**	**64,452**	**114,252**	**188,129**

Saving Tax-Free

With most ordinary savings accounts, you'll have to pay tax on your profits: income tax on the interest you earn and, in some cases, capital gains tax on the growth in value of the underlying investment. These taxes slow down your accumulation of money. However, you can help your money grow faster by taking advantage of various schemes for accumulating savings tax-free, including NISAs and National Savings and Investments plans.

✄ Alvin says . . .

On July 1, 2014 all existing and new ISAs became NISAs (New Individual Savings Accounts) with a higher contribution limits and greater flexibility. There is no longer a difference between the amount that can be contributed to a cash NISA (for savings) and a stocks-and-shares NISA (for investing). The government raised the limits substantially—to £15,000 for NISA's from July 1st, 2014. Under the new rules you can contribute up to the limit in a cash NISA or a stock-and-shares NISA, or you divide your contribution between the two accounts in any amount or percentage you want. You also move funds back and forth between the two accounts to suit your savings or investment objectives. And you can transfer money that's in old ISAs into either a cash or a stock-and-shares NISA.

How NISAs Work
A NISA, or *New Individual Savings Account*, is a special kind of account designed to let you save and invest without paying tax on the growth of your savings. A NISA is not a savings vehicle itself; instead, it is a 'wrapper' that can hold cash savings or investments (for

example, shares or unit trusts). The income and growth of a NISA are free of income tax and capital gains tax, and you don't have to declare a NISA on your tax return.

There are two types of NISAs: a *cash NISA* and a *stocks-and-shares NISA*. The cash NISA is for saving while the stocks-and-shares NISA is for investing.

HMRC sets a maximum overall limit that can be invested in NISAs during each tax year. (A tax year runs from 6 April of one year through 5 April of the next.) You are permitted to invest this total amount in a cash NISA, a stocks-and-shares NISA or divide the total contribution between the two accounts in whatever amounts or percentage you want. So, in each tax year a person can open one cash NISA and one stocks-and-share NISA. Under the new rules you can transfer money between the two accounts any time you want as your objectives change or divide the total contribution between the two accounts in whatever amounts and percentage you want.

To keep current on changes in the NISA limits as well as any changes in the regulations, products (for example, Junior ISAs) and other specific details, visit the website: www.hmrc.gov.uk/isa/

Advantages of a NISA

There are numerous advantages of having a NISA: you pay no taxes on the interest earned on savings or on the dividends and capital gains made on investments; you don't have to report your NISA accounts to HMRC; and you can withdraw money from a NISA anytime you need or want to. This combination of no taxes and a no-limit withdrawals policy has made NISAs a must-have saving and investment tool.

The basic kinds of accounts in which money in a cash NISA can be saved are:

- NISA bank and building society accounts
- Authorised unit trust cash funds
- National Savings and Investments (NS&I) Direct ISA (To learn more about the specific details of the NS&I Direct NISA, visit the website: www.nsandi.com/savings-direct-nisa)

Money deposited in a stocks-and-shares NISA can be invested in products that include:

- Shares in companies
- Corporate bonds
- Government bonds (gilts)
- Unit trusts
- OEIC (open-end investment companies)
- Investment trusts
- Investment funds
- Life insurance policies (with-profits, unit-linked or investment-linked policies)

Opening an NISA

You can open a NISA with a *NISA manager*, which is an organisation approved by HM Revenue & Customs (HMRC) and authorised by the Financial Conduct Authority (FCA). NISA managers include banks, building societies, investment firms, stockbrokers, insurance firms, solicitors and financial advisers. Not all NISA managers offer all kinds of NISAs. So, if you want to deposit your NISA money into various kinds of savings and investment plans, you may want to use more than one NISA manager. There's no problem with this at all.

What type of NISA is best for you? It depends on many factors. In later chapters, I'll explain how to think about different kinds of investments and how to decide what forms of investments make sense for you, based on your age, your financial goals, your personal risk tolerance and other considerations. For now, I'll offer the following rules of thumb:

- When building up your four-to-six-month cash emergency/reserve fund, put your money into a virtually risk-free savings vehicle. For this purpose, a cash NISA is best. As explained earlier, a bank or building society account works well for this purpose.
- Once you've accumulated your emergency/reserve fund, consider depositing money into a stocks-and-shares NISA, especially if you are trying to grow your money for long-term goals such as retirement. This kind of investment vehicle carries greater risk than a cash NISA (since stocks and shares go up and down in value) but it usually offers a higher rate of growth over a long time period.

National Savings and Investments
If you've reached your annual limit on NISA payments, consider using one of the National Savings and Investments plans as an additional source of tax-free money growth. These are tax-free forms of saving that include Premium Bonds, Index-linked Savings Certificates, Fixed-Rate Saving Certificates and Children's Bonds. They don't need to be listed on your tax return. You can

invest in these tax-free on top of any amounts you put away in a NISA, even if you've reached the maximum annual limit of your NISA contribution. Not all of these products are continually on offer and there are periodic changes to product features as well as available interest rates. For up-to-date information, visit the website:

www.nsandi.com/savings

Setting and Pursuing your Personal Saving Goals

Once you have your four-to-six-month cash reserve fund, you're ready to begin saving for other goals. Use these goals to determine the amount of money you want to save by a certain date. These will usually include both short-term and long-term goals.

Short-term goals are those that can be reached through six to sixty months of saving. Typical short-term goals include buying a car, refurbishing your home, taking a special holiday or buying new appliances.

Long-term goals are those that you will need to save towards for five years or longer. Typical long-term goals include buying a home, starting or buying a business and funding your retirement. Many parents also want to save to pay for their children's university education. This is important because the British government has become less generous with educational support and university fees increased greatly in 2012 and are likely to increase further in the years to come. Just as Americans have done for decades, people in the UK need to begin including the cost of university for the kids into their long-term financial goals.

> **▷◁ Alvin says . . .**
>
> Remember – saving towards your personal goals should follow on the building of your four-to-six-month cash reserve. This fund should be kept in a separate account and it shouldn't be touched except in a true emergency. A sudden overwhelming desire to get away for a long weekend to the Canary Islands does not qualify as an emergency!

A Plan for Beginning Savers

If you're new to the saving game, here's my recommended plan:

- Set at least one long-term and one short-term goal, but no more than three of each.
- Put a price on each – a pound value you want to accumulate.
- Decide how long it will take to accumulate this amount and develop a monthly savings plan to reach that goal.

Use the form on page 110 as a template to develop your savings plan. There's a filled-in sample on the following page to show you how it's done. For simplicity's sake, I suggest you ignore the (positive) impact of interest and other income on your savings. (Remember that interest rates will vary over the course of your savings plan.) Just calculate the amount you need to save each month by dividing the total you want to save by the number of months between today and your target date. The interest you earn on your savings will actually shorten the process, which means you will be able to buy the new car or take that special holiday a few months earlier than you now hope. Or, if you keep saving for the fully allotted time, you'll have a little extra money to spend (which always seems to find a purpose).

You'll notice that the sample plan does *not* include retirement as one of the long-term goals listed. There's a special reason for this. Nearly everyone would list retirement as a long-term goal and it's one of the most important reasons to save. But retirement planning is a rather complex process. Deciding how much money you'll need to live on after you stop working (considering such factors as inflation over the coming years) and then figuring out how much you need to save to make that possible (while considering additional help such as government assistance and company pensions) takes several steps and some detailed mathematics. I'll walk you through the entire process in chapter nine and, after working through that chapter, you'll have a complete retirement savings plan.

So for now, omit retirement from your savings plan. We'll deal with that important goal later.

YOUR SAVINGS PLAN

Date

_____

Short-term goals

Goal	Cost (£)	Time frame	Per month
1.			
2.			
3.			

Long-term goals

Goal	Cost (£)	Time frame	Per month
1.			
2.			
3.			

MONTHLY SAVINGS TOTAL

_____

_____

YOUR SAVINGS PLAN

Date 6 January 2014

Short-term goals

Goal	Cost (£)	Time frame	Per month
1. New cooker and fridge	800	10 months	80
2. Special holiday	3,500	18 months	194
3.			

Long-term goals

Goal	Cost (£)	Time frame	Per month
1. Vacation condominium deposit	30,000	10 years	250
2. University for baby Lara	25,000	17 years	123
3.			

MONTHLY SAVINGS TOTAL £647

First Steps towards Building Your Personal Wealth

If you follow the steps I've outlined so far in this book, your personal financial status will steadily improve. First, you'll reduce (and then eliminate) your outstanding credit card and other consumer debts. Then you'll begin to save some of your monthly income. In time, you'll build up a four-to-six-month cash reserve as protection against emergencies. And once that fund has been accumulated, you'll begin to focus on and save for other personal goals.

These stages will take time. For almost everyone, they will require some months of effort and self-discipline; for some (especially those who have fallen into serious debt) they will require a few years. But as you go through these stages, many good things will begin to happen to you.

Some of these improvements will be intangible. Your stress level will go down. You'll probably have fewer rows with your partner. You'll sleep better at night. And when you do indulge yourself, you'll find that you can enjoy spending money with less guilt and greater pleasure. As anxieties about money recede and your ability to concentrate on the things you care most about grows, you may find yourself experiencing greater success and satisfaction in your career, your hobbies and your family life.

There will also be some very tangible results. One of the most important will be the growth of your personal wealth. The best way to measure and track this improvement is by creating a Personal Balance Sheet.

Your *Personal Balance Sheet* is a tool for measuring your wealth. It's called a *balance sheet* because it involves listing all your assets (that is, everything of value that you own) and balancing them against your liabilities (that is, money you owe to others).

The balance sheet is a basic tool of business. Every public company must make its balance sheet available to investors and a company with a strong balance sheet (that is, a good accumulation of valuable assets, (including cash on hand) has much better future prospects than a company whose balance sheet is awash in debt.

The same is true for individuals. Drawing up your Personal Balance Sheet today will give you an idea of where you stand in your progress towards accumulating wealth. And it will help you gauge how far you need to go in order to have a level of wealth that will make you feel truly secure for the future.

Use the form on pages 114–116 to develop your Personal Balance Sheet. This exercise is more easily done using a spreadsheet program in which you use or adapt the Personal Balance Sheet form as a template. As usual, I've provided a filled-in sample on the following pages which you may find helpful. It may take you an hour or two to complete this exercise. Most of that time will be spent tracking down figures, such as your current bank balances and the amount due on your home mortgage. As you'll see, the maths required is simple: addition, subtraction and one division (when we show you how to figure your current asset ratio). Use a calculator or spreadsheet and you'll whizz through this exercise easily.

YOUR PERSONAL BALANCE SHEET

Date

Assets

I. Liquid assets (i.e., cash and assets that can be easily sold for their full cash value).

Cash on hand   £

Current account balance

Savings account balance

Shares (current value at which they can be sold)

Bonds (current value at which they can be sold)

NISA (cash/stocks & shares) balances

Unit trusts (current value at which they can be sold)

Other liquid assets

LIQUID ASSETS TOTAL: £

II. Illiquid assets (i.e., assets that may be harder to sell for their full cash value). For each item, list the *liquidation value* – the amount you could realistically get if you had to sell it quickly.

House   £

Other property

Cars

Jewellery

Household goods

Art, antiques, collectibles

Other illiquid assets

ILLIQUID ASSETS TOTAL: £

TOTAL ASSETS (LIQUID + ILLIQUID) £

Liabilities

III. Short-term liabilities (i.e., debts to be repaid within five years or less).

Bills you currently owe £

Credit card balances

Store card balances

Car loan balance

Current bank overdrafts

Revolving credit line balances

Money owed to friends or relatives

Other short-term debts

SHORT-TERM LIABILITIES TOTAL: £

IV. Long-term liabilities (i.e., debts to be repaid in longer than five years).

Home mortgage balance £

Second mortgage balance

Other long-term debts

LONG-TERM LIABILITIES TOTAL: £

TOTAL LIABILITIES (SHORT- + LONG-TERM) £

ANALYSING YOUR BALANCE SHEET

A. How healthy is your financial status today? One key measure is your *current asset ratio*, calculated by dividing your total liquid assets by your total short-term liabilities:

$$\frac{\text{Total Liquid Assets}}{\text{Total Short-Term Liabilities}} = \underline{\hspace{3cm}} = \underline{\hspace{3cm}}$$

Your current asset ratio should be positive (i.e., it should have a value greater than 1.0). The higher the ratio, the better. A good target is 4.0.

B. How bright is your long-term financial picture? One key measure is your *net worth*, calculated by subtracting your total liabilities from your total assets:

Total Assets − Total Liabilities = \underline{\hspace{3cm}}

Your net worth should be positive (i.e., your total assets should be greater than your total liabilities), and it should be steadily increasing over time.

YOUR PERSONAL BALANCE SHEET

Date: *6 January 2014*

Assets

I. Liquid assets (i.e., cash and assets that can be easily sold for their full cash value).

Cash on hand	£468
Current account balance	1,750
Savings account balance	7,570
Shares (current market value)	0
Bonds (current market value)	0
NISA balances	11,590
Unit trusts (current market value)	7,200
Other liquid assets	0
LIQUID ASSETS TOTAL:	£28,578

II. Illiquid assets (i.e., assets that may be harder to sell for their full cash value). For each item, list the *liquidation value* – the amount you could realistically get if you had to sell it quickly.

House	£200,000
Other property	0
Cars	3,500
Jewellery	1,000
Household goods	1,500
Art, antiques, collectibles	0
Other Illiquid assets	0

ILLIQUID ASSETS TOTAL:	£206,000
TOTAL ASSETS (LIQUID + FIXED)	£234,578

Liabilities

III. Short-term liabilities (i.e., debts to be repaid within five years or less).

Bills you currently owe	**£**970
Credit card balances	1,459
Store card balances	475
Car loan balance	4,210
Current bank overdrafts	350
Revolving credit line balances	0
Money owed to friends or relatives	250
Other short-term debts	0
SHORT-TERM LIABILITIES TOTAL:	£7,714

IV. Long-term liabilities (i.e., debts to be repaid in longer than five years).

Home mortgage balance	**£**152,530
Second mortgage balance	0
Other long-term debts	0
LONG-TERM LIABILITIES TOTAL:	£152,530
TOTAL LIABILITIES (SHORT- + LONG-TERM)	£160,244

ANALYSING YOUR BALANCE SHEET

A. How healthy is your financial status today? One key measure is your *current asset ratio*, calculated by dividing your total liquid assets by your total short-term liabilities :

$$\frac{\text{Total Liquid Assets}}{\text{Total Short-Term Liabilities}} = \frac{£28,578}{£7,714} = 3.70$$

Your current asset ratio should be positive (i.e., it should have a value greater than 1.0). The higher the ratio, the better. A good target is 4.0.

B. How bright is your long-term financial picture? One key measure is your *net worth*, calculated by subtracting your total liabilities from your total assets:

Total Assets – Total Liabilities = $£234,578 – 160,244 = £74,334$

Your net worth should be positive (i.e., your total assets should be greater than your total liabilities), and it should be steadily increasing over time.

Net Worth: Your Financial Marker

I have been using the term *wealth* to refer to the level of financial security you have. Maybe the word makes you a little uncomfortable: 'Wealthy? Me? Never!' But don't associate *wealth* only with multiple staffed properties, flying on private jets and Christmas holidays on a large boat in the Caribbean. Any positive sum at the bottom of your balance sheet constitutes wealth – your wealth – which is worth nurturing and building. You may start small but there's no reason why you can't finish (relatively) big – not necessarily in the league of Richard Branson, J. K. Rowling, François Pinault or Oprah, but big enough to make a wonderful difference in your life and the lives of those you love.

The key financial marker for tracking the growth of your wealth is your net worth. As the balance sheet exercise shows, your net worth is the difference between your total assets and your total liabilities. Obviously it's important for that to be a positive number, to begin with. Once you've attained that, your objective should be to have your net worth grow steadily, month by month and year by year. It is the growth in your net worth that will eventually make possible all your short-term and long-term goals, from a new car or a remodelled kitchen to a comfortable, secure retirement.

Four Keys to Building Net Worth

There are many ways to make your net worth grow. Every item shown on your balance sheet has an impact. But for the vast majority of people, there are four keys to the growth of net worth:

- Sticking to a regular programme of saving
- Keeping short-term liabilities under control
- Owning property that gradually increases in value
- Owning shares or other investments that gradually increase in value

So far in this book, we've considered the first two items on this list. In the chapters to come, we'll delve into the latter two.

4

PROPERTY CHOICES

The Financial Impact of Buying or Renting Your Home

Climbing the Property Ladder

The largest and most significant purchase most people ever make – by far – is the home they live in. For most people, their home (whether house or flat) is the largest item on the asset side of their personal balance sheet. Many consider their home to be their primary investment. (This is *not* the best way to think about it, as I'll explain shortly.) For all these reasons, your decisions about property ownership are among the most important financial decisions you'll ever make. This is why I'm devoting an entire chapter to this subject.

The most fundamental decision concerning property is whether to buy or to rent your home. If you're like most people in the UK, your strong bias is towards buying. Nearly everyone I speak to either owns a home (or two), is planning to buy a home or is desperately yearning for the chance to do so. Half the people I meet in the UK seem to feel driven to urge *me* to buy property there too. It is a national obsession.

This bias towards buying isn't wrong. There are distinct benefits to owning a home as opposed to renting. An important psychological benefit is knowing that you are in control of the place where you live. The greatest financial benefit is the potential growth of your home's value and therefore the growth in the *equity* you own in the house, which can be very beneficial, especially over the long-term.

Here's how it works. Most people borrow part of the purchase price of their home getting a *mortgage*, a long-term loan used for buying property. Because the mortgage is secured by the value of the home, the bank or building society has a claim on a portion of the home's value equal to the amount of the outstanding loan.

As the homeowner pays off the mortgage, the percentage of the home's equity that the bank has a right to shrinks and the percentage owned by the homeowner increases. Eventually, when the mortgage is completely paid off, the entire value of the home belongs to the homeowner. The house is theirs, free and clear, representing a large amount on the asset side of their personal balance sheet.

The good news doesn't stop there. In most places, but not all, houses and flats have tended to increase in value over time. This means that when you're ready someday to sell the home you own the chances are good that you'll profit from the sale, perhaps handsomely. You may want to use this profit to buy a larger, nicer home (this is called trading up), perhaps to accommodate a growing family or simply to provide a more enjoyable lifestyle. Some people repeat this process several times until they're ready to scale back to a more modest home – after they become empty nesters, for example – and the profits realised from the sale of their most expensive home help swell their retirement nest egg (or their kids' inheritance).

Many have benefited from climbing the property ladder

in this fashion. It's a financial strategy that works well when used with care. So *most* people should plan on owning the home in which they live – eventually.

But this doesn't mean that everything – including financial safety – should be sacrificed in the interest of buying a home *now*. I've found that many young people in the UK are too eager to hop aboard the property ladder. Under pressure from peers or parents, or led astray by advice from many different sources, they borrow heavily to buy a house they can't really afford. Unable to keep up the payments they fall behind in all their obligations, running the risk of ruining their credit rating for several years and perhaps having to sell the property under duress.

So, rent a home until you can really afford to buy. Money you spend on renting is *not* 'thrown away', 'tossed into a black hole' or simply 'put into someone else's pocket', as some people like to claim. Instead, think of it as a necessary living expense during the years when you are saving to be able to buy a home.

No Deposit? No Way

I strongly urge you not to hop aboard the property ladder until you've saved enough to put down a significant deposit on your home. You can then take out a mortgage to pay the balance of the purchase price.

As you may remember, it was once possible to borrow the entire purchase price for a home. This was known as a *100%* or *No-Deposit Mortgage*. It meant you could buy a property without depositing any money at all. Those days are g-o-n-e! Today the maximum loan-to-value (LTV) mortgage you can get is generally 95%.

(Individual banks can make their maximum LTV lower, typically at 80–90%.) While a 5% deposit makes it somewhat easier to get on the property ladder, borrowing such a large percentage can be risky. If property values fall shortly after you buy and you need to sell your home at that time, the home may be worth *less* than the amount you owe on your mortgage. This is known as *negative equity*. As a result, you may find yourself in debt that you can't get out of so easily. Also your borrowing costs are likely to be a lot higher. In general, the higher the LTV, the higher the interest rate you will pay on your mortgage.

When people buy property they believe or hope the average house prices in their area will have increased from the year before, though the levels will vary widely depending on where you buy or live. In some years the increase has been huge but during other periods house prices have trended lower. This is something that many people are reluctant to believe, even in the face of hard statistics. (The Council of Mortgage Lenders (CML) publishes data showing average house prices each year going back decades at its website: www.cml.org.uk.)

If you bought a house at the top of the market and then had to sell it when prices were low, you would have suffered a big loss. And it's possible, but not that likely, that the amount you'd still owe on your mortgage loan after selling the house would be *greater* than the amount you'd realise from the sale. You'd have to make up the difference from your own pocket.

So, contrary to general belief, house prices do carry some risk of decline. That's why paying up front for a significant percentage of your home's equity is far safer than borrowing without a deposit.

How Much Mortgage? How Much Home?

All right, I've convinced you that borrowing up to the full value of your home is foolhardy. But what amount *should* you borrow? How much mortgage debt is a reasonable amount? There are some rules of thumb that are commonly applied to mortgage debt. Some of these reflect the common practice of mortgage lenders (primarily banks and building societies):

- If you're single, you can usually get a mortgage equal to 3.5 to four times your annual salary. Thus, if you have an annual salary of £35,000, you can probably qualify for a mortgage loan of up to £140,000 (since 35,000 x 4 = 140,000).
- If you're a couple buying a home, you can usually get a mortgage equal to 2.5 times your total salaries. Thus, if you have an annual salary of £35,000 and your partner has an annual salary of £25,000, you can probably qualify for a mortgage loan equal to £150,000 (since 35,000 + 25,000 = 60,000, and 60,000 x 2.5 = 150,000).
- Your monthly mortgage payments should equal no more than 30 to 40 per cent of your take-home pay. Thus, if you have a monthly take-home salary of £3,000, your monthly mortgage payment should be no greater than £900 to £1,200.

These rules of thumb are all right. But I recommend that you be a bit more conservative, especially if you're a first-time homebuyer with no experience of owning property *or* if there's any doubt in your mind about your employment prospects. (And very few people today can honestly say that there's *no* chance they'll be laid off from their jobs or have a drop in income at some point in the future.)

Buying a property by depositing 20 per cent of the purchase price (and therefore taking out a mortgage equal to 80 per cent of the purchase price) will reduce the cost of your mortgage. (Remember, lenders do charge extra interest when there's a small homeowner's deposit because the risk of default on the loan is greater.) It will also help ensure that you won't be biting off more than you can chew. You should certainly steer away from following the prevailing wisdom, which is to mortgage yourself to the max. That can be a prescription for disaster, especially if or when there's a downturn in the economy.

Don't forget that there are many other costs involved in buying a home, including legal fees and stamp duty (property purchase tax). These can add up quickly, draining your bank account. You also need to limit what you spend on home-related items. For example, after buying your home, don't rush out to remodel, add a room, redecorate or buy a houseful of new furniture. If you borrow or use your credit cards for these purchases you'll be carrying even more expensive debt, which could cause financial problems sooner than you think.

Maybe you'll feel a little disappointed after doing these calculations. Maybe you were expecting to spend a lot more on a house, despite the possible risk. Time for an attitude adjustment. Remember the concept of the property ladder: most people trade up from one property to another, living in two, three, four or more homes over the course of a lifetime. It's silly to assume that your first or even your second home will represent your dream house. Instead, be patient. Buy the home you can really afford and let the usual growth in property values, combined with your rising income and savings, gradually lift you to the next level.

Believe me, you'll get much more pleasure out of living happily in a modest house than you'd get out of living in a palace burdened with excessive debt and constant anxiety. I'll discuss Help for First-Time Buyer and Help to Buy schemes later in this chapter.

⪢Alvin says . . .

The amount you borrow should be limited to no more than 80 per cent of the value of the home you're buying. In other words, be prepared to put down a deposit of (at least) 20 per cent of the cost of the house or flat. Thus, if you've saved £40,000 for your deposit, you can afford to buy a house that has a total value of £200,000 (since 40 = 20 per cent of 200). With a 20 per cent deposit (and a good credit history) you will usually qualify for a competitive mortgage interest rate.

Plumbing the Mortgage Mystery

There are many different kinds of mortgages; the varieties are limited only by the ingenuity of banks and building societies. Eager to develop new lending 'products' they can offer or sell, these financial firms are forever devising new variations on the old mortgage theme. Many prospective homebuyers find the proliferation of mortgage types (and the terminology that goes with them) confusing. In this section, I'll try to bring some order to the cacophony of words you'll hear.

Fundamentally, you need to know the difference among three kinds of mortgages: the *repayment mortgage*, the *interest-only mortgage*, and the *endowment mortgage*. The most common is the repayment mortgage. Here's how each works.

- With a *repayment mortgage*, you make a single monthly payment that includes both interest on the loan and a portion of the capital (that is, the amount you originally borrowed). The loan will be entirely repaid at the end of the *mortgage term*, a pre-set length of time which typically ranges between ten and thirty years.

- With an *interest-only mortgage*, during the term of the mortgage, you pay only the interest on the original amount you borrowed. The capital owed remains constant. At the end of the term, the borrower has to repay the entire amount of the capital. Interest-only mortgages tend to be most popular when interest rates are low because the monthly interest payments can be quite modest and manageable. Most lenders have lower LTV maximums on interest-only mortgages and require borrowers to have an investment plan in place in order to pay off the capital at the end of the mortgage's term. The most common investment plan used to be an endowment (discussed next) but borrowers now use other options, such as a stock-and-shares NISA which has lower fees than an endowment.

- With an *endowment mortgage*, you give the bank two payments every month. One pays only the interest on your mortgage loan. The other provides money that is used to buy into a unit trust or other investment vehicle that invests in the stock market. The hope is that the total value of the invested funds (the 'endowment') should grow to equal the principal you owe by the end of your mortgage term. [NOTE: An endowment mortgage used to be thought of as a type of interest-only mortgage. In fact, the terms were often used as synonyms. Currently, they are viewed as separate types of mortgages.]

An endowment mortgage includes life insurance coverage that will pay off the debt if you die during the term of the loan. This is called a mortgage protection policy. Here's the key thing to understand: the endowment mortgage concept relies on the stock market investment growing in line with projections made at the time you take out the loan. Since the performance of stock investments varies, three possible situations may result:

- If the investment grows as predicted, it will cover the capital you owe and at the end of your mortgage term you and the bank will be all square.
- If the investment does *better* than anticipated – if the stock market enjoys a period of significant growth, for example – then your endowment will have earned extra money and, at the end of your mortgage term, you'll receive a lump sum payment for the difference.
- But if the endowment does *worse* than anticipated, you'll end up with insufficient funds to pay off the mortgage. Therefore, you still owe money. This is known as an *endowment shortfall.* When that happens, many people remortgage their homes – that is, they take out a fresh loan to cover what they owe and they start the repayment process all over.

🎀 *Alvin says . . .*

If you have an endowment mortgage, the company that handles the investment part of the scheme (usually referred to as the *endowment company*) should keep you informed as to how your investment is growing by sending you a *re-projection letter*. This letter tells you whether your endowment policy is on track to pay off your mortgage loan or whether there is a risk that the policy will not pay off the whole loan. If there is such a risk, take action! The Money Advice Service website offers sound, practical advice on its website:

https://www.moneyadviceservice.org.uk/en/articles/
dealing-with-an-endowment-shortfall

Because of mis-selling and unexpected shortfalls, endowment mortgages have garnered a bad reputation and are unpopular.

🎀 *Alvin says . . .*

A repayment mortgage is the best choice for most people. Because it involves less risk, it is simply more sensible for the typical homeowner. It pays to be conservative with your personal finances and even more so when you're dealing with something as psychologically important as your home. If you are convinced that an interest-only mortgage is right for you, then make sure you understand all of the provisions and risk associated with it.

Playing Investment Plan Roulette

When weighing mortgage options, many people feel attracted to the interest-only mortgage because the monthly payments are less than with a repayment mortgage. During the 1990s, when the stock market rose rather steadily, endowment mortgages were a popular choice. Back then few people with endowment mortgages had experienced shortfalls when the loan came due. But more recently the stock market has provided a bumpy ride. As a result, many endowment borrowers have been (or soon will be) left without enough money from the endowment to pay off the remaining mortgage – a painful dilemma to face.

According to the FCA, many people with interest-only mortgages are facing a similar prospect: they will not be able to pay off the capital at the end of the mortgage.

Staying on Track

If you take out an interest-only mortgage, then your lender, in accordance with FCA regulations, must make sure you have an investment or savings plan in place to pay off the capital when the mortgage ends. The lenders must also contact the borrower at least once during the term of the mortgage to make sure the repayment plan is still in place. The plans that banks will accept vary and your choices will be affected by the individual bank's loan-to-value (LTV) requirement which is likely to be stricter than for a repayment mortgage. Here are a few of your options:

- Put money into a stocks-and-share NISA to accumulate the needed capital. However, the money is invested in the stock market and there is no way to guarantee that the investment will grow enough to meet the required capital payment at the end of the mortgage.
- Make extra payments to reduce the amount that will

be due at the end of the mortgage term. It's important to make sure there are no penalties involved in making these additional payments.

- Switch to a repayment mortgage. The monthly payments will undoubtedly be more, which will make this option unaffordable for some people. However, if you can make this work, then it is a lower risk choice that will give you some peace of mind.

There are other options available so it's important to talk to your mortgage lender to get a full list of your options and to understand them clearly.

Other Mortgage Choices You Must Make

Once you've decided between a repayment mortgage or an interest-only mortgage, your choices aren't finished. You'll need to make decisions concerning the interest rate you pay on your loan, the term of the loan and other special mortgage features.

Interest Rate Options

How mortgage interest rates are determined varies from one type of mortgage to another. Here are brief descriptions of the most common types of mortgage interest rates, with an explanation of how each one works:

- *Variable rate*. This is the most typical mortgage type. The interest rate varies from time to time. It tends to rise and fall when the Bank of England changes the base rate. However a bank or building society can increase or decrease its variable rate by more or less than the change in the Bank of England rate, or when there is no change at all. Be aware that the variable rate varies between banks and building societies.

- *Tracker rate.* Similar to a variable rate, but it mirrors the movements of the Bank of England base rate. If the Bank of England increases its interest rate, then a tracker has to follow, and the same is true if the Bank reduces its rate or leaves it at the same level.

- *Fixed rate.* Here you pay an interest rate that is guaranteed not to change for a set period of time, typically from two to five years. A few lenders offer 10-year fixed-rate mortgages. During that time, you can be certain that your monthly payments won't change. Fixed rate mortgages are most likely to have an early repayment penalty or early repayment charge (ERC) if you wish to switch or pay off your mortgage before the end of the fixed term. These penalties can be high.

- *Capped rate.* In this hybrid mortgage rate, the interest rate varies but it cannot increase above a specified level (although it may fall if other interest rates decline). Because you enjoy a degree of protection against the risk of higher rates, the capped-rate deal will probably be set at a slightly higher interest rate than with a fixed-rate mortgage although this may vary from lender to lender.

- *Discount rate.* You receive a discount on the standard variable rate for a set period. Not all lenders offer a discount-rate loan any more because tracker rates have become more popular. Ask about it when talking to prospective lenders.

Which of these mortgage rates is best for you? There's no one-size-fits-all answer. It depends on a number of specific variables including current interest rates and the likelihood that those rates will rise or fall in the coming months and years, the length of time you expect to own your home and your degree of risk tolerance (that is, your psychological and emotional willingness to place a financial wager on the economic future).

Consumer interest rates in the UK have varied substantially over the past three decades and longer. These rates charged consumers by banks, mortgage lenders and other financial institutions are strongly influenced by the base rate set by the Bank of England, although other factors also influence the rates charged. Its website shows how the base rate has changed over the years. These interesting and informative statistics can be accessed at:

http://www.bankofengland.co.uk/statistics/Pages/default.aspx

You will see that the rate swings have sometimes been substantial. If you want a forecast about what's likely to happen with the economy and what interest rates are likely to be in the future, you can probably get one from a financial adviser, your bank manager, or the financial media. Unfortunately, these forecasts are about as accurate as forecasts of the weather in the UK – not very. As the American baseball player Yogi Berra, famous for his fractured words of wisdom, once said, 'It's very hard to make predictions, especially about the future.'

My best advice on the subject: if you feel interest rates are likely to go up, look for a fixed-rate mortgage, taking into account how much more you may have to pay for a fixed-rate mortgage compared to a tracker rate, for example. There have been times in recent years when five-year-fixed-rate mortgages have been much cheaper than variable-rate mortgages and not much more expensive than tracker-rate mortgages. However, at other times fixed-rate deals can look uncompetitive. Work out how much of an interest rate rise your budget can take (if any at all) and whether you are the kind of person who will worry if rates rose, even if you can afford it. If so, opt for a fixed-rate mortgage. Don't forget to factor in mortgage fees, broker fees (if you're using a broker) and booking fees. Also, check how much the early repayment charges would be in case your plans change and you need to get out of your fixed-rate deal early. In general terms, the smaller the mortgage you have and the shorter the fixed-rate term you're going for, the more important it is to factor in any fees and charges. If you feel interest rates are likely to go down, choose a variable-rate mortgage, such as a tracker mortgage. If you want above all to protect yourself against a major upward swing, consider a capped-rate mortgage (although these are quite rare).

Mortgage Term Options

As I've mentioned, the term of your mortgage loan is the length of time you'll take to repay it. Naturally, the longer the term, the smaller your monthly payments. However, since you will be making many *more* payments with a longer term, you'll end up paying a lot more in total.

You can save enormously by borrowing for the shortest length possible. You will have to pay more each month but it will save you tens of thousands of pounds over time. Furthermore, you'll be thrilled when you finish paying off the loan at age 45 rather than age 60 and you'll enjoy many more years of financial freedom as a result. So a 20-year mortgage is a much better choice than a

30-year mortgage. And a 15-year mortgage is better still if you can afford it.

However, if it's your first steps on the property ladder, taking a short-term mortgage could be risky. Your financial circumstances could change suddenly and you could end up unable to make the payments. A better strategy might be to take out a mortgage with a 25-year term, but set your payments at a level to repay the loan in 15 years (assuming the overpayments would not trigger any penalties). The higher payments will reduce your total interest costs; however, if your financial circumstances change, you switch to making the lower interest payments required on the 25-year mortgage. If, for example, a couple has to live on only one income (instead of two) for a while, then the lower mortgage payment may prevent them from defaulting, which in turn would wreck their credit and trigger a repossession action.

How you can save with a shorter mortgage term

Suppose you are borrowing £150,000 at an interest rate of 4.25 per cent. The following chart compares the monthly and lifetime cost for a repayment mortgage at various term lengths.

Term (years)	Monthly payment (£)	Lifetime cost (£)	Amount saved (£)
30	767.30	276,260	0
25	842.98	252,894	23,366
20	960.95	230,628	45,632
15	1,163.92	209,506	66,754
10	1,576.73	189,568	89,692

The chart on page 129 offers a vivid illustration of how great the difference can be. Imagine how much you can save in interest costs if you are able to make one extra mortgage payment each year. Can't you think of any better uses for that money than handing it over to your mortgage lender?

Opting for the shortest possible mortgage term will mean that your mortgage payments may be a bit steeper than you'd like, especially at first. But if you're like most young people, you can expect (or at least hope) that your income will gradually increase over the years to come, even following a recession or a period of stagnant economic growth. Remember the economy is cyclical, involving periods of contraction, recovery, expansion, and prosperity. (I know this from direct experience because I have lived and worked through at least three significant recessions, including when I graduated from university and jobs were scarce.) The monthly payment of £500 that's quite painful today (when your annual income is, say, £25,000) will feel much more bearable when your income has increased to £43,000. And when, thanks to your hard work and diligence, your income has grown to £60,000, you'll wonder how £500 ever felt like such a burden.

Other Mortgage Variations

There are several mortgage options available. However, banks increase and decrease their availability depending on the economic conditions at the time and on how restrictive they are being about lending. Here are three other mortgage options you may want to consider if they are available and suitable to your financial situation:

- *Cash-back mortgage.* With this type of mortgage, the borrower get a modest (e.g., £400 cash 'gift' at the time the mortgage is made. Some people choose the cash-back option in order to have extra funds for improving their new home but the mortgage is likely to be a less-competitive, higher interest-rate choice compared with a more traditional mortgage. Instead of being tempted by the 'gift', save your pounds until you can afford to decorate out of the money you've accumulated in the bank.
- *Flexible mortgage.* This offering has also been substantially curtailed by lenders. It allows the borrower to vary his or her repayment schedule. For example, you can pay back your mortgage earlier with no penalty (known as *overpayment*) or take a 'payment holiday' when unexpected financial difficulties arise for a given month. These mortgages can be useful but be wary about overpaying too much without double checking how easy it will be to borrow the money-back if you need it. Some lenders have changed the rules. People who have overpaid may find out they can't have the money back.
- *Current account mortgage.* Here your savings, mortgage and current account are consolidated into a single account. You're given an equity line of credit against the value of your property. Your savings are used to reduce the amount of your mortgage. (In some accounts, the savings amount is nonetheless posted separately from the mortgage.) Your total pay cheque, when it enters the current account, is also automatically applied against the mortgage. Both of these features

131

reduce the mortgage balance on which you pay interest. Then, when you start paying your monthly bills, you tap first into the equity amount released by your pay cheque. This is not a bad system, especially for artists and other self-employed people who may need access to the equity line to help them live through the ups and downs of their income. But it requires real self-discipline. If you overspend you are dipping into your home equity and your savings (if any). The account makes this mistake easy to do by showing a large available balance, posing an enormous temptation. In a worst-case scenario, you could fritter away the equity in your home without even realising it.

- *Offset mortgage.* Here your mortgage and your savings account, which must be at the same bank, are linked using an offset mortgage account. You earn no interest on your savings; however that money is used to offset (i.e., lower) your outstanding mortgage balance. You only pay interest on the difference. If, however, you continue to make your payments at the amount of the actual mortgage balance, not the lower net balance, you will pay off your mortgage more quickly. This option may be suitable for homeowners who want to make sure their savings are accessible during the time they are repaying the mortgage, yet have the benefit of a lower overall interest cost. If they had used the money to overpay their mortgage and then needed the money, they would have to try to borrow back the funds and there is no guarantee that the lender would permit this. If the interest rate on a regular mortgage is exceptionally low, the interest-saving benefits of an offset mortgage are less. In such a case it might be better to keep your money in a regular savings account or NISA.

There are many other types of mortgages available in the UK. Websites like www.moneyadviceservice.org.uk offer good up-to-date information about the types of mortgages, the rates currently available and the loan-to-value (LTV) requirement. I must admit that I do enjoy reading about them and pondering the creativity involved in conceiving and bringing these new products to the market. However, when it comes to mortgages, I am a firm believer in the KISS concept: 'Keep it simple, stupid.' I think this is especially true if you are a first-time buyer. I think it is wise to understand your mortgage totally and mitigate the possibility of any nasty surprises. As you grow more knowledgeable about the risks associated with these more complex mortgages then you can consider them. Personally, I don't like any type of mortgage that is likely to keep me awake at night with even a little worry.

Schemes for First-Time Buyers and Others

As property prices have risen higher and higher over time and as mortgage lenders have become choosier about who they lend to, there has been much discussion about the difficulty young people have or will have getting on the property ladder. In particular, many parents who accumulated most of their net worth through property feel that their children should be buying their first flat or house as soon as they get their first significant job or graduate from university. They deeply, sincerely believe that if people don't buy when they are young adults they will never be able to afford to get on the property ladder. The peer pressure around this issue in the UK is unrelenting. In fact, this premise about property has become a widely accepted truth.

In response to this widespread concern, the government introduced several Affordable Home Ownership Schemes:

New Buy. Permits anyone – not just first-time buyers – to put down a deposit as little as 5% of the property's value when buying new-build flats or houses from builders whose developments participate in the scheme. In early 2014, a variation of the scheme became available across the whole UK housing market, including older houses.

Help to Buy – Equity Loan. Permits first-time buyers and people who want to move to another house to put down a minimum deposit of 5% on new-build homes. The property must be the buyer's only residence. The homebuyer must live in the property; it cannot be rented out. Interest-only mortgages are not permitted. The schemes are interesting in that the governmental agency involved, Homes & Communities Agency (HCA), retains a stake in the property you buy in exchange for the loan it makes to you which helps you to buy the property. When the purchaser of the home puts up 5%, HCA makes the qualifying person or couple an equity loan equal to 20% of the purchase price. This loan is secured by the house, which the HCA has a claim against. In effect, this enables the purchaser to put down 25% of the price of the property and get a repayment mortgage for the remaining 75%. When the property is sold, the HCA is entitled to a percentage of the property's sale price equal to the percentage of the original equity loan still outstanding.

Help to Buy – Mortgage Guarantee. Permits any homebuyer to purchase a new or existing home with a 5% deposit. The government provides the lender with a guarantee on a percentage of the mortgage (typically between 5% and 20%). The homebuyer must live in the property (it cannot be a second home) and it cannot be rented out.

The government is continually refining these current schemes and providing updated information about them. It is also creating new schemes to help people get on the property ladder. Up-to-date details, good explanatory tables, and informative question-and-answer (Q&A) sections about the schemes can be found at the websites below:

www.gov.uk/affordable-home-ownership-schemes/overview

www.newbuy.org.uk

www.helptobuy.org.uk

Don't be shy about asking questions. As a first-time buyer, this is the largest purchase you will have made. You want to make sure you understand all of the costs and potential risks associated with your mortgage. Also there is one key question you need to ask yourself: how long are you planning to live in the property. Given the small deposit required, the longer you plan to live there the better. This will give the property time to appreciate so that it builds up some equity, which increases your overall net worth as well as your financial security.

Your Mortgage Checklist

When applying for a home mortgage, be sure to consider each of the following items. Taken together, they can make an enormous difference in the lifetime cost of your home:

- Make sure your credit and your finances are in good shape. Get a copy of your credit report and review it to make sure there are no problems with your credit history that can be negatively interpreted by lenders. Make sure all of your credit or store card payments are up-to-date. Close any accounts you are not using. The fact that you could potentially use the credit lines on these accounts may cause the lender to lower the amount it believes you can afford as a mortgage.
- Be clear on what you need and want from your mortgage. Do you want to repay the loan as quickly as possible or do you need to keep your monthly payments as low as possible? You can't do both.
- Shop around for the best deal. Packages from different lenders vary widely. On a £100,000 mortgage, saving a single point on your interest rate could save you £18,000 over a twenty-five-year term.
- Let lenders know that you are comparison-shopping. Some may sweeten the deal – for example, by refunding your legal fees or survey costs – to get your business.
- Also, shop around for other home-buying services. For example, before choosing a solicitor, ask about fees. You may be able to save if your mortgage lender agrees to use the same solicitor as you. Ask about policies and restrictions your lender may impose.
- Understand how the interest rate on your loan will be

determined and how it may change when benchmark rates change.

- Make sure that every fee and charge associated with your mortgage is clearly explained and reflected in the paperwork. An itemised list is often the clearest way to capture and see all of them.
- Some lenders will automatically tack on a life insurance policy to your mortgage loan. Ask whether this is required. If not, you may be able to save money by omitting the policy.
- If you are considering working with a mortgage broker, ask whether they work with all the lenders or are restricted to a handful of different lenders. If the answer is 'yes' to the latter choice, then you may be missing out on the best deal.
- Ask about schedules and dates. Make sure your timetable for closing the deal and moving into your home matches the capabilities of your lender.
- Don't sign any mortgage document until you understand what you're signing and approve of the terms. Ask for an explanation of any clause you don't comprehend and insist that everything you're told orally be reflected in writing.

For further information, consult the Council of Mortgage Lenders. They offer a range of useful publications on home buying. Their website can be found at:

www.cml.org.uk.

For easy reference purposes, key items to consider when applying for a mortgage are summarised in the chart that follows.

YOUR MORTGAGE CHECKLIST

When applying for a home mortgage be sure to consider each of the following items. Taken together, they can make an enormous difference in the lifetime cost of your home.

☐ Be clear what you need and want from your mortgage. Do you want to repay the loan as quickly as possible, or do you need to keep your monthly payments as low as possible? You can't do both.

☐ Shop around for the best deal. Packages from different lenders vary widely. On a £100,000 mortgage, saving a single point on your interest rate could save you £18,000 over a twenty-five-year term.

☐ Let lenders know that you are comparison-shopping. Some may sweeten the deal – for example, by refunding your legal fees or survey costs – to get your business.

☐ Also shop around for other home-buying services. For example, before choosing a solicitor, ask about fees. You may be able to save if your mortgage lender agrees to use the same solicitor as you. Ask about policies and restrictions your lender may impose.

☐ Understand how the interest rate on your loan will be determined, and how it may change when benchmark rates change.

☐ Make sure that every fee and charge associated with your mortgage is clearly explained and reflected in the paperwork.

☐ Ask whether you must purchase home insurance through your mortgage lender. If so, you may lose most or all of what you save on your lower mortgage interest in the form of higher insurance premiums.

☐ Some lenders will automatically tack on a life insurance policy to your mortgage loan. Ask whether this is required. If not, you may be able to save money by omitting the policy.

☐ If you are considering working with a mortgage broker, ask whether they comply with the Mortgage Code. If the answer is no, don't use them.

☐ Ask about schedules and dates. Make sure your timetable for closing the deal and moving into your home matches the capabilities of your lender.

☐ Don't sign any mortgage document until you understand what you're signing and approve of the terms. Ask for an explanation of any clause you don't follow, and insist that everything you're told orally be reflected in writing.

☐ For further information, consult the Council of Mortgage Lenders. They offer a range of useful publications on home buying. Their website can be found at www.cml.org.uk.

Ask the Tough Questions, and Insist on Getting Answers

In any case, when you're mortgage-shopping, be certain you fully understand your options. Both the charges you are accepting and the commitments you are undertaking should be crystal-clear before you sign any document.

Your banker may be a wonderful person but sometimes they may not be great communicators. (If they were they'd be teachers, politicians or hosts of advice programmes on radio and television!) Your banker may fail to explain the penalties, such as the prepayment penalties, with sufficient clarity. Sometimes this is because he or she doesn't fully understand the rules himself or herself. In other cases, he or she understands the mortgage contract but has forgotten how to explain it in terms ordinary humans can follow. Don't be shy about asking for an explanation and ask again until you *really and clearly* understand the answer.

> ### ✉ *Alvin says . . .*
>
> Get it in writing. When you have complicated questions about the provisions of your mortgage, have the lender point out the answers to your questions on the contract itself and ask him or her to explain underlying key provisions. (Then take the time to read them.) Does this sound pushy? Maybe so, but remember that lenders are competing for your business. Make it clear that you are prepared to visit the banks or other lenders in the area if you're not satisfied with the terms of the service you receive and you may be pleasantly surprised by the change in attitude.

Overpaying and Remortgaging

Overpaying Your Mortgage

I've mentioned that some people like to have the option of overpaying their mortgage – that is, making more than the minimum payment each month as often as they can afford to do so. The advantage of overpaying is that you save enormously on interest over time, even when your extra payments are relatively small. Eventually, you can pay off your mortgage some months or years ahead of schedule and begin living a mortgage-free life earlier than you expected.

There is, however, a subtle disadvantage to consider. When you make extra mortgage payments, you are placing your cash into an investment vehicle (your home) that is considered *illiquid* – that is, sometimes difficult to sell. In a worst-case scenario, you might need access to the cash that is locked up in the value of your property during a time when house prices are falling or the economy is in turmoil, causing banks to tighten their lending and credit requirements. Under these circumstances, it may be better to have the cash sitting safe and sound in a building society account.

Refinancing Your Mortgage

The issue of penalties for early repayment is relevant to another mortgage strategy question – namely, when to consider *refinancing* or *remortgaging*.

First, a bit of background. As I've mentioned, like other interest rates, mortgage interest rates charged by banks and other lenders vary from time to time. In times of inflation, the rates tend to rise; in times of price stability or when the Bank of England eases (i.e., increases) the money supply to stimulate the economy, interest rates tend to fall. When mortgage rates fall, people who've taken out loans at relatively high rates of interest begin to think seriously about refinancing; that is, replacing their higher-interest loan with a new loan at a lower rate. This means, in effect, paying off the old loan using money borrowed at the new, lower rate. The idea is to save money by reducing the monthly interest charges you pay.

Is refinancing to save on mortgage interest a good idea? It can be. You will definitely save on interest payments when interest rates go down significantly. But there is a downside. Many UK lenders impose penalties for early payment of your original loan on a fixed interest rate mortgage. These penalties can be quite steep. For example, if you refinance during the first five years of the mortgage term, you may have to pay a full year's interest as a penalty or up to five per cent of the amount you borrowed. It's important to know what penalties your bank imposes and to take them into account in deciding whether or not it pays to refinance. You also need to consider the costs involved in taking out the new mortgage. The application fee, valuation fee and solicitors' fees may amount to £700–800 or even more. However, some of the usual mortgage charges may *not* apply if you remortgage with the same lender that gave you your original loan. And if you switch lenders, the new firm may willingly waive or pick up some of these charges as a reward for bringing them your business.

A key consideration is how many months or years it will take you to recoup the cost of the prepayment penalty as well as any fees associated with the refinancing. This is a simple calculation. Calculate the difference between your former higher payment and your new lower mortgage payment to find out how much money you are saving each month. Then divide the total prepayment penalty and fees by the amount of your monthly savings. The resulting figure is the number of months it will take you to negate or offset the total cost of the penalty. Generally speaking, if you can recoup the cost in three years or less, then it is probably a good decision to remortgage and pay the penalty. If it takes more than three years to recover the penalty, then it may only be a good idea if you can lock in the lowest possible mortgage rate for five to ten years, although ten-year fixed-rate mortgages are not plentiful.

So, the key lesson here is to take nothing for granted. Ask about the deals you can get. And, as always, don't rely purely on oral responses. Get the answers in writing so you know you can depend on them.

⋈ *Alvin says . . .*

When interest rates fall, consider refinancing your mortgage. But be sure to consider:

- The cost of early repayment penalties
- The cost or fees associated with taking out the new loan
- The time and effort involved in making the switch
- The number of months or years it will take you to offset the total prepayment penalty and other fees because of the money saved on the lower monthly mortgage payment

The Gold-Plated Castle

You know the old saying, 'My home is my castle.' It captures a very common attitude. If it means simply that your home is a cherished refuge from the troubles and worries of the outside world, that's wonderful. But if it means that you feel entitled to decorate it in a style befitting a Renaissance warrior prince, think again. Your home may be your castle – but does it have a moat wide enough and deep enough to keep creditors from knocking on the door?

This isn't an idle question. Refurbishing or redecorating a home to a good standard can easily increase the value of the property way beyond the amount of money that has been spent. This is one of the reasons, perhaps the primary one, why decorating is enormously popular in the UK and why many of the families strain their finances by succumbing too often to the lure of new furniture, drapes, rugs, appliances and a new conservatory. I recommend that you treat decorating as a step-by-step process. Don't give in to the temptation to use your credit cards to do the whole house at once. The pressure of carrying the debt incurred in spending money on fix-ups is likely to negate the pleasure you'd otherwise derive from living in the house.

The home-as-castle attitude leads to over-spending and over-borrowing. It also helps produce renovations whose value is unlikely to be gained back when it comes time to sell. Thoughtfully planned DIY projects can enhance your home's value. But many people fix up their homes in ways that are so, well, unique (a polite way of saying 'overly personal' or 'odd') that whoever buys the house from them will probably want to rip out the insides and start all over again. Those who make this mistake will almost never get back the money they've spent on renovations.

Property as an Investment

Is property a shrewd investment? It depends on how you define the word *investment* and what you hope to gain from the money you spend on a home.

Unlike most of the things you buy for your own use and enjoyment – cars, clothing, furniture, appliances – property does tend to increase in value over time, provided it's well-maintained and located in an area where other people want to live. There are exceptions, however in different regions of the country. Also, the property market, like any other market, is subject to downturns. If you need to sell your home during a slump, you may actually lose money on the deal.

However, most people find that they can sell their homes for more than they paid for them. By that definition, then, a home can be a good investment. And in certain places at certain times, the growth in the value of houses has been so rapid that some lucky people have found themselves enjoying enormous windfalls. Maybe you've heard stories about people who bought houses for £30,000 or £40,000 during the 1960s and were able to sell them for many times that amount today. For these people, a home turned into a fabulous investment that may have helped to secure a comfortable retirement.

Can you 'Retire on the House'?

Despite the stories you may have heard, it's a bad idea to try to build a personal investment programme totally around your home. This is true for several reasons:

- The super-fast growth of home values during the 1960s and 1970s as well as during the late 1990s and early 2000s was an aberration, not the norm. You can't automatically expect the same kind of growth in the future.
- Unlike other investments, the home you live in doesn't produce income. When you own shares, you usually receive dividends; when you own bonds, you receive interest payments. But a house or flat doesn't send you any cheques (unless, of course, you rent out a room). In fact, you have to spend money to heat, light, maintain, refurbish and repair it. I know quite a few people who maintain their property minimally while they live in it. I suppose this is done in order to keep their ongoing costs low. They only do the major work and decorating when they are planning to sell the property and want to get the maximum price they can – including all of the recent costs of upgrading the place.

- As your home's value increases so do the values of other properties. So, when the time comes to sell your home, you'll probably find that buying the *new*, usually smaller, home into which you'll move eats up most of the profits made from selling the old home, unless it is part of your financial planning to considerably downsize when you retire.

For all these reasons, don't expect to 'retire on your house'. Life just doesn't usually work that way. Instead, buy a home you can enjoy living in and take care of it in a way that enhances your comfort and pleasure. If you profit handsomely when you sell it, fine. (Later in this book I'll outline the kind of investment portfolio you *should* be developing to fund your retirement and other long-term goals.)

Buying to Let

What about investing in properties other than your own home? Here, the picture is a little different.

Buying property to rent out is very popular, especially among older people. My friend Sheila, a public relations and communications specialist for public and non-profit organisations, is saving her pounds in hopes of buying a place to rent out as an ongoing source of income. She is pursuing this dream even though she herself lives in a rental property! For Sheila, buying property isn't a matter of owning her own castle; rather, it's a business venture. She knows and accepts a basic truth about buy-to-let: it is a strategy for capital growth more than income. She hopes that when she eventually sells the property it will have increased in value substantially over the time she owns and rents it out.

If you dream of becoming a property mogul, approach the process of properties in a total business-like manner. Do a lot of homework before you buy. Make certain that you're buying a property that is likely to command a worthwhile rent: one in a location and with an architectural style and amenities that will be popular among the mass of renters.

If you plan to handle the property directly, rather than using the services of a property manager, then be prepared for the complications of being a landlord. You'll be responsible for all the various nuisances involved: the paperwork related to leases and taxes; collecting rent regularly (and when necessary pursuing negligent renters for the money); keeping the property in repair; complying with all the government and local authority rules and regulations; working with contractors and utility companies and so on. When the heating breaks down or the roof springs a leak, *you* will be the person who gets the irate phone call – and you can count on it happening most often after midnight on Saturday!

When considering the profit potential in managing property, weigh all the costs involved. They will probably be greater than you expect. Wear and tear on an apartment can be high and the expense of repainting, refinishing floors and fixing wiring and plumbing between tenants can be shocking. And you should assume that the property will be vacant for an average of two months a year. If you can't carry the expenses without income for that long, you could easily get into trouble.

Having offered all these warnings, let's end on a more positive note. For those who are prepared to do all the necessary homework and to spend the time required to maintain the property and deal with tenants, investing in property can be a fine source of income and growing wealth. If you buy a well-chosen flat or house, mortgage it conservatively and collect a rent that's large enough to cover the mortgage cost and all other expenses as well as providing a significant profit, you can do well. You may be able to buy a second property with the profits thrown off by the first and then eventually a third property and a fourth. Some people end up building modest property empires that they devote full-time to managing.

If this idea appeals to you, go for it! But expect it to be just as much work as any other full-time job.

Buying with a Partner

One final point about buying property. If you're part of an unmarried couple that plans on buying a home together, you should really have a partnership agreement that includes a clause about how the property will be handled if the relationship breaks up. More once-loving people end up fighting over property than any other subject (save children).

In the next chapter, I'll offer more advice about how to manage the volatile combination of love and money.

Alvin says . . .

Expect the rules and requirements for mortgages to change, primarily trying to prevent practices that caused problems in the past. One FCA rule requires lenders to determine if the borrower can afford the mortgage if, for example, payment were to increase. This means that lenders must delve more deeply into the borrower's income and spending. This rule is designed to prevent people from borrowing more than they can afford in a market where property values and interest rates may change in unexpected ways.

5

Financial Partnership

Love, Marriage, Family and the
Money Choices They Bring

The Talking Cure

I'm no expert on love and romance. Like most people, I've had a few heartthrobs and heartbreaks. One thing I *do* know, however, is the effect of money on a love relationship. At its worst, I can tell you, it's far from pretty.

Experts say that most personal problems – spats over the children and the in-laws, arguments about careers, even sexual differences – can be overcome with a little goodwill and compromise. But conflicts involving money are different. For most couples, these are harder to resolve. One reason is that attitudes towards money are deep-seated, largely unconscious and often virtually non-negotiable. So disagreements about how money should be earned, managed, spent, saved, invested and passed on can be almost impossible to reconcile.

Therefore, it's important to talk about your differing attitudes in regard to money *before* making a serious life commitment to one another, whether through marriage, living together or some other big joint step such as buying a home, having a child or chucking it all to move to Tahiti. This is not to say that talking about money *afterwards* isn't important and valuable too – of course it is. And if you find that you've become involved in a serious relationship with someone without having talked through your financial attitudes, don't despair; you can deal with those issues now. My point simply is that sooner is better, before assumptions harden into positions that must be defended at all costs.

All these years later, I still remember one couple on my TV programme who discovered that they had radically different points of view about money which they'd never discussed in five years of living together. Just a week after we filmed with them, she left him, convinced that their differences about money could never be overcome and that her personal financial well-being was in danger from her partner's seeming indifference. Is this an extreme case? Yes, but don't think it could never happen to you.

Your Money Partnership Quiz

On pages 152–154, you'll find the 'Your Money Partnership Quiz'. Make two copies: one for yourself, one for your partner. Answer the questions separately (no peeking at your partner's responses). Then set aside an hour or two to go through the questions together and *seriously* discuss the areas of agreement and disagreement that you uncover. You'll learn a lot about the values you and your partner hold in regard to money, the (often unspoken) assumptions you each make and the dreams, fears and desires you each have concerning money.

You'll also learn a bit about how to listen to one another and talk to one another in a mutually respectful, sympathetic way. These skills can go a long way towards helping you keep your relationship strong and healthy, even when serious arguments about money arise.

YOUR MONEY PARTNERSHIP QUIZ

Each partner should answer the following questions individually. Then review and discuss your answers together. There are no right or wrong answers. Instead, the quiz is designed to launch a conversation between the two of you about your attitudes towards money and your financial goals, dreams and desires. The objective is to learn about yourself and your partner, and to lay the foundation for developing a money plan for life that you can *both* be happy with.

YOUR CURRENT MONEY SITUATION

☐ How satisfied am I with my current income?

☐ How satisfied am I with my career and income prospects for the near future (one to three years)? How about for the longer term (three, five, ten or twenty years)?

☐ Are there things I would like to do to improve my career and income prospects? If so, what are they? Am I taking steps to pursue those goals?

☐ How satisfied am I with my current degree of financial security?

☐ How satisfied am I with my current saving patterns?

☐ How much money do I have set aside for an emergency? Is it enough?

☐ How much debt do I currently have? Is my current debt load comfortable or is it too great?

☐ How satisfied am I with my current spending patterns? Why?

☐ What would I like to spend less money on?

☐ What would I like to spend more money on?

☐ What do I wish I could buy that I can't currently afford?

☐ How much money do I have invested in shares, unit trusts, bonds or other financial investments?

☐ How satisfied am I with the current returns on my investments? Why?

HOW YOU MANAGE YOUR MONEY

☐ Do I enjoy managing money? Specifically, how do I feel about paying bills? About saving? About investing?

☐ Would I like to turn over the management of my money to another person if I could?

☐ Where do I turn for advice and information about money?

☐ Do I have a professional money adviser? If so, am I satisfied with the help he or she gives me? Why or why not?

YOUR FUTURE FINANCIAL PLANS

☐ What plans do I have for a family? Do I plan to have children? If so, how many? When?

☐ If I plan to have children, do I expect to have enough income to raise them in a style I consider appropriate?

☐ What 'special things' (beyond basic food and shelter) would I want to provide for my children? Which are most important? Do I expect to be able to afford them?

☐ What level of income do I hope to enjoy ten years from now? Twenty years? Thirty years?

☐ What lifestyle would I like to enjoy ten years from now? Twenty years? Thirty years?

☐ How long do I intend to keep working?

☐ What is my idea of a rewarding retirement?

☐ Where do I hope to live in retirement?

☐ What activities do I hope to pursue in retirement?

☐ How much income will I need to enjoy my desired retirement lifestyle?

☐ How much savings will I need to make my desired retirement lifestyle possible?

MONEY AND YOUR PARTNERSHIP

☐ To what extent do my partner and I share income and expenses?

☐ Am I satisfied with the current sharing of money rights and responsibilities between me and my partner? Why or why not?

☐ What money matters, if any, would I prefer not to share with my partner? Why?

☐ Do I have any other emotional or psychological concerns related to money that this quiz has not uncovered? If so, what are they?

Your Family Money History

Another valuable exercise is shown on pages 156–158. This involves creating Your Family Money History. It's a process you can work through together with your partner. It includes creating a simple 'genogram' or family tree, for you and your partner. This is a starting point for an in-depth discussion of the role money played in both your families and how this influences your present attitudes towards money.

A couple of points regarding the creation of your genogram:

- In a traditional family tree, squares are used to symbolise males and circles to symbolise females. If you or your family are part of a non-traditional partnership (two males, for example), simply ignore the shapes of the symbols.
- If births, remarriages, adoptions or other events added additional members to any generation of your family, just add squares or circles as needed to include all the relevant family members.

As you'll see, the purpose of the genogram is simply to provide an easy way to talk with your partner about the ways in which money was handled in your family and the meanings money took on over time.

YOUR FAMILY MONEY HISTORY

Create a simple 'genogram' for yourself and your partner. Fill in the names of the family members as shown in the sample genogram (family tree) on page 157. The two boxes at the bottom of the diagram represent you and your partner. Prior generations appear above. Draw horizontal lines to represent marriages or other committed partnerships. Draw vertical lines to represent parent-child relationships. Add brothers, sisters, aunts, uncles and other relatives to the genogram as appropriate, depending on which family members were significant in your upbringing and family history.

Your Money Genogram

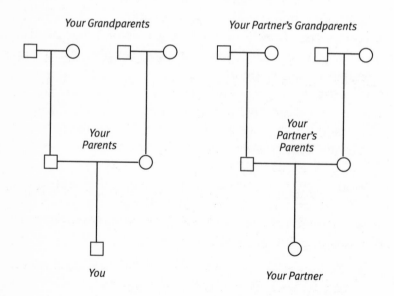

You

Your Partner

Your Money Genogram · EXAMPLE

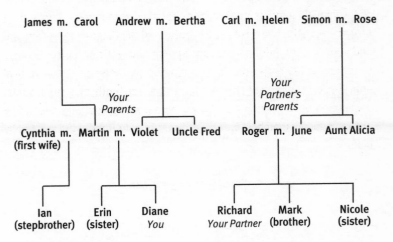

Next, for *each* person named on your genogram, answer the following questions as fully and accurately as you can:

1. What work did s/he do?

2. How did s/he use money? Was s/he a 'saver', an 'investor', a 'spender', or a combination?

3. What kind and amount of assets or property did this person accumulate?

4. What stories regarding money and this person were told in your family?

5. Is there any money connection between this person and you (for example, by way of gift, loan or inheritance)?

6. Do you consider this person a role model, good or bad, for the handling of money? Why or why not? What lessons can you learn from this person's personal history?

7. How did this person's work, property, giving, spending, or other money activities impact the rest of the family?

Family Money Patterns

As you work your way through the Family Money History with your partner, you'll find yourself discussing how money was earned, accumulated, invested, enjoyed, used and lost in your families. You may remember events, family stories and sayings that you haven't thought about for years and you'll undoubtedly discover things about your partner that you never knew. Among the themes you may want to explore as you carry out this exercise are:

- How was money viewed in the families you and your partner grew up in? Was it a source of worry, tension and discord? Was it a source of happiness and pride? Was it viewed as something to hoard against disaster or something to spend freely, even carelessly? Or was there a good balance between saving and spending, as well as between accomplishing short-term and long-term goals?
- Was money discussed openly (for example, around the family dinner table)? Or was it regarded as a 'secret' to be talked about only behind closed doors by your parents?
- What were the preferred 'truths' about money that you inherited from your family? Were there certain sayings or lessons concerning money that were passed on from generation to generation? (For example, did you hear sayings like, 'A penny saved is a penny earned', 'Take care of the pennies and the pounds will take care of themselves', or 'The rich get richer, the

poor get children' when you were growing up? Did they unconsciously influence the ways you feel about and behave with money?

- What rights and responsibilities regarding money did children have? Did they receive pocket money or allowances? Was money given as a 'treat', a reward for good behaviour, or a 'bribe' to win affection? Were they expected to earn money? To save money?

- What assumptions were made about the differing roles of men and women in regard to money? Was one sex expected to assume the responsibility of earning money? Did one sex manage the family finances? Did one sex handle most of the shopping and spending? Did one sex handle the investing? Did family stories, jokes and remarks convey any stereotyped assumptions about money and men, or about money and women?

- How did money figure in the family history? Was there a 'family fortune', either in the past or present? If so, how was it amassed? Who controlled it? What disputes about money occurred in the family? How were they resolved? Were there certain family members with notable attitudes towards money or relationships towards money? Was there a family member generally regarded as a 'miser', a 'spendthrift', a 'worry-wart', a 'financial genius', a 'money magnet', a 'squirrel', a 'generous giver' and so on?

- How did money figure in the important family events? How was money used or regarded in connection with significant holidays (Christmas, for example) or family milestones (weddings, anniversaries, births, deaths)? What messages about the importance or meaning of money were conveyed by these activities?

As you talk with your partner about these questions, you may find patterns emerging. Money habits (like other ways of behaving) tend to run in families. If your father was a feckless dreamer, forever throwing money away on get-rich-quick schemes that 'can't fail' – but always did – look back a generation or two. It's likely you'll discover that *his* father, or perhaps an uncle or a grandfather, exhibited much the same behaviour. Uncovering patterns like these can serve as an early warning device about your own tendencies. Chances are good that the idiosyncrasies of your family members will reappear in your own life at some point.

When I was around ten years old, my mother inherited a small sum from her uncle. About six months later, I heard my grandmother ask what had become of the money. Mother admitted that it was all gone. I still remember the tone of disappointment and frustration in my grandmother's voice as she asked, 'Didn't you save *any* of it?'

I mention this episode because I can see in all my brothers and sisters – including me – the same tendency to quickly spend any money that comes into our hands. For all of us, saving is a constant struggle. Recognising this as an inherited trait makes it a little easier to deal with and keep in check. Nonetheless, you must never forget that it will always and ultimately be your responsibility to fix the situation and remain in control.

Talking about Money

The Money Partnership Quiz and the Family Money History are designed to provoke an in-depth conversation about money with your partner. For many people, it will be the first such conversation ever. And you may find that it raises some uncomfortable issues. You'll probably uncover differences in your attitudes towards money, your desires and fears, and your experiences in handling money. That's all right! Differences can be the spice in a relationship, provided you approach them in a spirit of mutual acceptance, honesty and respect.

Try hard to avoid blaming, criticising and attacking. There is no one right way to manage money and virtually everyone is gifted with *some* valuable talent or attitude in regard to money. Even in the classic case where a frugal, highly responsible, conservative person is partnered with someone who cannot keep track of money for more than five minutes and is much better at spending money (usually on needless things) than at earning or saving it – even in a case like this, *both* partners should realise that they can learn useful lessons from one another. Frugal Fred can teach Spendthrift Susan the pleasures (such as feeling financially secure) of accumulating money and gaining control over her impulses; but Susan can also teach Fred about the fun of (occasionally) tossing self-control to the wind and using money simply for the joy it can bring to oneself and others.

Don't use the facts and stories that emerge from your Family Money History dialogue as tools of arguments. Believe me, you'll be tempted to do so! The next time your partner does something that annoys you, you'll want to blurt out, 'You *would* squander half your bonus on a night out with the boys – it's just what your granddad used to do!' or, 'No wonder you can't stop buying shoes – you're just picking up where your mum left off!' When this urge surfaces, bite your tongue. When family secrets are turned into weapons, it only fosters mistrust. Deal forthrightly with your current disagreements and don't drag the past into the conversation – as relevant as it may seem.

Above all, don't allow money differences to turn into a battle for control of the relationship. The goals and dreams that each of you harbour are important and worthwhile, and the best shared money plan is one that gives you *both* a chance to make those dreams come true.

▶◀ *Alvin says* . . .

- Use the Family Money History exercise as a chance to explore your assumptions, feelings and beliefs about money.
- Approach your differences with your partner in a spirit of openness and acceptance; no one has a monopoly on financial wisdom.
- Your goal should be a money plan that satisfies both of you, not a 'victory' in a struggle for control and power.

Sharing the Responsibilities

The overall responsibility for your shared financial future must be 'owned' by both partners. It's foolish and unrealistic for anyone to say (or feel), 'Oh, I never have to think about money – Jane [or Harold] handles everything.' This doesn't mean, however, that both partners must participate equally in every money activity. One outcome of your shared money conversation should be an honest appreciation for the unique skills and interests that each of you has. Try to talk through what you both enjoy doing with money and use the insights you develop to decide who should do what in your partnership. Of course, issues such as the amount of time you each have available should also be taken into account. You need to determine which partner is best equipped to:

- Pay the routine bills (mortgage or rent, heating, telephone, credit cards). If you use direct debit, make sure the dates work best with the cash flow into your bank accounts
- Shop for food and other routine items
- Monitor and reconcile your bank, credit card and store card account(s)
- Handle spending money (possibly including giving an 'allowance' to the other partner)
- Shop for special purchases (major gifts, furniture, appliances)
- Save for short-term goals (holidays, for example) and long-term goals (a home deposit or retirement)
- Make investment and asset allocation decisions
- Monitor investment accounts
- Deal with banks, brokers, insurance companies and financial advisers

In most relationships, these chores will be divvied up between the partners. In some cases, a chore will become a shared responsibility, perhaps with one partner taking the lead. For example, consider the important issue of making investment and asset allocation decisions. You might agree that you will research investment ideas and make *tentative* plans but that you must run your decisions by your partner before actually writing a cheque to the broker – with the understanding that they will not second-guess you unless they have some distinct concern, special knowledge or insight to offer.

Exactly how you divide up the money chores is

completely up to you, of course. And you may want to change the division of labour from time to time, as your interests, abilities, needs and time availability change. This is an important and natural part of any mature relationship anyway. There are just two important rules to remember:

- Be certain there's a clear understanding between the two of you as to who is responsible for a particular task and what approval (if any) is needed from the other partner. This is the only way to avoid needless misunderstandings and rows: 'But I thought *you* were handling the insurance bills!' 'Wasn't it clear that I expect to be consulted any time you want to spend more than £100?'
- Don't allow yourself the luxury of total, blissful ignorance concerning any money activity. The fact that your partner handles the monthly bills (for example) is no excuse for you to be unaware of how much they amount to and how they impact your budget. Remember that separation, divorce, disability and death are unfortunate, unpredictable facts of life. If you suddenly find yourself having to handle *all* the financial chores, you want to be at least generally familiar with what's required. So make it your business to share the basic information about every money activity with your partner at least every quarter or twice a year.

When I meet a young couple today, I must say I'm always surprised when I find out in casual conversation that one partner has decided that handling money is the *other* partner's responsibility. Sometimes they make this decision and cling to it even when they know that their partner is undisciplined, disorganised, bad with numbers or otherwise unfit to manage their joint finances. Today it is essential to share the responsibility for your finances, to build on each other's strengths and to help each other improve their weaknesses. This way you grow together in your skills at handling money as well as in your progress towards your financial objectives and dreams.

Putting it in Writing

Once you've gone through the exercises described in the earlier parts of this chapter, you're just a short step away from creating a full-blown partnership agreement, setting out the financial rights and responsibilities that you and your partner will take on.

I can hear your objections already: 'A *contract* defining our love? How cold! How unromantic!' And you may want to add, 'We don't need some kind of financial agreement, anyway. We have so little it wouldn't even be *worth* fighting over.'

I understand your feelings. I've been young and in love, and I know that young partners are rarely preoccupied with legal and financial matters. And the media do encourage us to think of 'cohabitation agreements' and 'pre-nuptial contracts' as the special prerogative of the rich and famous. Their divorces certainly get front-page coverage repeatedly in the tabloids and on celebrity-oriented television programmes. While you probably don't have assets like Posh and Becks to worry about, you should still think about establishing a partnership agreement. It is important for both unmarried and married couples, especially if:

- One or both partners have significant net worth (£100,000 or more) or significant annual income (£70,000 or more).

- Either of you has children from a previous partnership.
- Either of you has inherited assets (cash, shares, property).
- Either of you owns a business.

The partnership agreement is simply a way of setting down on paper the plans and understanding you've reached together through the open discussions we've described in this chapter. Creating it will have several powerful benefits:

- Putting your agreement in writing forces you both to think clearly about how you want to handle your money matters and to express your understandings with no ambiguity or confusion.
- It also forces you both to think through *all* your financial rights and responsibilities without ignoring or forgetting any of them.
- Having a written document to refer to prevents future rows due to honest forgetfulness about what you've agreed.
- In the event of a break-up, the agreement provides a basis for splitting your assets and liabilities fairly, preventing needless (and expensive) wrangling.
- It will also help to protect children and others who may have a legitimate claim on part of your resources.

Frankly, creating a partnership agreement is also an important stepping-stone in the development of a lasting relationship. The process calls for honesty, trust, respect and generosity from both partners. If you can work through the process together and emerge with an agreement you are both happy with, your love will be greatly strengthened. And if you discover that the process is impossible because you have disagreements that are simply too deep-seated to resolve – well, maybe you need to question whether it makes sense to plan a lifetime commitment to a partner whose basic values you don't and can't share.

You may think that the amount of money or other assets you have doesn't justify the bother of producing a written agreement. Maybe so. But many couples are a little startled to discover how *much* they've accumulated when they take the time to produce a written list or personal balance sheet.

Furthermore, there are almost certainly assets of emotional and psychological significance that ought to be handled appropriately, even if their monetary value isn't enormous. (Think about the ring you inherited from a dear, close relative; that painting you bought during your first holiday together; or your pet budgie, for that matter. Is it really clear who ought to have it if you two break up?)

Finally, having an agreement as a basis for your financial future is important even if you feel fairly poor today. Perhaps the little business you launch tomorrow may grow into a tidy, profitable operation over the next five years. If that happens, your agreement will spell out who owns what portion of that business in the event that it becomes an issue. And it'll be relatively easy to revise the agreement as needed should your circumstances change dramatically – far easier than starting from scratch.

For all these reasons, it's worthwhile to create a partnership agreement even if the two of you have only modest financial means.

Partnerships and the Law

What I've been referring to as a partnership agreement actually includes several components. They're listed in the checklist on pages 169–70. Taken together, the various documents that go into the partnership agreement serve to spell out how the financial rights and responsibilities of the two partners will be shared and how assets and liabilities should be handled in the event of a break-up or the death of a partner.

You'll need the help of a lawyer in putting your wishes into legal written form. But you can save time and money by thinking and talking through the details with your partner before visiting a lawyer, who can then use his or her legal knowledge to create documents with the proper form and wording.

YOUR PARTNERSHIP AGREEMENT CHECKLIST

Most committed couples should put in writing the following kinds of financial partnership documents. The advice of a lawyer is strongly recommended and all relevant documents should be considered together, so that the provisions of one document do not clash with those of another:

☐ Cohabitation agreement (if unmarried) or pre-nuptial agreement (if married). This document spells out who will pay for which living expenses, who controls which assets (such as individual or joint bank accounts), who is responsible for debts incurred by each partner, what should happen if one partner is disabled or otherwise unable to contribute financially and how assets will be divided in the event of a break-up.

☐ Post-civil partnership agreement (also called a post-nuptial agreement). Unlike a pre-nuptial agreement, a post-nuptial agreement is legally binding. It also may cost a few thousand pounds to properly set up. Post-nups don't have to cover all of your assets. You can use it to protect what your children from a previous marriage will inherit, assets that you have inherited, as well as your ownership in a business you had before the marriage. If, however, the post-nup is clearly unfair to one party, the courts may choose not to enforce it.

☐ Agreement concerning titles and deeds to any properties. This document spells out whose name (or names) will appear on the titles and deeds for any land, houses, flats or other properties you own.

☐ Wills for each party. These documents spell out what should happen to your assets upon your death. With the help of a lawyer, committed partners should make wills that are designed to work together, so that children or other dependants will be properly taken care of no matter whether Partner A dies first, Partner B dies first or both partners die at the same time (as in a car crash, for example). More on wills in Chapter 10.

☐ Parental responsibility agreement. This document spells out how children of either or both partners should be cared for in the event of a break-up or the death of either or both partners.

Cohabitation agreements (between unmarried couples, including same-sex couples) and pre-nuptial agreements (between married couples) have somewhat different legal statuses in the UK today. Cohabitation agreements are generally considered legally enforceable, on the grounds that two unrelated persons who enter into a contract together deserve to have their wishes recognised and enforced.

By contrast, pre-nuptial agreements may or may not be upheld by a court. (Pre-nups are not enforceable in England and Wales but are legally enforceable in Scotland.) The reason for this is that, over the centuries, an extensive body of law has grown up which spells out how courts are supposed to divide property and income, and to provide for the maintenance of children in the event of a divorce. Courts are supposed to consider the assets and the requirements of both parties, the needs of children, the standard of living to which all parties are accustomed, the length of the marriage and other factors in determining a fair divorce settlement. The terms of a pre-nuptial agreement will probably influence the settlement but they may not control it.

However, courts have been showing an increasing readiness to give weight to pre-nuptial agreements when making divorce settlements. Post-nups are already legally enforceable as long as they are not unfair to one party. If you and your spouse do agree on fair divorce terms as embodied in a pre-nup or post-nup, the chances are good that the acrimony and cost of your break-up can be greatly reduced.

Playing Fair

I've been touting all the good things a partnership agreement can do for your relationship. But these benefits
will be negated if you don't handle the process in a way
that is fair to both of you. Here are some tips to follow
to make sure that your agreement is truly mutual:

- Be sure your legal advice is even-handed. Choose your
  lawyer together. He or she should be equally sympathetic and attentive to the interests of both partners.
  If you have any concerns about the fairness of the
  agreement, or if you have large or complicated interests
  that are important to protect, consider having a lawyer
  for *each* partner – at least to review and bless the
  finished document.
- Work to equalise the balance of power in your relationship. Neither partner should accept any agreement
  under duress. If there is any provision you feel uncomfortable with or don't understand, don't go along for
  the sake of harmony. Insist on having your questions
  answered (by a professional if necessary) and make
  certain that the final agreement respects your legitimate concerns.
- Be prepared to compromise as needed. In the best
  agreement, neither partner gets everything he or she
  wants. Instead, both partners should expect to give up
  some things in return for getting others.

When Baby Makes Three (or More)

When I meet couples with a newborn baby or with one on the way, I'm often amazed at how ill-prepared they are to deal with the financial realities of parenthood. Maybe the denial they experience is a hormonal thing. Whatever the cause, many young parents seem to assume they can go on living with a child just like single people, making no changes in their spending or saving patterns, as if the baby were a lifestyle accessory rather than a living, breathing human being with steadily increasing needs and wants.

The fact is that raising a baby – or two, or three – from birth to university is very expensive. One financial services company, Liverpool Victoria (LV=), has published and disseminated data for the last decade that shows the amounts you can expect to spend on raising a child to age 21. Liverpool Victoria's data shows a nearly 60 per cent increase over the decade between 2003 and 2013, with total costs slowly but surely approaching £250,000. This amount varied by region and socioeconomic status. For example, the Child Poverty Action Group (CPAG) reported in the same year that the total cost is nearly £150,000 to raise a child from birth to age 18 (this estimate does not include university fees and other associated costs).

The drivers of the increase are not surprising. Below is data from the Liverpool Victoria report showing the percentages of increase in selected categories over the decade since the company started calculating the costs:

Education (private school costs not included)	up 123.5%
Furniture	up 66.9%
Childcare and babysitting	up 60.9%
Holidays	up 41.3%
Pocket money	up 31.6%
Food	up 29.2%

Feeling frightened yet? The responsibilities of parenthood are very serious and a baby is something that must be planned and saved for. However, I would take figures like those shown above with a grain of salt. For one thing, remember that the total cost of child rearing (whether it amounts to £250,000, £150,000 or some other total) isn't demanded in a lump sum in the delivery room but, rather, is paid out in dribs and drabs over eighteen or more years. These expenses tend to increase gradually over time. During the first year of life, the cost of nappies, juice, cereal and a few items of equipment can usually be kept within affordable limits; by contrast, the clothes, shoes, toys and activities of a twelve-year-old can be quite expensive – and even more so as they get older. Hopefully your career, and the income it generates, will grow as your baby does.

The largest single expense in data reported is for education. And that number does not include private education. Strictly speaking, private education is not a necessity but rather a luxury, since state schools are available free of charge to all. Does the quality of a private education justify the additional financial burden it imposes? Only you can answer that question.

Investigate the schools in your area, gather the opinions of other parents (and their children) and weigh the trade-offs you'll have to make to invest several thousand pounds a year in tuition. In the end, the choice you'll make will be a personal one.

For what it's worth, I'm convinced that the most important factor in a child's success is not the kind of school he or she attends but the attitudes instilled by the parents. If you raise your youngster to love reading, to be curious about many subjects and to aspire to an interesting career, the chances are good that he or she will get a lot out of school no matter what kind of school it is.

The cost of a university education, however, is an obligation I'd take very seriously. Today, most of the lucrative careers require a university degree and tuition costs (as well as living expenses during three or four years of college) continue to rise steadily. If you're a parent (or a prospective parent), university expenses ought to find a place in your list of long-term savings goals or your child's long-term savings goals.

Fortunately, you'll have eighteen years in which to amass the amount needed and there are tax-free plans available that make saving for a child's education easier. These include Junior ISAs, National Savings and Investments (NS&I) Children's Bonds (which accumulate interest tax-free until your child is twenty-one years old) and various tax-free savings plans offered by friendly societies (that is, mutually owned assurance companies). Investigate these and begin saving sooner rather than later. The more time you allow for the brilliance of compounding to work on the money you save and capital growth to increase the value of the money you invest, the easier it'll be to amass the sum (even when you start by saving and investing small amounts) needed to pay for the years of schooling.

> ### 🎀 Alvin says . . .
>
> Grandparents and parents should consider opening a Junior ISA (called a 'JISA') for their young ones. This could be a one-time lump sum at the child's birth or small contributions periodically over years (up to the annual limit set by the government). Over the long-term, investing this money prudently in the stock market, even using low-cost tracker funds, offers an opportunity for growth and dividend reinvestment that could yield the money to pay university fees or provide the deposit for the purchase of a young adult's first property.

The majority of people won't be able to save enough to pay for the total cost of their children's university fees. This means the children will have to take out loans to pay for their education. Going into significant debt to pay for advanced education that is unlikely to yield significant financial benefits for years has remained a highly emotional discussion in the UK since university fees were first introduced. I feel it's the new financial reality that everyone must accept and find ways to make it work, rather than resist. There will not be a return to the 'good ole days' of free university education in the UK, and so a more proactive approach is to start creating a personal financial strategy that will work for your family and your children.

Having been born and gone to college in the US, I have only known an educational system in which, unless you were rich or very well-to-do, one would most likely have to go into some debt (i.e., take out a student loan) to pay for one's education. I considered the borrowed money an investment in myself. I understood that paying back the loan would be a burden in exchange for the long-term benefits that a good education provides. I did not know exactly how I would use my education, but I did clearly understand that it gave me an elastic skill – i.e., how to think in different ways – that I could adapt to different opportunities that came my way. This same skill will help distinguish anyone in his or her career over time and open the doors to opportunities they often could not have imagined at the time they graduated from university. Each person has to remember and believe in this as he or she is taking out the loan to cover the university fees and then paying them back.

Before the child leaves for university, the parents should sit down with him or her and establish an itemised budget for each semester or each year. This should be done whether or not the child is borrowing money to pay for university fees. For those young people who are not borrowing money, the budget will be their first attempt to manage their money and live within their means – an important life lesson. For people who are using loans, the budget will provide them with a realistic view of how much they will need to borrow and the lifestyle choices they will have to make during their university years so that they don't run out of money or borrow excessively. Remember to build in some entertainment and treats for yourself. All studying and no play can make for a dull young adult.

The process of applying for student finance packages is detailed in step-by-step instructions at a useful website:

www.gov.uk/student-finance

Note that the process is different if you are a student from Northern Ireland, Scotland and Wales. The website provides access to the different procedures.

The website covers the types of financial resources available to pay for one's education. They include different types of loans, grants, scholarships, bursaries, awards and allowances. Some are from the government; some are from your university; and some are from your local authority. (Funding is also available from charitable grants. These can be researched on Family Action's website: www.family-action.org.uk.) The government's site clearly explains the differences, the qualifications needed, the amount you will receive, and the application process for each; it also contains links to other sites that may be sources of additional funding for your education. Loans must be repaid after graduation; however, the other types of financial help do not have to be paid back.

One of the most useful tools at the website is the calculator that enables one to determine approximately how much of a loan and maintenance the student will qualify for. If there's a shortfall in what the student needs, the website can be used to find other sources of money to apply for that probably won't have to be repaid.

At this point, it is important for parents to understand that students need to take control of their finances and begin making decisions for themselves.

What the Student Needs to Know

Depending on your circumstances, your temperament, and your self-discipline, you may want to take a part-time job while you are at university. For some people this may be too much for them to handle, especially if their courses demand a lot of study time. When I was in university I always worked a summer job in order to save up the money to cover some of my living expenses during the academic year. Here again, it's important to refer to the budget that you created for yourself (with your parents' assistance) before university and have refined during the time there. This will help you determine how much of your summer earnings you want to save. [Note: Use a cash NISA for your savings so you won't have to pay any taxes on any interest earned.]

During the academic year, it's important to remain self-disciplined about how you use the money allocated to cover your living expenses. If you have a maintenance grant, for example, this money will be paid into your account at regular intervals. With the substantial increase of the balance in your bank account will come the temptation to go out, to have a good time, to spend those pounds! The money will be burning more than a hole in your pocket; it will also be burning a psychological hole in your self-discipline. Resist the urge to intentionally or unintentionally squander the money and then have to struggle for the remainder of the term. Try the following in order to keep cash flow regular:

1. Keep the majority of the money in a savings account and make *one* transfer from it once a week (or once a month depending on your self-discipline).

2. Take advantage of the special low-cost student current (with overdraft protection) and savings accounts that most banks offer.

3. Transfer the same amount each time. This should be the budgeted amount of your living expenses for the designated period of time. This will regularise your cash flows and help to mitigate some of your spending impulses. Some people divide their money into daily envelopes of cash in order to avoid overspending. Use whatever strategy works for you.

4. Make sure you have a little financial flexibility built into your budget for a little spontaneity. Make sure that whatever you do will satisfy you enough so that you return to your self-discipline pleased with your choice and how good you feel about yourself.

5. Avoid using credit cards. Many parents give a credit card to their children who are in university to 'use in an emergency' unless they give their permission otherwise. Adhere to your parents' restrictions and don't use the credit card needlessly.

6. Take advantage of the student discounts available in the local area stores and businesses where your university is located.

7. Learn from former and current students. Websites like The Student Room (www.thestudentroom.co.uk) bring together millions of current and former students who share information about all aspects of their university lives and experiences. Perusing the website, I found the videos contain lots of practical and useful information, and the articles cover a surprising array of topics ranging from intimate personal concerns to global issues.

By handling your money well during your university years, you will remove one of the frequent sources of stress that affect people. There is no need for you to add this to the other academic and personal stresses (like dating and break-ups) that you will have during your university years.

While you are studying, your loans will be accruing interest at the rate of inflation (as measured by the Retail Price Index) plus a fixed percentage. Once you've graduated, this interest rate charged on your outstanding loan balances changes. Upon graduation you will have to repay your loans. This may take quite a few years depending on the amount you borrowed. I think it took me more than a decade after graduating from college to repay my educational loans.

The good news is that you don't have to start paying back the loans until your income reaches a certain threshold. Currently that is set at £21,000. If you are earning £21,000 or less, no repayments are required and the rate of interest charged on the outstanding balance drops to only the rate of inflation. No additional percentage is added.

Once your income is above £21,000, you are required to pay nine per cent per year of any amount over the threshold. So if you are earning £27,000, your income is £6000 over the threshold. Nine per cent of £6000 equals £540. That's the amount of your loan you must repay over the course of the year. The monthly payment would be £45, which is £540 divided by 12 months. Through your employer, this money is automatically deducted from your pay in the same way that taxes are.

When your income goes over £21,000 the additional points are added to the inflation rate, increasing gradually until your income reaches £41,000. At this income level and above, the interest on the loan accrues at the same rate it did while you were studying – that's the inflation rate plus a fixed percentage.

Again, it may take many years to pay off your loans depending on how much you borrow. Add to that the cost of bank loans associated with attending graduate school and a recent college graduate with a Master's Degree can end up paying two loans as soon as they begin working. [NOTE: Educational loans from banks are repaid in the traditional way, not based on your income as educational loans from the government are.]

A good education gives you skills that will serve to open doors to many opportunities for you over your lifetime. It won't provide a smooth, steady path to ever-greater responsibilities, success and pay. Virtually no one's career, with or without an education, works that way. However, with your education you increase the likelihood that you will be able to turn those opportunities into success – personally and financially. And at some point in your life and career, you will look back and think the loans (plus interest) you used to pay for your education were a small price indeed for what it yielded.

Affluenza: the Spreading Blight

One of the biggest financial problems I see among some teenagers and young adults grows out of the increasing *prosperity* of many British families. In the first edition of this book, I called this *affluenza*: the sense of entitlement that infects the money attitudes of many well-off and wannabe-well-off families. Today, the term is a pseudo-psychological condition, widely associated with the defence of a US teenager in Texas who was charged in a drink-driving manslaughter case and given a light sentence. A psychologist testified that affluenza – that is, the teenager's very privileged and pampered upbringing – inhibited his ability to see the real-life consequences of his irresponsible behaviour.

Personal prosperity results in a paradox because most parents are of two minds: they want their children to benefit from the greater incomes they've achieved and the relative wealth they've accumulated, yet they don't want their children to be spoiled, spending frivolously and excessively, unwilling to work hard, unable to cope with adversity and unrealistic in their expectations. For these families, achieving the right balance is an ongoing challenge.

I still vividly remember a family who had received a large payoff from selling a successful window-glazing business. I interviewed the three grown-up sons, all of whom were either non-working or working at undemanding jobs. Curious, I asked them point-blank, 'Do you think that your family's financial good fortune has taken away your own sense of ambition?' Without hesitation, they all answered, simply and honestly, 'Yes.'

One symptom of affluenza is the drop-off in employment by teenage youngsters. Fewer kids work at part-time jobs as a way of earning pocket money or saving for tuition. Instead, some just look to their parents for the money. Things have changed a lot from my own boyhood in the 1960s and 1970s, as well as from the lives of friends and acquaintances who grew up in the

1980s when lots of kids from many socioeconomic backgrounds worked at fast-food shops, groceries, car washes and other local places. Nowadays, many teenagers, especially those with well-off parents, actually look down on such work as beneath them.

Don't misunderstand me, I don't advocate paid employment for every teenager. Part-time work can cause problems, especially if it interferes with school work or with worthwhile activities such as sports and clubs. But it can have many good effects as well. Looking back, I can see that part-time jobs helped my friends and me to learn such lessons as the importance of hard work, the discipline of budgeting and saving, and the pride of achieving a goal through our personal efforts. Along with classroom schooling, this was a good training ground for adult life.

So, when your children reach their teenage years, don't dismiss the notion of part-time work or encourage them to regard the idea as something unpleasant or unworthy of them. In moderation, it can be a wonderful training ground for money lessons they'll benefit from for a lifetime.

Early Lessons in Money Management

In any case, I *do* advocate having children help around the home from an early age – not for pay, but simply as a way of shouldering part of the responsibility for keeping the family going. The smallest youngsters can help to set the dinner table, take out the trash and make their beds. Older kids can be assigned such chores as caring for the family pet, washing the car, doing the laundry and helping with the grocery shopping. Is this financial advice? Strictly speaking, no. But when kids learn from an early age that life involves responsibilities as well as fun, they develop attitudes that will make them smarter handlers of money.

It's also beneficial to give kids regular pocket money and to require that they manage some of their own recurring expenses through that allowance. For example, they might be expected to use their allowance to pay for bus fares, cinema tickets, games, toys, or school supplies. The lessons this teaches are many: how to create and stick to a simple budget; how to save money towards a goal; how to choose among competing priorities; how to shop and spend wisely.

Almost every youngster will make a financial blunder or two. Ten-year-old Matt may get to a video game arcade and, caught up in the excitement, spend more money than he can really afford; fifteen-year-old Nancy may blow her allowance on a shopping trip with friends and wind up with no money to pay for next week's lunches. When this happens, bail them out – one time. Take the opportunity to teach them a lesson, (firmly but not heavy-handedly. Then, if the problem recurs, make the child fix it. Perhaps Matt can earn a little money by walking the neighbours' dogs for a week; Nancy can do some babysitting. If he or she has no choice but to borrow money from Mum or Dad, handle it as a business transaction: write up the debt and the repayment schedule and make your youngster stick to it.

If instead you simply provide your child with the money he or she needs to undo the mistake, or make a loan and 'forget' to insist on repayment, you will be teaching exactly the *wrong* lessons. You'll convince your child – unconsciously, but powerfully – that no matter how irresponsibly he or she behaves, there will always be someone around to pick up the pieces. Remember the woman in Chapter 2 who had run up significant store card debts, but she knew her Dad would pay them off? That's the direction you are heading in.

I've met many thirty- and forty-year-olds who are still trying to unlearn this faulty childhood lesson; for example, the adult going through a divorce whose first instinct is to move back in with his or her parents or to borrow money from them so as to avoid having to scale back a comfortable lifestyle.

Set the Right Example

Most importantly, parents should teach their kids how to handle money responsibly through the power of personal example. This means getting your own act together: identifying and exorcising your own financial demons, getting debt under control, launching and maintaining a savings programme along with all the other steps I've discussed (and will discuss) in this book. Children are amazingly observant. If they see you thinking before you spend and making careful, deliberate plans for saving money and building the family wealth, they will learn to behave in the same ways without a lot of scolding. If they see you doing the opposite, they'll likely do so too.

One way in which too many parents send the *wrong* message to their children centres around gift-giving. I interviewed one mother who admitted – proudly! – that she'd bought a gift for each of her three children every single week of their lives, a six-year-old habit by the time I met her. 'I love to see the look in their eyes when I hand them a present,' she declared. Meanwhile, perhaps unsurprisingly, the family didn't have a penny in savings.

Gift-giving has a way of getting out of hand, especially

on birthdays and at Christmas time. We all love giving (and receiving) gifts. A thoughtful, appropriate present is a lasting source of happiness that deepens the bond between people. But the orgy of buying we see at Christmas time is another thing altogether. When a child (or an adult, for that matter) is swamped with ten or fifteen expensive toys, games and other presents, the real meaning of the holiday and the true joy of exchanging gifts are both lost. Each individual gift is diminished in value. Often, a week after Christmas, the child is hard-pressed to remember more than one or two presents and he or she may not even know who gave them what. Overwhelmed with competing demands on his or her attention, the child responds by becoming bored. Half the toys end up broken; the other half wind up under the bed or in the back of the closet. What a waste of energy and money!

I'm sure that most parents are at least somewhat aware of this pattern. Why do they continue to give in to the madness? I put part of the blame on advertising and our consumerist media. But only a small part. The real responsibility lies with parents. In too many cases, they equate gifts with love – at least unconsciously – and lavish their children with presents as a way of proving their devotion. And perhaps they hope to buy an equal amount of love from their children in return.

Once again, I'm wading into deep psychological waters. Hopefully, the exercises you've done to examine your own money attitudes and the role of money in your upbringing have given you some awareness of the existence of emotional patterns like these. If you've fallen victim to this syndrome, make a vow to change your behaviour, beginning with the next holiday season or birthday. Buy a few meaningful gifts and then spend time with your family rather than spending more money on them. The result may be a day that goes down in family lore as the best ever.

The Costs of Divorce

I can't conclude a chapter on financial partnerships without a word on the costs of divorce.

You've probably heard some of the statistics. They're fairly staggering and consistent. Over 40 per cent of all UK marriages can now be expected to end in divorce. As a result, a great number of families are headed by just one parent and the vast majority of these are single-mum families.

The rising rates of divorce entail serious social costs. There are many studies trying to quantify the effects. In the US, where the problem has been studied in depth, statistics show that fatherless children are five times more likely to commit suicide, nine times more likely to drop out of school, ten times more likely to abuse drugs and twenty times more likely to end up in prison. Anecdotal evidence suggests that the impact of divorce is similar in the UK.

Aside from this, however, there's no doubt that divorce involves heavy costs on the individual level. To begin with, the process of divorce is a burdensome one: the average legal fees incurred by each parent undergoing a divorce are substantial – tens of thousands of pounds. And over the long-term, every member of a broken family is apt to suffer financially. It's obviously far harder to maintain two households than one on the same income and many divorcing mothers (who generally obtain custody of young children) are forced to return to the workforce sooner than they expected or, if they've been working all along, to get second jobs to make ends meet.

Some groups, including those with fundamentalist Christian views, use these facts to support their contention that divorce should be made far more difficult to obtain. I don't agree. For some people, divorce is the only way out of an impossible situation. For some women in particular, it may save them from serious physical or mental abuse. Forcing people to stay in bitter, destructive marriages is not the answer to the problems of divorce.

Instead, my advice for minimising the destructive effects of divorce on your life is consistent with my general suggestions for managing your financial partnership:

- Look before you leap. Make choices about marriage with your eyes wide open. In particular, be certain that you and your partner have compatible attitudes towards money before you tie the knot. That way, you can at least minimise the chances that financial troubles will lead to a break-up.
- Use a thoughtful and fair pre-nuptial or post-nuptial agreement to guard the wellbeing of both partners and of any children in the event a divorce becomes inevitable.
- While you're married, stay informed about your family finances, keep debt under control and maintain a healthy savings plan. This will help reduce your chance of becoming so dependent on your spouse (or anyone else) financially that you have no choice but to remain trapped in a destructive relationship. It will also enable

you to stay on track financially if a break-up does happen.

- Make divorce a last resort. Be willing to try counselling or psychotherapy as long as there is hope of saving your marriage. And have the maturity to balance your personal quest for self-fulfilment with the inevitability of compromise and sharing that marriage entails.

Love is wonderful. But it's no excuse for behaving in ways that are unrealistic, immature or self-destructive. Thinking hard about the financial impact of your life decisions will help prevent money matters from becoming the cause of a marital break-up – and give your love for one another a far better chance to thrive.

6

INVESTMENT BASICS

First Steps in Building Your Personal Wealth

Saving, Investing and Speculating

Many people think of *saving*, *investing* and *speculating* as being the same thing. In fact, they're quite different:

- *Saving* is putting money into a virtually risk-free financial vehicle, where it can grow slowly and safely over time.
- *Investing* is putting money into financial vehicles with some degree of risk in the hope of seeing the money grow significantly over time.
- *Speculating* is putting money into financial vehicles with a high degree of risk in the hope of enjoying rapid growth.

Both saving and investing *should* have a place in your personal money plan and speculating *may* have a place (though a limited one). But you need to be conscious of the purpose as well as the potential rewards and risks of each of these activities. The failure to delineate and understand these distinctions clearly leads to serious investment mistakes. In particular, it leads people to take greater-than-necessary risks with investment vehicles they assume are safe – especially the stock market.

Savings Come First

As I've already suggested, your *first* financial goal should be to build up savings to protect yourself in case of an emergency. In Chapter 3, I urged you to set a goal of accumulating the equivalent of four to six months' living expenses. This money is your emergency fund. It should be put into an interest-bearing account with little or no risk, such as a savings account at a building society or a cash NISA. Your goal is to have this money earn the highest rate of interest available at the time.

Don't plan to invest (and certainly not to speculate) until after you have accumulated your emergency fund. Moreover, the money you use for investing should be separate from it.

Basic Investment Vehicles

Once you've accumulated your emergency cash fund and are ready to consider investing, you'll find that there are many choices of investment vehicles – that is, types of investments (also called *securities*). Those suitable for most people are:

* *Shares.* A share is a security representing part-ownership in a company. When you purchase a share, you are buying a small part of the company and are entitled to a portion of its profits. These profits are generally paid to the shareholders annually in the form of *dividends*. In addition, if the revenues and profits of the business increase over time, then the market value of the company's shares should also increase in value above the price you paid for them. If this happens, they can then be sold at a profit, known as a *capital gain*.

- *Bonds.* A bond is basically an IOU. When you buy a bond, you are lending money to a company, a government agency or another institution. The institution that issues the bond promises to pay you a fixed amount of interest at regular intervals over a set period of time (the *term*). It also promises to repay the amount borrowed (the *principal*) on a fixed date, which is known as the *maturity date* of the bond.

- *Unit trusts.* A unit trust is a portfolio of securities (usually shares or bonds) created by an investment company or other registered financial services company. When you invest in a unit trust, you are buying a portion of that portfolio and you will share in the dividends or interest, as well as the increase (or decrease) in value of the collective investments. The portfolio can be managed or unmanaged. If it is managed, then a professional called a *portfolio manager* or *investment manager* selects the stocks and/or bonds that are bought into and sold out of the portfolio in accordance with the trust's stated investment objectives (such as income or capital growth). If the unit trust is unmanaged, its objective is to provide the same total investment return as a designated index, such as the FTSE 100 Index. Hence the underlying portfolio consists of the shares that make up the specified index. Unmanaged unit trusts are widely referred to as *tracker funds.*

- *OEICs (Open-ended investment companies).* An OEIC is also a collective or pooled investment that, instead of being set up as a trust, is set up as a limited liability company. OEIC investors buy into a portfolio that offers returns in the form of dividends, interest and capital gains like all pooled investments. The critical difference between a unit trust and an OEIC is how their respective prices are quoted. A unit trust price is a two-sided quote, consisting of a *bid price* (at which a customer's sell order is executed) and an *offer price* (at which a customer's buy order is executed). In contrast, an OEIC has only one price. It is the *net asset value (NAV)* of the underlying portfolio and it is calculated at noon each business day. All customer orders to buy or sell are executed at the NAV. If the order is entered before noon, then the current day's NAV is used. If the order is entered after noon, then it is executed when the next day's NAV is calculated. Commissions are added to the NAV when a customer buys an OEIC or they are subtracted when a customer sells an OEIC. Customers find an OEIC's one-price structure easier to understand. As a result, many unit trusts are converting to OEICs. For simplicity's sake and because their basic underlying structures are so similar, I will discuss unit trusts and OEICs together.

- *Exchange-traded products (ETPs).* While exchange-traded products are a type of pooled investment, I put them in a separate category because they trade on a stock exchange like ordinary shares. (Unit trusts and OEICs do not trade on a stock exchange. They are bought from and sold back to the financial service firm that created the portfolio.) This popular type of security offers many of the features of a unit trust (such as diversification and low costs) and each share represents part ownership of the underlying portfolio and its return; however, ETPs can be bought or sold throughout the trading day.

Within these categories, there are many variations: numerous kinds of shares, bonds, unit trusts, OEICs and ETPs, each designed to cater to a particular type of investor or investment objective. As you'll see, they range widely in their suitability for the average investor. So, don't assume that all investments in a single category are similar. The wise rule is: know what you are buying.

There are also many other kinds of investments you'll see touted. Some are *derivatives*, such as options and futures, while others like spread betting and real estate investment trusts (REITs) are quite complex. Generally, these are quite speculative (that is, high-risk) and *not* suitable for the beginning investor.

Some people consider such things as wine, antiques, fine art, precious metals, rare books and postage stamps as investments. These, too, should *not* be chosen as investment vehicles by the average person. Most of those who sink their money into such collectible items lose more than they gain; the only ones who profit (besides the dealers) are a few collectors with deep knowledge of the field, inside connections and good luck. Of course, if you love pictures or pottery or Persian rugs, by all means buy some and enjoy them. If they grow in value, wonderful! But don't bet your home or your retirement on them.

Later in this chapter, I'll discuss, in detail, shares, bonds, unit trusts and ETPs, which are the investment vehicles of choice for the overwhelming majority of prudent people. But first let's evaluate how ready you are to take those first steps into investing.

> **⋙ *Alvin says* . . .**
>
> Remember – money in savings should be insulated from short-term loss. Money put in investments must be amounts that you *can* afford to lose (at least in part).

Realities of Risk

When the time comes to consider investing, many people completely ignore the risk factor. Even worse, they ignore their own emotional reactions to risk. To see what I mean, try the following simple test.

Imagine I gave you £1,000 in cash as a gift, free and clear. You are on your way to your favourite store to spend this windfall on whatever your heart desires. Now imagine that, when you arrive at the store, you discover that you somehow lost £200 on the way. (Maybe it slipped out of your purse or wallet.) How badly would that loss bother you?

If your answer is, 'Not very much – after all, I still have £800,' then imagine the amount you lost was £300. How do you feel about *that*? What about £400? What about £600? At some point, you'll find that your sense of anxiety and dismay (even in thinking about this imaginary situation) kicks in. The higher the figure, the greater your emotional risk tolerance.

Here's another way to think about risk. Imagine that you've accumulated £1,000 in a safe and secure savings account. You know exactly what you are going to purchase with the money. However, instead of your money growing, it's shrinking. How would you feel if it shrank from £1,000 to £800? Would that loss in buying power make you feel unsettled and nervous? What if you could only purchase £700 of what you wanted with the £1,000 you had saved? Would you feel cheated that your money had lost so much of its value?

When I use these tests with typical investors, it becomes clear that most are not nearly as risk-tolerant as they believe and that they don't understand the different types of risk that affect their money. Being too conservative over the long-term can be as risky as being too speculative in the short-term. If you want further help in determining your own attitude towards risk, try one of the risk self-assessment quizzes or evaluation forms available on many financial websites, or ask the financial services firm you use if it has a risk-assessment quiz or tool that it recommends.

I think a prudent first step in considering your personal investment strategy is to ask yourself, 'How much risk am I willing to accept?' But what exactly is risk? Many definitions have been suggested but the most commonly used one is this: *risk is the possibility of financial loss*. If I had a pound for every time somebody asked me to recommend a totally risk-free security, I would almost be as rich as J. K. Rowling. If I actually found one (which would require more than a little bit of sorcery) I would most certainly be richer than Ms Rowling and qualify for an OBE! In truth, *no* investment is completely free of risk. No matter what investment vehicle you put your money into, there is always at least a small chance that you may lose some or all of your money. But the degree of risk varies greatly from one type of investment to the next. For example, if you invest in the shares of a small, relatively unknown new company, the possibility that the company will go bankrupt and that you will lose your entire investment is quite significant. By contrast, if you invest in gilts – that is, bonds issued by the British government – the possibility of loss from a decline in value of the security is very, very slight. It would probably take some kind of worldwide financial disaster to cause Her Majesty's government to refuse to pay off its debts, in which case collecting the interest on your bonds would probably not be your only worry!

Alvin says . . .

Risk, in reality, is far more complicated than the risk of losing a certain percentage or amount of your money. It's also about the loss of the value of your money. It's important to distinguish between two key words: the *amount* of money and the *value* of money. The value of your money in the safe, interest-bearing bank account is not protected against effects of inflation. Over time, as the amount of money in your account is earning interest and increasing, its real value in terms of purchasing power may be declining due to inflation. So, while the *amount* of money in the bank is safe, its *value* is not.

The risks involved in investing, therefore, run along a spectrum from very high to very low, depending largely on the kind of investment vehicles you choose. The Risk Pyramid on page 199 offers one possible presentation of the risk spectrum, from a building society savings account to derivative instruments such as futures and options. (Don't worry if some of the terms on this chart are unfamiliar to you now; I'll explain them later.) Depending on your personal risk tolerance, you may choose to spend most of your time at the bottom of the pyramid (in the low-risk arena) or venture more boldly towards the middle and top of the pyramid with at least a portion of your money.

There *is* a rationale for accepting somewhat greater risk: namely, the potential for greater gain. But for now, I want to stay focused on the downside of risk, since I believe so many investors, especially novices, underestimate this.

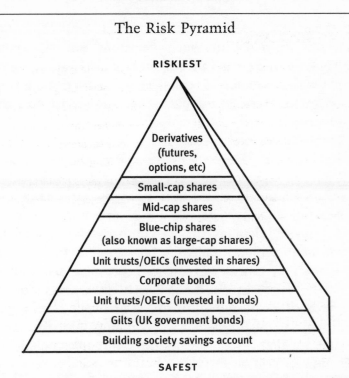

The Risk Pyramid

RISKIEST

Derivatives (futures, options, etc)

Small-cap shares

Mid-cap shares

Blue-chip shares (also known as large-cap shares)

Unit trusts/OEICs (invested in shares)

Corporate bonds

Unit trusts/OEICs (invested in bonds)

Gilts (UK government bonds)

Building society savings account

SAFEST

I've not included Exchange Traded Products (ETPs) in the Risk Pyramid because the risk profile of each depends on the index or commodity whose performance it is seeking to match. An ETP that seeks to match the performance of a broad market index would have risk characteristics of a unit trust, while a gold ETP would have the characteristics of a commodity future.

Kinds of Risk

In fact, the concept of risk is a little more complicated than the risk spectrum might suggest. There are actually several distinct kinds of risk, each of which can affect the value of your investments in different ways. It's important to know a little about each kind of risk so that you can make intelligent decisions, not only about *how much* risk you can accept but also about *which* kinds of risk you need to consider when developing your investment strategy for both the short-term and the long-term.

The kinds of risk include:

- *Company-specific risk.* This is the possibility that shares or bonds issued by a particular company will decline. This may happen for a variety of reasons: a drop in the demand for the company's key products, bad management, increased business competition, an ill-advised company expansion, excessive debt and so on. If you've invested substantially in the shares or bonds of a specific company whose value falls, you may lose your money. If the company declares bankruptcy, then all of the money you invested in the company will be lost.
- *Sector risk.* This is the possibility that shares in a particular *business sector* or industry will decline due to factors specific to that industry. Recall what happened to the shares of banks and other financial services companies in 2007 or the shares of companies in the food sector during the horsemeat scandal. If you invest heavily in one or two sectors, you may lose a lot of money if those shares tumble. Most sectors rebound eventually but it may take years.
- *Market risk.* Also called *systematic risk*, this is the possibility that an entire investment market – the stock market, for example – will suffer a decline, causing you to lose all or part of your investment no matter how diversified your holdings are. In fact, such

declines do happen, as we saw starkly in 2007. They're often referred to as *bear markets* and they occasion much wailing and gnashing of teeth among investors. Bear markets pass in time, giving way to renewed price increases. But if you need to cash in your investment during such a period, you may suffer a real and unavoidable loss.

- *Inflation risk*. Also called *purchasing power risk*, this is the possibility that the money you've invested will lose part of its value over time due to an increase in the prices of the goods and services we use every day. If your money is not growing at a rate that keeps pace with or exceeds the price increases then the buying power of the money you have in the bank is declining while, at the same time, the actual amount of money you have may be relatively the same or growing modestly. During a high-inflation period (such as that experienced in the 1970s), otherwise sound investments may grow more slowly than the inflation rate. As a result, people may find that their overly conservative investments have in fact slowly dragged down the real value of their money. It's impossible to forecast future inflation rates precisely or when a period of inflation is likely to begin in an economy but inflation does need to be considered when developing a long-term investment plan.

- *Currency risk*. This risk primarily affects investments in foreign companies, although it can also affect investments in UK companies with large overseas operations or whose revenue comes from sales in country-specific markets. Currency risk is the possibility that the value of your investment will decline due to changes in the relative value of a foreign currency against the pound.

For example, suppose you buy shares in a Japanese company. If the value of the yen suddenly collapses, you may find that the value of your shares declines dramatically even though the Japanese firm may be as well run and solvent as ever. Additionally, if the company pays the dividend, its value would be lower because the depreciated value of the yen (the currency in which the Japanese company would pay its dividend) would buy fewer pounds. Alternatively, if the yen rose in value then this would benefit you, the investor, because any dividend payments in yen would be worth more in pounds.

- *Political risk*. This is another risk related to international investments. It is the possibility of losing part of your investment due to governmental instability. When you invest in countries that are politically secure, with strong legal systems and free-market traditions (such as the United States, for example), political risk is minimal. But when you invest in countries that are struggling to establish secure, law-based, free-market systems (such as some countries in the Pacific Rim, for example), political risk may be a significant factor. In a worst-case scenario, a ruling government could choose to nationalise all businesses within the country. This would result in a total loss of every investor in those companies because their stocks and bonds would be suddenly worthless.

Most people are more risk-averse than they realise. What happened to many investors during the bear market in stocks that began in 2007 and during the recession that started nearly at the same time offers a vivid illustration of my point. Quite a few of my friends and acquaintances who had planned to retire in between 2010 and 2013 found that they could not because the value of the unit trusts or OEICs in which they had invested their retirement money over the years had declined substantially in value. They now had substantially less money than they had envisioned. In addition the recession caused unemployment and wage stagnation. Each person, in his or her own way, had to confront the reality that they would most likely have to work longer (if they still had a job) than they had planned before they could retire; or, if they decided to go forward with their retirement plans, had to downsize their dreams to fit their new economic circumstances. This was definitely not the 'golden years' dream they had planned for. The bear market also affected the investments they had made for their children's or grandchildren's university fees and expenses. Understandably, some of these people are angry, even bitter. 'Why didn't the professionals or someone tell us the market was doing to drop?' is a question I still hear often.

I wish for my sake, yours and that of my friends, that every bull and bear cycle of the investment markets could be precisely predicted. Not only is it impossible to do so consistently and accurately but investors also often don't want to believe or hear the predictions for fear of missing out on the gains. As we've seen in both the stock market and the property market, a prolonged period of substantial growth causes people to conclude that it will continue. Or if there is a downturn, people expect the markets will rise back to their old price levels quickly and go even higher. This optimism can become its own blinder, subtly slowing the frequency with which people monitor and adjust their investments and seducing people into thinking they are more risk-tolerant than they are. Markets move in cycles. For every rising period (and the optimism that comes with it), there will eventually be a period of decline or stagnation (that can result in realised losses and sometimes cynicism). It's important to maintain a realistic sense of what it will feel like to lose real money before you invest. If you're nervous about it, think twice about investing in shares or any other vehicle that carries significant risk. However, you can also decide to do what I did when I had doubts: to educate yourself about stocks and bonds. Remember, you are not going to invest all of your money, only a portion of it that you are comfortable exposing to the risks and rewards of prudent investing – not speculation. (In Chapter 7, we'll show you a risk-free way to try your hand at share investing, which will permit you to experience the highs and lows of the market, see first-hand how you react and, perhaps most importantly, start your own education.)

The Paradox of Risk

Since risk is the possibility of loss, most investors are eager to reduce their risk exposure. And there are various ways of minimising your exposure to each kind of risk. For example, it's possible to reduce your stock-specific and sector risk by spreading your investment money among shares and bonds in various business sectors or among two or more different markets. This strategy is known as *diversification*. Since stock markets and bond markets often move in opposite directions, you can reduce both stock-specific and sector risk by investing part of your money in a group of shares and part in a group of bonds.

For example, if some of your money is invested in shares of consumer products companies (such as retailers and food suppliers), you may want to invest a separate sum in shares of industrial companies (such as aerospace manufacturers and information technology firms) or new technology companies. The chances are good that, when one sector is down, the other may be up, thereby reducing your chance of suffering a catastrophic investment loss.

But here is the paradox of risk: *in general, the greater the risk you are willing to take on, the greater the potential gains you may enjoy.* In other words, for most investments, the size of the potential upside is closely related to the size of the potential downside.

The paradox of risk means that a very conservative strategy, designed to virtually eliminate risk, is likely to yield steady but very modest gains. By contrast, a very risky strategy – one that accepts high risk in hopes of a big payoff (for example, spread betting) – could produce results ranging from spectacularly good to horrendously bad, depending on your timing, your cleverness and your luck.

⋙*Alvin says* . . .

For most people, neither complete risk avoidance nor complete risk acceptance is appropriate. Instead, a strategy somewhere in the middle range, which accepts some degree of risk while partly protecting your assets (widely referred to as *preservation of capital*) is the best.

Adjusting Your Risk to Your Time Frame

Of course, all that we've just discussed is still only the start of the risk conversation. It leaves open the question: *Exactly where on the risk spectrum do I fall?* As we've seen, the answer to this question depends in part on your psychology. Any investment mix that would make it hard for you to sleep at night is wrong for you. But the answer should also depend in part on your age and your financial objectives. Here's why.

Ideally, you should adjust your risk tolerance depending on the time frame of your main investment goals. Suppose you are investing mainly for a short-term goal: a new car, say, or a once-in-a-lifetime vacation to South America planned for next year. In that case, it makes sense to avoid high-risk vehicles because if you suffer a loss you'll have little time in which to make it back.

By contrast, suppose you are investing mainly for a long-term goal: your retirement in ten, twenty or thirty years, for example. In that case, you can afford to incur somewhat greater risk. Why? Because the stock market tends to move up over time. Even if the market goes though a bearish period, the chances are good that the market will recover and rise again before your retirement rolls around.

For the same reason, many investors like to adjust their investment strategy as well as the mix of securities they hold over time, as dictated by the changing time frame of their personal financial goals.

⬅️*Alvin says . . .*

Remember the two basic rules of risk management:

1) Don't take on more risk than you can handle psychologically. If you start to worry or can't sleep, then you have mostly likely taken on more risk that you can handle emotionally.

2) For short-term goals you should choose low- or no-risk investments; for long-term goals you may choose higher-risk investments.

Doing Your Homework

Another issue that every would-be investor must consider is this: *How much homework are you willing to do before you invest?*

Smart investing isn't easy. Everyone wants to meet an investment wizard, a highly talented and clever adviser who can show you how to triple your money, risk-free, overnight. But there is no one who can honestly make and deliver on such a promise consistently. People in search of this kind of certainty go badly wrong, mistakenly relying on rumours about 'sure bets' they hear from friends and business associates or on 'hot ideas' published in newsletters and on websites.

It *is* possible to improve your investment choices but this isn't by discovering a magic formula or a market wizard. The truth is more mundane. If you're willing to learn the basic principles of investing, to work on developing a personalised strategy that makes sense for you, to read the reports compiled by investment analysts and to follow company news and share prices in the financial press, then you're ready to invest. Remember, investing will never be both easy *and* profitable – one or the other, yes, but not both.

Ready to Invest?

Let's say you're financially ready to invest; that is, you've squirrelled away your emergency cash fund in a safe and secure place and have accumulated an additional sum for investment purposes. And let's say further that you're ready to do your homework about the basics of investing and to work on developing an investment strategy that makes sense for you and for your personal risk tolerance.

If both are true, then you're ready to think seriously about investing. In the pages that follow, I'll lay out some of the facts you need to know to create your own investment strategy. I'll start with shares, partly because they are such an important investment vehicle, partly because understanding shares will make it easier to understand bonds, unit trusts and exchange-traded products.

Basic Facts about Shares

As I've explained, shares represent partial ownership of a company. They are issued by companies to raise money (referred to as *capital*) and they are subsequently traded among retail and institutional investors on *stock exchanges*, which are marketplaces established for the purpose. Share prices rise and fall along with the company's prospects and a large part of the art of share investing lies in learning how to spot companies that are demonstrating strong and continued growth, or those that are ready to expand and become more profitable. As these expectations are realised, the shares of such companies will usually respond by rising in value, to the benefit of the investors who own them.

When you own shares in a company you are entitled to some of the company's profits, which are paid out in the form of dividends. Some companies pay out a substantial portion of their profits to their investors, which means that dividend payments are high. Others retain a large percentage of their profits, investing the money in its own future growth by buying new equipment, increasing research and development, or expanding into new marketplaces, for example. These companies pay smaller dividends or none at all; investors hang on to these shares in the hope that their market price will increase as the company grows. Depending on your investment goals, you may prefer to invest in *high-dividend* shares (often called *income* or *high-yielding* shares) or in *capital growth* shares.

If you want to buy shares, you'll need the help of a *stockbroker* (also simply called a *broker*). This is an individual or company authorised to trade shares on the exchange. The broker is paid a fee, called a *commission*, for this service. Some brokers do nothing more than carry out customers' orders to buy or sell shares; these are called *execution-only* brokers. Others also provide investment ideas and financial guidance; these are called *advisory* brokers. Advisory brokers generally charge higher fees than execution-only brokers. (I explain more about the types of brokers and the services they offer in Chapter 11.)

Many people, especially in the UK, still assume that the stock market is not for them. They think the stock market is only for insiders, 'old money' types or the rich. (In this respect, the British are behind the Americans, who have a better understanding of the benefits and risks of the stock market.)

Nonetheless, British stock markets have become much more accessible to individuals in recent years. More accounts and schemes have been introduced like stocks-and-shares NISAs and self-invested personal pensions (SIPPs) that encourage people to invest for the long-term and receive tax benefits. All of the major newspapers publish daily reports and columns about the overall investment markets and the performance of specific companies. Other information and news organisations offer information and insights important to the retail investors like you and me. Also, the London Stock Exchange has created trading systems like the Order Book for Retail Bonds (ORB) that makes it easier for small investors to buy and sell gilts and corporate bonds. Additionally ORB provides issuers of corporate bonds with a well-established way of distributing their securities to retail investors interested in buying the company's bonds. As a result of the developments in the UK markets, in areas from improved online brokerage to new types of investment products, investors experience more customer-friendly service as well as more competition, more price transparency, and openness among financial services firms.

Opening a brokerage account at a financial services firm of your choice is a fairly simple and easy process. You fill out a form requesting information like that listed on pages 211–214. Note that it includes basic questions about your financial status and the level of investment risk you're prepared to assume. This information will help your broker, if you are using one, to recommend investments that are suitable for you. But remember! The main responsibility for picking (if you are doing it yourself) or approving (if you are working with a broker) investments you can live with is yours and yours alone.

OPENING A BROKERAGE ACCOUNT

This checklist shows the kind of information typically requested when opening a brokerage account. (Adapted from the account opening form used by Killik & Co.)

PERSONAL DETAILS

- ☐ Full name, current address, phone number (home, mobile, business) and email address
- ☐ Date of birth
- ☐ UK National Insurance number
- ☐ Nationality
- ☐ Country of residence
- ☐ Country of taxation
- ☐ Marital status

BANK ACCOUNT DETAILS

- ☐ Principal bankers
- ☐ Branch
- ☐ Account title
- ☐ Account number and related details (such as the Swift code)

FINANCIAL INFORMATION

- ☐ Occupation
- ☐ Position held
- ☐ Nature of employment (full-time, part-time, contract, retired)
- ☐ Annual income (gross)
- ☐ Value of investments and savings
- ☐ Financial knowledge and experience, including the types of

investments you are familiar with and the typical value and frequency of those transactions

☐ Level of investment knowledge and experience (e.g., little or no experience, fairly experienced, to market professional

☐ Investment objectives (e.g., income balanced, growth, aggressive growth)

☐ Level of risk you are prepared to accept on individual stocks to meet your overall objectives, taking your whole porfolio into account.

LEGAL REQUIREMENTS

The Money Laundering Regulations require all financial institutions to verify the identity of their clients. Accordingly, your broker will require two of the following items – one item from each list. Photocopies are not acceptable unless certified by a lawyer, banker, or a regulated professional person.

Personal Identification – one of the following (among others):

☐ Your current signed passport

☐ EEA member state identity card

☐ Northern Ireland Voter's Card

☐ Current UK or EEA photo-card driving licence or current full UK driving licence (provisional licence will not be accepted)

☐ An HMRC Tax Notification (valid for the current year)

☐ Residence permit issued by Home office to Nationals on sight of own country passport.

Address Verification – one of the following (among others):

☐ A bank, building society or credit union statement or passbook issued in the last 3 months

- ☐ A recent utility bill (up to 3 months old)

- ☐ Your most recent mortgage statement from a recognised lender

- ☐ EEA member state identity card

- ☐ HMRC Income Tax bill or coding notice issued within the last year (if not already used to verify name)

- ☐ A local authority tax bill (valid for the current year)

AUTHORITY TO DEAL

In addition to receiving instructions from you, you can also authorise your spouse, agent or other person to provide investment instructions on your behalf. If you wish to do so, provide that person's name and sign the authorisation statement.

SIGNATURE

In signing the new account form, you declare that:

- ☐ This application form has been completed to the best of my knowledge and that the information provided is accurate.

- ☐ I/we acknowledge receipt of the brokerage firm's Terms & Conditions and Rate Card and have read and agreed to the terms.

- ☐ I/we understand the applicable risk ratings and will notify my broker in writing of any material or significant changes in my circumstances.

- ☐ I/we understand that the brokerage firm will classify me/us as a 'Retail Client' [NOTE: Under FCA rules there are three categories of clients: retail, professional, or eligible counterparty.]

- ☐ Unless indicated otherwise, I/we expressly invite unsolicited communications (i.e., telephone calls). Personal visits will not be made without prior approval.

Your signature indicates your acceptance of these terms.

OTHER INFORMATION ABOUT YOUR FINANCIAL SITUATION THAT HELPS THE BROKER TO GIVE SUITABLE ADVICE

- ☐ Type of account (e.g., individual, joint, company, pension, etc.)
- ☐ Value of property
- ☐ Amount and type of outstanding mortgage as well as other loans
- ☐ Whether or not you have financial dependants (children)
- ☐ Details of any committed (cost of living) and anticipated expenditures (e.g., school fees)
- ☐ Details of any critical events (e.g., upcoming retirement)
- ☐ Whether you have a will
- ☐ Whether you want your account managed on an advisory or managed (discretionary) basis
- ☐ Whether you want dividends and interest accruing on securities or cash to be retained, paid into your bank account, or paid into your brokerage account
- ☐ Whether you want online access.

Categories of Shares

To help investors better understand the basic characteristics of different companies' shares, equity securities
are widely grouped together in the following ways:

- *Capitalisation* – the total market value of a company
  based on its outstanding ordinary shares. The capitalisation is calculated by multiplying the current price
  of a company's ordinary shares by the total number of
  shares outstanding in the market. Depending on the
  size, a company is labelled as being *mega-cap, large-
  cap, mid-cap, small-cap* or *micro-cap*. Generally
  speaking, a mega-cap company is one whose capitalisation is in excess of £5 billion while a micro-cap has a
  capitalisation of £250 million or less. The amounts
  associated with the other sizes will vary somewhat
  depending on the research organisation's or the analyst's
  definition. Large- and mega-cap companies are well-
  established businesses in major industry sectors that
  have demonstrated the ability to successfully expand
  the business, grow profits and create new product over
  time. Other capitalisations are typically associated with
  younger companies in new or emerging sectors. Mid-cap
  stocks tend to be somewhat more risky than blue chips.
  Their share prices are likely to rise and fall more
  quickly and unpredictably. However, at any given time,
  much of the nation's (and the world's) economic growth
  is concentrated in strong mid-cap companies. Small-cap
  and micro-cap companies have a higher degree of risk
  associated with them, especially the risk of the business failing.
- *Stage of the business's development or growth* – this
  classification includes a range of mature companies

with strong cash flows and the ability to pay dividends regularly, to young companies whose market share or turnover is growing strongly but the company may not be turning a profit yet. Names associated with this grouping are *blue chip stock, income stock, growth stock, emerging growth stock, aggressive growth stock* and *penny stock.* Blue chip and income stock pay dividends and are unlikely to fluctuate wildly in price. (This is referred to as having low volatility.) They appeal to a conservative investor who is interested in steady income and preservation of capital. The various types of growth stocks often don't pay a dividend but they do offer a chance for modest-to-substantial capital appreciation as the company fortunes improve and the value of its common stock rises accordingly. Penny stock is by far the most risky type in this grouping. It gets its name from the fact that the per-share price is very low, often under £1. [NOTE: This grouping is synonymous with another category, micro-caps.] Too often, people want to invest in low-price shares, assuming they are a real bargain. This leads them to invest in a company that is small and often new. But low price isn't the key: quality is. Most inexpensive shares (like most small, new companies) are quite speculative. A few of the companies that issue such shares will become very profitable and successful but most will not. Thus, buying cheap stocks is a little like buying lottery tickets: there's the chance of a great payoff but most people will lose their money and have nothing at all to show for it. As tempting as those low prices may seem, I urge you to steer clear of micro-caps and penny stocks, especially as a beginning investor.

- *Sensitivity to the economy* – companies in this group benefit in different ways as the economy changes. Cyclical stocks prosper when the economy is doing well but see turnover and profits fall when the economy does poorly. Countercyclical stock fortunes move opposite to changes in the economic cycle. When the economy is in a recession, for example, individuals will shop at more bargain-oriented stores and buy more basic products. Companies in this business sector or that produce such goods are likely to see their turnover rise. Defensive stock and interest-sensitive stock are other shares in this group. The former includes companies such as health care, pharmaceuticals and consumer staples (food, household products, spirits) whose products people continue to purchase regardless of the state of the economy. Banks and other companies that depend on lending and borrowing are prime examples of interest-sensitive stocks. Their profits rise and fall depending on the profit margins they make on loans.

A single company can be described using terms from all of these groupings. For example, Unilever is a mega-cap, defensive income or blue chip stock because of its global size, its products and the regularity of its dividend payments. The primary benefit of these groupings is that they give an investor a quick thumbnail sketch of the company's financial position as well as its growth prospects through changing economic conditions.

Going with the Big Names
Many new investors feel most comfortable starting off with blue chip or income shares. The leading UK blue

chips belong to the FTSE 100. This is a collection of one hundred companies representing Britain's largest industries by capitalisation. Their share prices, combined according to a complex formula, make up the FTSE 100 Index which is reported on the news and in the financial pages as a convenient way of measuring the progress of big business and the current state of the economy in the UK. Some of the familiar company names included in the FTSE 100 are BT Group, Diageo, Vodafone, BP, GlaxoSmithKline, Unilever, Tesco, Sainsbury's, Burberry Group, Aviva, Experian and Hargreaves Lansdown.

Market Sectors

Analysts also break down the stock market into industries or business sectors. To give you a feeling for the breadth of the sectors, here's a random sampling of the sectors into which the companies that trade on the London Stock Exchange (and also included in the FTSE indices) are divided:

- Mobile telecommunications
- Pharmaceuticals and biotechnology
- Electronic and electrical equipment
- Construction and metals
- Technology hardware and equipment
- Mining
- Oil and gas production
- Personal goods
- Life insurance
- Aerospace and defence
- Food and drug retailers
- Gas, water and multi-utilities

As you can imagine, the names given to the sectors change as the companies in them evolve, diversify, merge or are acquired. New sectors are created as entrepreneurs create new, viable business enterprises. Different sectors tend to react in distinct ways to changing economic conditions. When the financial crisis started in 2007, financial services companies across the board experienced big drops in their prices. At the same time, young companies involved in social networking saw their share prices rise on the public's enthusiasm about this new business area and then fall, sometimes quickly, as revenue-generation projections disappointed analysts and others. As mobile technology expanded with the introduction of increasingly powerful handheld devices, companies involved in all aspects of that business, from chipmakers to the owners of intellectual property related to the software, experienced growth, even as the overall economy was sluggish, still struggling to come out of the recession.

When considering a share purchase, it makes sense to evaluate both the industry sector and the individual company. First, consider the overall strength of the sector and the likelihood that it will grow in sales and profits in the coming years. Then consider the individual company. How does it compare to other companies in the sector? Is it one of the best-managed, highly innovative, most profitable and fastest-growing companies in the sector? If so, it stands a good chance of outperforming the rest of the sector. (I'll provide many more tips about choosing individual shares in Chapter 7.)

Investing Overseas

Investing in the shares of companies in other countries is an increasingly important consideration given today's globalised economy. Emerging markets, in particular, offer investors a way to diversify their holdings to include expanding and growing companies whose shares may provide a better return than those of businesses in the UK. The emerging markets are frequently grouped together using an acronym such as BRIC (for Brazil, Russia, India and China), MIST (for Mexico, Indonesia, South Korea and Turkey) and CAPPT (for Chile, Argentina, Peru, the Philippines and Thailand). Selecting specific companies in these markets requires a great deal of expertise, both business and cultural.

The easiest way to invest internationally is through a unit trust, OEIC or country-specific ETF. The portfolio manager (usually a team) of an actively managed fund will be knowledgeable about the economy of the country and key businesses there; however, this individual will also have access to in-depth research that will help identify investment opportunities that will meet the fund's investment objectives. Importantly, you should not choose to invest abroad just because it's the hot strategy of the moment. You should at least have some interest in the country or that sector of business in the local economy. Your decision to invest internationally must be part of a larger, diversified investment strategy. Consider investing some portion (5 per cent to 15 per cent perhaps) of your money in the shares of foreign companies, in emerging markets and in my own native land, America.

Learning More about Shares: Third-Party Information Providers

There are many excellent sources of information on shares (including a specific company's own Investor

Relations area of its website where analytical data is free). Depending on the provider's site, you will be able to access important details such as:

- The corporation's address, phone number, areas of business, directors and other basic information including selected news items for the past 12 months
- Price graphs, showing normalised EPS
- Price-earning growth and gearing
- Share capital, holdings and directors' dealings
- Summary of historic data
- Key data about the company's finances
- Broker's earning estimate
- Real-time or slightly delayed price quote
- Up-to-the-minute commentary about current and anticipated market conditions

Third-party information vendors seek to provide you with as much data as possible to help you in stock selection, whether you work alone or with a stockbroker. *Investegate* (www.investegate.co.uk) is a free, reliable service used by both professionals and the public to research companies across the broad market. *Stockopedia* (www.stockopedia.com) charges the retail investor a modest up front and monthly fee for access to key data. Other vendors include: *Bloomberg* (www.bloomberg.com), *Morningstar* (www.morningstar.co.uk), *The Motley Fool* (www.fool.co.uk), *ADVFN* (www.advfn.com), *Yahoo! Finance UK & Ireland* (uk.finance.yahoo.com), and the expensive *Company REFS* (www.companyrefs.co). Some vendors, like Morningstar, also offer educational tools that will help you improve your knowledge about shares overall. All strive to make sure the information they provide is both useful and accurate. You can also call your broker, if you already have one, and ask him or her to send you the latest analyst's report or summary on a company you're interested in.

The Bond Alternative

As I've explained, a bond is essentially an IOU. When you buy a bond, you are lending money to a company, a government or other organisation. The borrower promises to pay interest, usually a set amount, to you at regular intervals (semi-annually or annually) for a set period of time (known as the bond's *term*). This is why a bond is referred to as a fixed income security. On a specific date (the bond's *maturity date*) at the end of the term, the borrower promises to pay back the bond's *principal* or *face value*. This is often (although not always) the same as the amount originally borrowed.

As an investment, bonds are generally considered lower risk than shares. There are several reasons for this. For one thing, the amount of income you'll enjoy from your bond is spelled out in advance, in the form of the fixed-rate of interest promised by the bond issuer. (This rate is referred to as the *coupon*.) Bond issuers are obligated to make these payments when they are due; if they miss a payment, they are said to be in default.

A second reason bonds are considered relatively low-risk is that the price does not fluctuate like common shares. The market price of bonds is affected by changes in interest rates. In fact, bond prices move in the opposite direction of interest rates. As interest rates move up, the market prices of bonds will drop. As interest rates move down, the market prices of bonds will go up. Because interest rates change or fluctuate little or not at all from day to day, the market prices of bonds tend to move very little. In short, bonds are less volatile than shares and are therefore considered less risky.

Bonds are also considered less risky for a third reason. When a company goes bankrupt and its assets are sold off, the law generally stipulates that the claims of bondholders take precedence over those of shareholders. Hopefully, bankruptcy will never strike any company you invest in but if it does you will be better off as a bondholder, since ordinary shareholders come last in line among those to be paid off and typically get nothing.

Of course, bonds are not completely risk-free – no investment is. As I've mentioned, companies do go bankrupt and sometimes the bondholders are left high and dry or paid back just a fraction of their investment money. Even governments occasionally default on their debts. Think of the fears associated with several countries in the Eurozone during the recession that began in 2007. Most nations will do everything possible to avoid default since it can make the cost of any future borrowing very expensive. Bond buyers will demand higher coupon rates to compensate for the risk. Obviously the British government is one of the most stable and secure in the world and the risk of default on UK-issued bonds is very, very small.

Bonds also carry other, more subtle forms of risk. After they've been issued, bonds can be bought and sold on a stock exchange (like the London Stock Exchange) or other type of trading market (generally through a broker or dealer, like shares). The price of a bond on this *after-market* will fluctuate from time to time, mainly moving opposite to changes in interest rates as I mentioned before. Here's how this works. Suppose you own a bond that is paying interest at an annual coupon rate of 5.5 per cent. If interest rates rise so that comparable bonds are paying (say) 6.5 per cent, your coupon will become less desirable to other investors who would only buy it at a lower price to compensate for the unattractive coupon rate. As a result, the market price of your bond will fall. On the other hand, if interest rates fall to (say) 4.5 per cent, your 5.5 per cent coupon rate will look very attractive and the market price of your bond will rise as investors are willing to pay more for the better coupon rate. Thus, the market value of bonds is subject to what is known as *interest rate risk*.

Bonds are also subject to *inflation risk*. Another name for this is *purchasing power risk*. When inflation accelerates, the cost of everyday goods and services increases. Therefore, a fixed-rate of interest that you receive from a bond will buy less of the things you want and need. In short, the money's buying power is eroded. Here is a simple example. If you own a bond with a 4 per cent coupon and inflation is rising 6 per cent annually, the interest payments you receive will actually be *losing* value every year. At maturity, when the bond's principal is repaid, the money you receive will buy fewer groceries, petrol and haircuts than it would have when you initially invested the money.

In the investment markets, risk and reward are always intertwined. Being too speculative can expose your money to the market risk, that is, wild price fluctuations and even bankruptcy in the bond markets. Being too conservative can expose your money to the risk of loss from inflation over time. Below are three time-tested, classic ways to think about investing in individual bonds in different interest rate environments.

1. If interest rates are low, do not invest in bonds with long-term maturities. If you do, you will expose your money to inflation risk over time. Instead, invest in shorter-term bonds that will allow you to take advantage of higher yields if interest rates begin to rise. One sensible strategy is called *laddering*. Rather than invest all of your money in bonds with a single maturity date, you buy bonds with several different maturities from short-to-intermediate-term, perhaps no longer than four or five years. If interest rates start to increase, you will be able to purchase the new, higher-coupon bonds when the short-term bonds you already own reach their maturity and the principal is returned to you.

2. If interest rates are high, invest in long-term bonds. Not only will you be locking in a high coupon rate but you also give yourself the opportunity to make capital gains on the bonds. Remember that bond prices move opposite to changes in interest rates. If interest rates move lower, then the market price of the bonds you own will rise, perhaps significantly above the principal amount if there is a long time to maturity. Therefore, if you had to sell the bonds, you would make a capital gain – perhaps a higher amount of money than if you held it to maturity; however, you would also give up the higher coupon rate – and therein lies your dilemma. Most people, like my co-author

Karl, would hold the bonds to their maturity. In the 1970s, Karl bought long-term US Treasury bonds (the American equivalent of gilts) as investments for his children's university education. At the time, inflation was rampant and interest rates were very high. Accordingly, Karl's bonds carried a coupon of over 13 per cent. These bonds were still paying the same high rate of interest in the late 1980s, when other interest rates had fallen into single digits. In this case, market risk worked in Karl's favour and his investment suddenly looked brilliant.

3. Regardless of what the current interest rates are, if you have concerns over interest rates rising significantly in the near term, don't be afraid to hold some of your money in a deposit account (a type of savings account, usually with a fix period) or a cash fund (a short-term money market fund that holds highly liquid, short-term investments, until you feel comfortable with investing. Missing out on a few months of higher interest won't have a significant adverse effect on your portfolio. When you re-enter the investment market, do so carefully by investing in stages rather than putting all of your money to work at one time.

Types of Bonds

Just as there are many kinds of shares with differing degrees of risk (and potential reward), there are various kinds of bonds. Although as a generalisation it's correct to say that bonds carry lower risk than shares, there are exceptions at both ends of the spectrum. Some of the most important types of bonds are:

- *Gilts* or *government bonds*. These are bonds issued by the British government, considered extremely safe as investments. Every gilt has a so-called *par value* of £100. This is the amount you'll receive as a repayment if you hold the bond to maturity (that is, throughout its term). In addition, of course, you'll receive regular interest payments as long as you hold the bond. Most gilts have terms of five, ten or fifteen years and they can be purchased through a stockbroker, a bank or directly from the government at any Post Office.

- *Corporate bonds*. These are issued by companies as a way of raising capital. The risk you assume when you buy a corporate bond depends on the financial strength of the company that issued it. Bonds issued by large, profitable, long-established businesses in stable industries are almost as safe as government bonds, while bonds issued by small, new firms may be quite risky. The most risky corporate bonds are sometimes called *junk bonds* or *high-yield bonds*. (For obvious reasons, the bond salespeople prefer the latter, marketing-friendly term!)

The interest rates paid by bonds will usually vary directly with the degree of risk entailed. This risk is assessed by third-party bond rating agencies, primarily Moody's Investors Service and Standard & Poor's. Each of these independent companies uses its own proprietary analysis to assess which rating to assign to a company's or a government's bond issue. The letters or letter used is, in essence, a quick summary of the bond's creditworthiness, risk of default, and investment quality.

Moody's	S&P	
Aaa	AAA	
Aa	AA	*Investment Grade Ratings*
A	A	
Baa	BBB	
Ba	BB	
B	B	
Caa	CCC	*Junk or High-Yield Ratings*
Ca	CC	
C	C	
D	Default	

As shown in the illustration above, the first four ratings from Moody's and S&P are investment grade with little likelihood of default. Any bond rated below these is considered a junk bond. Bonds issued by blue chip firms pay relatively low interest rates; risky junk bonds promise high interest payments (but, of course, there's the chance the company may go belly-up and you may receive nothing at all).

Why Own Bonds?

There are several good reasons why an investor might want to own bonds. The most important are:

• *To generate low-risk income.* An investor who is mainly interested in preserving his or her capital while producing a reliable, steady stream of current income (rather than in building a nest egg for the future through growth) will probably want to put a significant part of his or her portfolio into bonds. Many retirees use government bonds or investment-grade corporate bonds for this purpose. If you don't need the income to live on, then the interest can be accumulated and used to buy more bonds.

- *To balance the risk involved in owning shares.* Generally speaking, ordinary shares increase in value as the financial outlook of the company that issued them improves through rising sales or increasing market share. Therefore, during hard times, when the national or world economy (or large sectors of the economy) contracts or growth slows, shares are apt to stagnate or fall in value. By contrast, bond values often increase at such times. Therefore, you may want to put some of your investment money into bonds to balance, or *hedge*, the risk associated with the ordinary shares in your portfolio.

Most individual investors select the bonds they will buy using two simple criteria: the bond's rating and its coupon rate. However, deciding what maturities to buy and how to properly diversify a bond portfolio is more complex and challenging. One easy way to get started in bond investing (this is also true for investing in stocks) is to buy shares in a unit trust or OEIC whose portfolio is made of these securities, and sometimes others. I'll explain how this works in the next section.

Your Best First Choice: Unit Trusts or Open-Ended Investment Companies (OEICs)

For most people, a diversified unit trust or OEIC is an excellent first investment choice. These are pooled investments in which a portfolio consisting of shares, bonds or both, is created and managed by a registered investment professional using the money of hundreds or thousands of individual and institutional investors who have chosen to invest in the fund. Shares of the unit trust or OEIC are easily bought directly from the company that manages them and you can start investing with a modest sum. The minimum investment depends on the fund's rules for the type of account (such as a stocks and shares NISA) that you have. You can even sign up for a savings scheme by which £20 or £50 per month is automatically deducted from your bank account and invested in the unit trust or OEIC of your choice. Best of all, these pooled investments offer the average investor a quick-and-easy way of achieving diversification – that is, of investing in shares in a wide range of different companies. This reduces the degree of stock-specific risk you are exposed to. When a particular company suffers a downturn, chances are good that other securities owned in the fund's investment portfolio will be moving up, thus making up for some of the decline. (Of course, when the entire stock market is going lower and lower, many unit trusts will decline in value as well.)

Both unit trusts and OEICs also employ professional management. The investment managers who buy and sell shares and bonds into and out of each of the fund's underlying portfolio spend all their time evaluating specific companies and their management, analysing the prospects in a business's specific sector, studying the economic environment and developing strategies they hope will produce profits for their investors. Although like anyone else they are fallible, they are probably better informed than the average amateur investor.

Naturally, the managers of the unit trust or OEIC expect to be compensated for their work on your behalf. They are paid in two basic ways. In the case of a unit trust, there may be an initial charge when you buy into the fund. This averages 5 per cent of the amount you invest. With both unit trusts and OEICs, the investment manager charges an ongoing annual charge, which is deducted in small increments from the total value of your holdings. The annual charge averages between 1 and 1.5 per cent of the fund's total value. You should pay attention to these charges when deciding on a unit trust or OEIC investment. All things being equal, a unit trust or OEIC that charges lower fees may be a more profitable long-term investment.

Types of Unit Trusts and OEICs

There are thousands of different pooled investments (unit trusts and OEICs) to choose from in the UK. Each is managed according to a stated investment objective. However, the many types of trusts and OEICs tend to fall into several general categories. What follows is a list of the most popular types, with some indication of the kind of investor who ought to consider each.

- *Bond funds* invest in bonds and other fixed-income securities rather than ordinary shares. Some concentrate on government bonds (gilts), others on corporate bonds. Buying bond funds can be a convenient, low-risk way of including some fixed income securities in your portfolio. Since bonds and shares generally move in opposite directions, this can help to balance some of the risk involved in owning shares. An important fact to remember when investing in a bond fund is that a portfolio manager typically does not hold the bonds in the portfolio to their maturity date, as an individual investor does. They are continually buying and selling bonds to improve the fund's investment return and also to reduce the adverse effects of interest rate risk. (Remember, the market price of bonds moves opposite to changes in interest rates.) Reducing the negative impact on a bond portfolio can be particularly challenging in a low-interest rate environment.

- *Capital growth funds* invest in companies whose share prices are expected to increase substantially. Companies in this fund's portfolio often pay little or no dividends because they are reinvesting their profits to expand their businesses. Investors with long-time horizons who are able to tolerate the inevitable ups and downs of the market should consider investing in capital growth funds.

- *Equity income funds* focus on companies that pay high dividends. These trusts or OEICs are a good choice for investors who seek a moderately low-risk investment that offers relatively high current income (though with limited long-term growth prospects). Thus, retirees often favour equity income funds as part of their investment portfolios.

- *Ethical funds* invest in shares of companies that meet specified moral or socially conscious criteria. For example, some ethical funds avoid companies that make military equipment, tobacco products or alcoholic beverages. Others choose companies with stellar environmental records or a strong track record of hiring and promoting women and minority group members. (Those that focus on environmental issues are often referred to as *green funds*.) Many ethical funds have performed well over time, so consider investing in such a fund if you have strong moral principles you'd like to back up with your pocketbook.

- *Global funds* (also known as *world funds*) invest in foreign shares and shares of UK companies that do significant business overseas. Depending on the mix of countries, regions and industries that are selected by the portfolio manager, global funds can have relatively strong, long-term growth prospects; but they can also be rather risky. Different areas of the world often have periods of rapid economic expansion and growth, especially compared to that of developed countries like the UK and the US. However, this period of positive investment returns is always followed by a period when the growth slows or the economy contracts, thereby causing share prices to fall, sometimes precipitously. An investment manager with deep experience in the specific global business sector, country or region is key, especially in profiting from and avoiding losses when there are changes in the economic cycle.

- *Index-tracker funds* are designed to follow the performance of a specific stock market index, such as the FTSE 100. The underlying portfolio typically consists of all of the securities in the exact percentages that make up the index. These funds are unmanaged. There is no portfolio manager who determines what securities to buy and sell. Instead, the investments in the fund's portfolio only change when the company that created the index adds or removes securities from the composition of the index. Tracker funds have generally outperformed most actively managed unit trusts and OEICs because they typically have relatively low fees and ongoing expenses, therefore more of the profit comes directly to the investor's fund. This makes them an attractive option for most investors, particularly small investors.

- *International funds* invest solely outside the UK. They have many of the same characteristics as global funds but are generally even more risky, largely because of the increased foreign exchange and political risk.
- *Regional funds* invest in shares of companies from a particular region of the world: Asia, the Pacific Rim countries, the former Soviet bloc or Latin America, for example.
- *Sector funds* invest in specific industries. These funds perform as well or as poorly as the industries they focus on. Some funds focus on new business areas like social networking, gaming and new forms of medical testing. Others look at traditional business sectors that may have fallen out of favour but that are likely to recover because of new product development or changes in customer demand. Remember that sector funds can have periods of boom (producing returns that are described as 'moon shots'), and bust (when investors can't say that four-letter word that begins with 's' fast enough). Don't invest money that you can't afford to lose in a sector fund. But if you feel strongly that a particular industry (whether it's social networking, gaming, pharmaceuticals, entertainment, health care or consumer goods) is due for a period of rapid growth then consider buying shares in an appropriate sector fund.
- *Small-cap funds* invest in smaller companies that are often in new, innovative business areas considered to

have strong growth prospects. Since the long-term performance of companies in this category is very hard to predict, these funds are relatively risky. In a bad year you could lose 20, 30 or even 50 per cent of your total investment in a small-cap fund. But in a good year you could double your money. You may want to invest a portion of your long-term money in a small-cap fund but, if you do, you need to be prepared for the share prices to move in ways that will sometimes feel like a ride on a roller coaster.

This is just a sampling of the types of unit trusts and open-ended investment companies (OEICs) currently available in the UK. New types of funds are being created all the time with new investment objectives and strategies, limited only by the ingenuity of fund managers (and of the marketing departments of the financial firms).

These products also serve as the basic model for creating or developing other investment products. Two features of both unit trusts and OEICs sometimes frustrate investors. First, they are redeemable securities, not tradable securities. These products do not trade on exchanges like ordinary shares and bonds. You can only redeem them – i.e., buy them from or sell them back to the firm that created the unit trust or OEIC, or with other financial firms that act as the creator's authorised sales agents.

The second feature that frustrates some investors is the fact that the market prices of both unit trusts and OEICs are set only once a day. This means that investors cannot buy or sell the funds during a volatile trading day to take advantage of the best prices or avoid significant losses.

In 1987, the American Stock Exchange in New York launched a new, tradable version of a pooled investment to relieve these frustrations. This investment product became known as an *exchange-traded fund* or *ETF*. It was the first product in a new category of investments now called *exchange-traded products* or *ETPs*.

Exchange-Traded Products (ETPs)

The first type of exchange-traded product was an exchange-traded fund (ETF). It was essentially a tracker fund (whose portfolio consists of the ordinary stocks of the companies comprising a specific index, such as the FTSE 250) whose shares could be bought and sold throughout the trading day, just like the securities of listed companies. This is possible only because of powerful, speedy computers. Remember that an ETF consists of two components: 1) the underlying portfolio of securities and 2) the ETF shares that trade on the stock exchange. Throughout the day as the securities in the portfolio are traded in the market, the computers calculate the net asset value (NAV) of that portfolio every few seconds. This value is disseminated across the securities industry. At the same time, the ETF shares are trading (separate from the underlying portfolio) and their current market price is being shown throughout the markets. Since the ETF shares are designed to track the underlying portfolio, the market price of the shares and the NAV of the portfolio should be the same or very close. Occasionally, on a very volatile day in the market for example, the two may begin to trade at different prices because different market forces temporarily affect them. When this happens, a special trader called an *arbitrageur* tries to profit quickly from the price distortion. Using a computer to place orders, this trader simultaneously buys the ETF component that is temporarily undervalued and sells short the component that is overvalued. Quickly (in less than a second, usually) the two prices become properly aligned again and the arbitrageur makes a small profit. Hence, the ETF trades at or very close to the portfolio's NAV all during the day. This feature, in combination with the liquidity of being listed on a stock exchange, has made ETFs the most popular and successful new security to be created in decades.

Also contributing to its popularity is the ETF's low expense ratio. Management fees (money paid to the portfolio manager, whether an individual or a team) are typically the largest expense of a unit trust or OEIC. Because an ETF's portfolio is based on an existing or customised index, there is no portfolio manager involved and therefore little or no management fees. This means that more of the net return or profit goes to you, the investor. Listed on the London Stock Exchange you can find ETFs that track many of the world's best-known indices and there are also many that have been created to track the performance of specific business sectors and regions of the world.

Two important variations of the ETFs have been developed that give investors access to other asset classes, namely fixed-income securities and commodities. exchange-traded notes (ETNs) offer investors the returns of a benchmark fixed-income index (such as the widely known Barclays Capital Aggregate Bond Index) or the more customised fixed-income strategy indices created by a financial services company. exchange-traded commodities (ETCs) seek to provide the price performance of a specific asset such as gold, oil, foreign currencies, or indices on other commodities. The shares of an ETC represent ownership in an underlying portfolio of the physical commodity (such as gold and other precious metals) or of future contracts on the commodities. ETFs, ETNs and ETCs as a group are referred to as *Exchange-Traded Products (ETPs)*.

Evaluating Performance

Many investors try to select a unit trust, OEIC or ETF on the basis of past performance. That is, they look at the price movement or total return over the past one, three or five years and use this to extrapolate future performance. The assumption is that the fund that has earned the greatest profits for investors in the recent past is likely to do the same in the future.

It's certainly worthwhile to consider past performance when evaluating a fund. (And managers whose funds have performed well will certainly encourage you to do so!) However, history shows that past performance is no guarantee of future returns. Only a few actively managed funds have been able to earn significantly better returns for their clients when compared to the overall stock market over time. This fact makes a strong argument for considering broad-based index or tracker funds as a core part of your investment strategy.

However, it's easy to give past performance more weight than it deserves. This is true for several reasons:

• Short-term performance is partly a matter of luck, good or bad. Quite often the fund at the top of its category in a given year does no better than middling or even below average in the following year, while last year's low-rated fund rises to the top of the heap.

- Fund managers switch jobs from time to time as in any industry. The fund that earned huge profits last year may be led by an entirely different portfolio manager this year, making past performance that much harder to replicate.
- Funds often rise or fall based on unpredictable or cyclical economic factors. Investment managers who looked like geniuses when the dot.com shares were booming or the price of gold was soaring suddenly looked like imbeciles when the bottom fell out of that marketplace. In truth, they were neither geniuses nor imbeciles; they just happened to be in the right place one year and in the wrong place the next.

Does this mean that the performance of unit trusts, OEICs and ETFs is purely a matter of dumb luck? Should you pick a trust simply by tossing a dart at the listings in the *Financial Times*? Not quite.

The largest provider of comprehensive information about unit trusts, OEICs, ETFs and other types of pooled investments is *Morningstar* (www.morningstar.co.uk). It provides information about the thousands of funds available to investors in the UK. Visit the website and use its clear, succinct educational tools. They start with the basics and allow you to learn more as and when you need it. You will increase your understanding of many different types of investment products. Read about the various fund types and try to compare your investment interests, objectives and risk tolerance with those of the funds you're considering. Pay careful and special attention to how Morningstar rates each fund, how it evaluates a fund's risk profile, the tenure of its fund manager and the fund's long-term performance. When you find a fund or two that's a good match, you may want to invest in it.

> ⧓ **Alvin says . . .**
>
> Several years of consistently above-average performance by a particular unit trust or OEIC should certainly earn your respect. If the same fund also charges fees that are at or below the average for the fund category and (most importantly) if the investment strategy currently being followed by the fund manager matches your own, then you may have found a trust that is worth buying.

From Unit Trusts to Shares

As we've discussed, investing in pooled investments (unit trusts, OEICs and ETFs) is a good starting point for most investors. However, at some point in your financial life, especially if you begin to accumulate a significant amount of investment money, you'll probably want to consider direct investment in shares. I'll turn to that topic in the next chapter.

7

INVESTING FOR LIFE

*Developing a Personal Strategy to Make
Your Money Grow*

Getting Started in Share Investing

I've suggested that the best place for most people to start
investing is with a unit trust, OEIC or broad market
index ETF. After a while, however, you may want to
'graduate' to investing directly in shares.

Most investors agree that *smart* share investing is
the best way to amass really significant wealth. For
one thing, the direct stock investor doesn't have to pay
the management fees and other ongoing charges that
investors in actively managed pooled investments must
bear.

Furthermore, the individual investor has a potentially
significant advantage over the professional investment
manager. A fund portfolio manager is under constant
pressure to invest since more money keeps flowing into
the fund from investors, particularly if the fund is
successful. This pressure makes it hard for a fund
manager to maintain a consistently successful track
record over time. By contrast, the individual investor can
simply refrain from buying shares until a really good
opportunity appears.

So when you're ready, investing to create your own

share portfolio can present some exciting opportunities. But how to begin?

There's one piece of advice offered by all the great share investors, from Warren Buffett (the legendary director of the ultra-successful holding company Berkshire Hathaway) to Peter Lynch (the exceptional former investment manager during the glory days of Fidelity's Magellan Fund): *invest in what you know.*

'How can I follow that advice?' you may wonder. 'I'm no financial expert. And when it comes to shares, I'm a novice. How can I invest in what I know?'

The answer is that you probably know more than you realise. Based on your career, your personal interests, the items or tools you use at home and work, as well as what you observe in your community, you in fact know quite a bit about the world of business. For example, you know:

- Which new products, clothing, services, tools, technology (hardware or software) or websites do you, your family and your friends love to use – and which ones you strongly dislike or think are mediocre.
- Which shops in your neighbourhood are always crowded – and which ones have fewer and fewer customers, even at peak shopping times.
- Which toys, games, movies, theme parks, music and clothing styles do your kids (if you are a parent) and their friends consider cool – and which ones they shun.
- Which companies in the industry you work in are well managed – and which ones are run by incompetents.
- Which businesses in your area are hiring workers and expanding – and which ones are contracting or shutting down.

Each of these facts represents a possible clue as to which companies are likely to enjoy growing sales in the future and which ones are apt to decline. As you'll discover, everything you know about the world of business can be applied to finding worthwhile companies to invest in.

Of course, before buying shares, you'll also want to increase your specific knowledge about the companies you are considering investing in. This is the process known as *fundamental analysis*. Although this is a serious discipline to which some experts devote a lifetime, it's not hard to learn and begin practising the basics. As you'll see, analysing and choosing shares isn't necessarily much more complicated than examining the pros and cons of a dozen different resorts and then choosing the place you'll visit on your next holiday.

If you are intrigued by the brief presentation in this chapter, there are many books (including my own *The Stock Market Explained*) that you can study for a more in-depth introduction to understanding how the market works and developing a share-investing strategy.

The Least You Should Know About Stock Analysis

There are many approaches to stock analysis. Every stock-picking expert – and many of those who'd like to consider themselves experts – have their own favoured methods. In this section, I'll suggest a few items I consider basic to any analysis of the fundamentals of a company and its shares. You can locate this information about a particular company in several ways. Sources such as Morningstar, Investegate, Stockopedia and others mentioned in the last chapter present all this information and much more. A lot of the data can be found in the share listings and the columns about investing in your daily newspaper and on financial websites, like The Motley Fool. And your stockbroker, if you have one, can probably provide you with analysts' reports on any company you are considering as an investment.

The key items anyone interested in investing should examine about any company include:

- *The story of the company.* This refers to the basic history of the company: the products or services it sells, the markets it serves, how it is organised, how creatively and progressively it is managed and what strategies it is pursuing to grow in the future. A convincing, positive story that makes sense in the light of everything you know about business is not enough in itself to make a company's shares worth buying but it's not a bad starting point.
- *The company's turnover and profit history.* Turnover (also known as revenue) refers to the company's total sales of products and services. Profit, on the other hand, is the portion of revenues remaining after operating expenses, interest payments and taxes have been deducted. Generally speaking, a company with a history of strong and steady growth in turnover over the past several years is a better investment prospect than one whose sales are flat or declining. It is also important to look at the *sources* of the increased turnover. If they come mainly from acquisitions of competing companies, there's a chance that the growth may soon falter because of the many unknowns associated with acquiring and integrating a new company. Similarly, the more consistent the company's profits

the better. And a pattern of steadily increasing profits over time is better still.

- *The company's earnings per share (EPS) and earnings growth*. Earnings are the amount of a company's profit that it has available to distribute to ordinary shareholders. Earnings per share (EPS) is this amount divided by the number of ordinary shares outstanding. This is 'the bottom line' for investors. Consistent annual growth in EPS over a period of five years or more is a sign of a strong company, especially if that growth comes from increased turnover or from improved company productivity and efficiency. Conversely, a decline in EPS may indicate problems within the company or reflect a slowdown in the overall economy.
- *Recent movements in the company's share price*. These will indicate how investors have reacted to recent developments in the company's business as well as to news about the current and future expectations of its sector and of the overall economy. All share prices have their ups and downs, but a generally upward trend is a sign that the marketplace has confidence in the company's management, its business strategy and it products; while a declining stock price suggests that many investors have doubts about the company's future or the continued success of one of its key money-making products. Of course, it's dangerous to assume that the share price trend of the past year will continue. When a basically sound company has a lagging share price it may mean there is a bargain to be had, while a high share price may be too high suggesting that the company may be heading for a sharp pullback. So look at past share price movements but analyse their meaning sceptically. Use this

information to get a better understanding of how news affects the company's shares.

- *Share price volatility*. When examining recent share price movements you should also consider the size of the up-and-down price swings exhibited by the shares over the past year. If you are uncomfortable with a high degree of risk, you may want to avoid shares that have a pattern of very large price swings (often referred to as high volatility). Instead, look for less volatile shares – that is, those with generally smaller price movements.

- *The stock's P/E ratio*. This refers to the ratio of the ordinary share's current market price to the company's annual earnings per share (EPS) – hence, price/earnings ratio or P/E. For example, if a company's shares are currently selling at a price of £24 and the company had earnings of £2 per share during the past twelve months, the P/E ratio is 12 [24 ÷ 2]. One way to understand this is to think of that twelve as representing the number of years it would take for you to recoup the cost of the shares from the company's earnings. The higher the P/E ratio, the more positive – some would say exuberant – are the expectations of most investors and analysts concerning the company's future prospects, particularly the growth of its earnings. They're hoping that earnings will grow at a rate that will enable them to earn back the cost of the initial investment more quickly. However, a high P/E ratio generally means that the share price will be more volatile. Any disappointing news about the company's earning growth will cause investors to sell in droves, driving the price of the stock down sharply. Adversely, positive news will prompt a wave of buying that can drive the price of the stock up quickly. Other investors like to buy shares whose P/E ratio is low compared to other companies in the same business sector. They feel that this indicates that the shares are a relative bargain. However, a low P/E ratio can also indicate that a company is heading for trouble. Investors may have sold off their shares, driving the price down, in anticipation of bad news about the company's earnings. A company's P/E ratio must therefore be analysed in the light of other news about the company's future financial prospects and relative to other companies in the same sector.

- *The company's dividend history.* Remember that dividends represent the portion of a company's earnings that the Board of Directors decides to pay out to investors. Examining the consistency and size of the dividend payout over the past several years can offer a partial indication of the financial health of the company. After all, only a company that is consistently profitable can afford to pay and periodically increase the dividends year after year. This is an especially important indicator if you are seeking shares primarily for current income.

- *The company's gearing (or leverage).* This refers to the amount of debt owed by the company. Owing some money isn't necessarily a bad thing; an expanding business often must borrow to finance the construction of new factories or stores, for example. But excessive debt is a red flag. Servicing the debt (industry jargon for paying interest on the money borrowed) can be a huge drain on a company's financial resources. This situation gets worse if turnover or revenues slow down for any reason. Since average gearing ratios vary greatly from industry to industry, the best way to evaluate a company's indebtedness is by comparing it with others in the same sector. Other things being equal, a company with less gearing (and therefore a stronger corporate balance sheet) is likely to be a better investment.

- *How share analysts view the company.* Finally, consider the opinions of the analysts who track shares and issue reports about them for brokerage houses, financial firms and information vendors (such as FactSet, Bloomberg, Morningstar and CompanyREFS) for which they work. Organisations like Yahoo! Finance and The Motley Fool also offer useful information and insights. The analysts' opinions are sometimes consolidated into a list on the websites of third-party information vendors and the financial press. Analysts' opinions are frequently referred to in newspaper articles as well as on television and radio shows where sometimes the expert is interviewed. Like anyone else, the analysts working in the City are human and fallible. They've been known to overrate a company because of a convincing presentation by a charismatic chief executive or fall prey to fads, crazes and manias (which occur in finance just as in other human activities). Nonetheless, you will find it informative and educational to read what the professional analysts have to say, especially *after* you've studied a company and drawn your own conclusions.

Does this list of indicators add up to a perfect formula for profitable share investing? Unfortunately, no. The factors that determine the ultimate success of a company (and therefore the value of its shares) are too complex and unpredictable to be easily reduced to a formula. Even the best investors (including Buffett and Lynch) have

> ⋈ *Alvin says . . .*
>
> Remember that when you buy shares you are buying part-ownership of a company. Since companies tend to grow along with the overall economy, national and worldwide trends will usually work on your behalf. History bears this out: over the decades, share values have generally trended upwards and no form of investment has yielded greater profits than share investing. So be diligent, patient and confident. In the long run, the share investor is swimming with the tide, not against it.

picked their share of losers. If you want to invest in shares, you'll need to study, experiment and learn from your successes and failures.

Think of it as being a bit like taking up golf or any other challenging sport. No one shoots a hole in one every time out. But those who take the game seriously and put in the necessary practice can expect to improve their performance steadily.

A Risk-Free Way to Try Your Hand at Share Investing

If you're intrigued by the possibilities of share investing but uncertain whether you're ready to risk real money in the markets, I have an ideal method to suggest that can bridge the gap. On pages 250–254, I present a risk-free plan for testing your aptitude for share investing. I call it the Portfolio Game. You can do something similar at many investment websites today. The advantage of using a website is that they provide price updates as well as relevant news and articles about the companies in your 'test portfolio' throughout the trading day.

THE PORTFOLIO GAME:
A BEGINNER'S PATH INTO SHARE INVESTING

1. PICK THREE SECTORS. Select three business sectors you are interested in considering for an investment. They may include the sector you work in, the sector someone close to you works in, a sector you are interested in, a sector you happen to be knowledgeable about, a sector you have heard is 'hot' or just a sector you'd like to learn more about. You can use the *Financial Times*, The Motley Fool or a financial services company's website to identify the names of various sectors. List your three sector choices below:

SECTOR A: _____

SECTOR B: _____

SECTOR C: _____

2. PICK FOUR COMPANIES IN EACH SECTOR. List four companies that are active in each of the sectors you've chosen. You can find these companies in several ways. If you already know a company in the sector, list it. You can also find names in the stock market pages of your daily newspaper, through Morningstar or another information provider, or by consulting a stockbroker. Don't worry yet about whether the companies you list are 'good' companies or not. Just choose them at random. List your choices below.

SECTOR A:	SECTOR B:	SECTOR C:
1.	1.	1.
2.	2.	2.
3.	3.	3.
4.	4.	4.

3. RESEARCH ALL TWELVE COMPANIES. Here's where you will have a bit of homework to do. For each of the twelve companies you listed, read the relevant research information provided at the Investor Relations part of the company's website, by Morningstar, The Motley Fool or other online research service that you like. You can also use information from a share analyst's report or an information sheet from a broker. For each company, fill out the Share Study Form shown on page 252. (Make as many photocopies as you need or use it to create a template using a spreadsheet program.)

4. PICK THREE POTENTIAL WINNERS. Based on what you've learned about the twelve companies, pick three (one from each sector) that you think have the best chance of increasing in value over the next six months.

5. 'PURCHASE' SHARES OF YOUR THREE POTENTIAL WINNERS. Pretend that you buy shares of each of your three favoured companies. Allocate the same amount of investment money to each. For example, if you want to 'invest' a total of £15,000, you will allocate £5,000 to each share. Then determine the number of shares that you can purchase with that amount of money. Simply divide the amount to be invested by the latest price per share. (If you were really investing, broker commissions would also be charged. For this exercise, ignore such costs.) Round off to the nearest share. For example, if you are investing £5,000 in a company whose most recent share price is £36, you will purchase 139 shares [£5,000 ÷ £36 = about 139].

6. TRACK THE PRICE MOVEMENTS OF YOUR 'PURCHASES' FOR SIX MONTHS. Use the Share Tracking Form on pages 253–254. Remember if you do this exercise using a website like www.morningstar.co.uk, then the prices will automatically be updated throughout the day.

THE SHARE STUDY FORM

Complete this form for each share you are considering.

1. Story of the company

   _____

2. Turnover and profit history

   _____

3. Earnings per share (EPS) history

   _____

4. Past price movement

   _____

5. P/E ratio. Compare to others in the same sector and to the overall market

   _____

6. Dividend history

   _____

7. Gearing (leverage). Compare to others in the sector

   _____

8. Analysts' assessments

   _____

SHARE TRACKING FORM

Name of company

Date purchased

Per-share purchase price

Number of shares purchased

Total invested

Week	Price per share (£)	Total value (price per share x number of shares purchased) (£)
1		
2		
3		
4		
5		
6		
7		
8		
9		
10		
11		
12		
13		
14		
15		

16	
17	
18	
19	
20	
21	
22	
23	
24	
25	
26	

Final per-share price

Final value of total investment

Increase or (loss) from initial value

Percentage increase or (loss)

(Mark any loss by enclosing it in parentheses.) Determine the percentage increase or (loss) by dividing the amount of the increase or (loss) by the initial investment value. The result will be a decimal value. Multiply that value by 100 to obtain a percentage. For example, suppose your initial investment of £5,000 grows in value to £5,470. The increase from the initial value is £470 [£5,470 – £5,000]. The percentage increase is 9.4 per cent, which is calculated as follows: [£470 ÷ £5,000 = 0.094; then 0.094 × 100 = 9.4%].

THE SHARE STUDY FORM

Complete this form for each share you are considering. (The information used in this example is for illustrative purposes only, to give you a sense of how you might focus on the information and what key data to pay attention to.)

1. Story of the company: *ABC Global Corp is an international company that makes food, home and personal care products – everything from soap to tea. Its product base includes products known worldwide that people use every day. How good is the company's management?*

2. Turnover and profit history: *After four years of decline, revenues rose last year from £26.9 billion to £29.7 billion. Profits have been up and down – last year went down from £2.8 billion to £1.7 billion. What caused the decline? Is the company ready to rebound?*

3. Earnings per share (EPS) history: *Shows steady growth over the past seven years, from 24.8 to an estimated 35.8 for this current year. How did earnings continue to grow when profits were down?*

4. Past price movement: *Over the past six months, fluctuated from a low of 478p to a high of 610p. Recently closed near its 6-month high and the overall price trend is upwards? Downwards?*

5. P/E ratio. Compare to others in the same sector and to the overall market: *Currently at 9 – pretty low compared to the sector and overall stock market. Does this mean that Unilever is undervalued relative to its competitors? Is it therefore a good time to buy?*

6. Dividend history: *Has paid dividends for more than a decade. The most recent annual payment amounts have been £8.01, £8.42, £10.7, £12.5 and £13.1 per share. Nice upward trend there! But can it continue with the increase given the variability of its turnover and profit? What might cause it to cut its dividend payment?*

7. Gearing (leverage). Compare to others in the sector: *Pretty high: 67.3 per cent! A bad sign?*

8. Analysts' assessments: *Consensus – 14 per cent growth in revenues, 15 per cent growth in earnings for next year. Do they see any danger signs in the company's future?*

SHARE TRACKING FORM

Name of company	ABC Global Corp
Date purchased	1 Jan 2014
Per-share purchase price	£5.40
Number of shares purchased	929
Total invested	£5,000

Week	Price per share (£)	Total value (price per share x number of shares purchased) (£)
1	5.42	5,040.06
2	5.70	5,300.43
3	5.62	5,226.04
4	5.84	5,430.62
5	5.88	5,467.81
6	6.08	5,653.79
7	5.94	5,523.61
8	6.16	5,728.18
9	6.00	5,579.40
10	5.92	5,505.01
11	5.81	5,402.72
12	5.85	5,439.92
13	6.12	5,690.99
14	5.86	5,449.21
15	5.67	5,272.53

16	5.47	5,086.55
17	5.13	4,770.39
18	4.95	4,603.01
19	5.03	4,677.40
20	5.28	4,909.87
21	4.86	4,519.31
22	5.10	4,742.49
23	5.22	4,854.08
24	5.30	4,928.47
25	5.50	5,114.45
26	5.62	5,226.04

Final per-share price	£5.62
Final value of total investment	£5,226.04
Increase or (loss) from initial value	£226.04
Percentage increase or (loss)	4.5

(Mark any loss by enclosing it in parentheses.) Determine the percentage increase or (loss) by dividing the amount of the increase or (loss) by the initial investment value. The result will be a decimal value. Multiply that value by 100 to obtain a percentage. For example, suppose your initial investment of £5,000 grows in value to £5,470. The increase from the initial value is £470 [£5,470 – £5,000]. The percentage increase is 9.4 per cent, which is calculated as follows: [£470 ÷ £5,000 = 0.094; then 0.094 × 100 = 9.4%].

Playing the Portfolio Game

When you play the Portfolio Game, you'll identify and research several companies (using the Share Study Form on **page 255**). You'll select and 'invest' in three companies on paper for four to six months without actually spending money. Choose an amount you might really invest – an amount it would hurt a bit to lose. Then you'll track the shares using the Share Tracking Form (pages 256–257). Look up the prices at least once a week, for example, every Sunday. (I like using Sunday for this purpose, since I'm sometimes moved to prayer by what I find!) On pages 255–257, you'll find filled-in samples to show what the forms might look like.

Many share investors like to create charts (that is, line graphs) that capture the up-and-down price movement of their shares. You can do this as you play the Portfolio Game if you like. There are many websites, apps and software packages that will help you do this but I still strongly recommend that first-time investors make charts by hand. You'll get a much better 'feel' for price activity that way. Charts are nice because they're visual, providing a vivid and concrete sense of how prices go up and down.

You may also want to jot down news events that may affect the price of your shares. (You can use the margins of the Share Tracking Form for this purpose.) Such news might include:

- Major pieces of economic news: a change in interest rates, for example, or an important government announcement about unemployment.
- Events related to a particular industry you are tracking: for example, a merger between two companies, or an

announcement concerning quarterly sales or profit results.

- Major price moves for the stock market as a whole.

Finally, you may want to jot a note about your emotional reactions, particularly if they are strong. If shares you 'own' are doing exceptionally well, you may want to record your jubilation on the Share Tracking Form ('Up 25 per cent in one week. The stock is on a tear!). If they take a tumble, record those feelings as well ('Lost one-fifth of my stake. This makes me very nervous. What will happen next week?'). The entire process of recording prices and making notes about your holdings shouldn't take very long. Expect to spend a total of between thirty minutes and one hour per week.

After four to six months, look back at your performance. How many winners and losers did you have? How much did your entire portfolio grow? You may discover that you're not really a very good share picker! If so, stick with unit trusts for now. Or you may find that your instincts were excellent. If so, consider taking the plunge carefully with some *real* money.

In any case, playing the Portfolio Game will give you a feeling for how events affect share prices. You'll begin to understand your strengths and weaknesses as an investor and you'll get a sense for how you react to ups and downs in the market. One of the keys to successful investing is the ability to keep your head and make rational decisions in times of euphoria and gloom. Naturally, your feelings as you play the Portfolio Game won't be as powerful as those you'll experience when the investments are real. But at least they'll give you some inkling of the highs and lows that share investors

experience and a sense as to whether you have the temperament to stay cool as you ride those inevitable waves.

Playing the Game in Real Time

One warning: it's important to play the Portfolio Game
in real time – that is, to track the share price movements as they actually occur, week by week. I've
suggested once a week so that you avoid the emotional
overreaction that can come with tracking a stock every
hour, twice a day or once a day. Some clever people
think that they can speed up the process of testing
their investment ideas by picking shares and then
tracking the price movements backwards by gathering
historical data. (This technique even has a name: it's
called *back-fitting*.) Resist this temptation. Back-fitting
is not the same as really living with the ups and downs
of the market. It's deceptively easy to pick shares that
have performed well in recent months (even to do so
unconsciously) and then congratulate yourself on your
investment wisdom.

▧ Alvin says . . .

Investing in shares requires optimism, especially in the long-term upward
movement of the stock market. The daily volatility can been unnerving,
even frightening, when prices plummet. The understandable reaction is
to sell, run away from the stock market and make sure you don't lose
more money. Pessimism can easily take hold. However, if you believe in
the long-term positive performance of the equities markets, then a
downturn may be a time to shop for bargains – undervalued companies.
Optimism enables you to override your fears, seeing the market's periodic
downturns as buying opportunities for the intermediate to long term.

Play the game looking forwards, not backwards. After all, that's what you'll have to do when you put real pounds on the line.

Developing Your Personal Investment Strategy

As you've seen, it's important to do your homework so that you choose your investment vehicles as well as your specific investments wisely. But research is not enough to make a successful investor. It's also necessary to develop an investment strategy – an overall approach that will guide you in managing your money and increase your chances of reaching your financial goals, no matter how the markets behave. In this section, I'll offer some hints about how to develop a strategy that will work for you.

Focus

A key aspect of your investment strategy is to set some reasonable limits as to how much of the market you will try to master. It's impossible to know everything about the whole stock market. There are just too many widely varying business sectors, interacting in complex ways with one another and with larger economic and social trends, for any one person to comprehend fully. So if you decide to get involved in shares, focus on a limited group of sectors that you understand and that appear promising in today's economy. Look for the best companies within those sectors, ones with strong business and financial fundamentals. Buy shares when their prices appear to be reasonable and hold them patiently for as long as the business prospects continue to look solid.

Also focus on a limited number of companies. For most people, five or six shares are enough to study at once. I have a friend who invests his money in no more than five stocks at any one time. John generally drops one company each year and replaces it with a different one whose prospects he's impressed with. I don't recommend this unusual plan to everyone but it has the advantage of being very focused. Because John keeps close tabs on just five companies at a time, he feels he has a manageable number of firms to be truly knowledgeable about.

In most cases, a focused approach will bring success in the long run. In fact (in a simplified form), this is how Warren Buffett made his billions. Of course, this approach is simpler to describe than to carry out. Otherwise, every share investor would be as rich as Buffett. But it does provide a proven framework for the ongoing learning you'll need to carry out if you hope to become a skilled and successful investor.

Remember to Diversify

As I explained in Chapter six, the share investor needs to guard against two kinds of risk in particular: sector risk and company-specific risk. The former is the possibility of loss due to the poor performance or collapse of a particular industry; the latter is the possibility of loss due to the underperformance or failure of a single company.

Both kinds of risk can be reduced through the strategy of diversification. This means making certain that your portfolio includes holdings from more than one company and more than one sector. If you select shares from companies whose business fundamentals are quite different, it's likely that a decline in one company will be offset by an increase in others, reducing the risk of an overall loss to your portfolio.

Therefore, as you buy shares, be aware of the need to diversify. Don't exclusively buy shares of companies in the same industries, or in closely related ones: computer hardware and software, for example, or retailing and fashion. Otherwise, when one falls, your whole share portfolio is apt to collapse along with it.

⧓ Alvin says . . .

Diversification isn't easy to achieve through the purchase of individual shares. Traditional thinking has held that you need to own shares in at least eight to ten different companies in different sectors in order to be sufficiently diversified. When the stock market is particularly volatile you need to own even more shares. It takes a fair amount of money to buy that many shares. As noted, it's also hard to focus on that many companies and their stories at any one time. Therefore I suggest you continue to hold on to your unit trust or OEIC investment during your early years as a share investor. Your unit trusts and OEICs will broaden your holdings, giving you the diversification you might otherwise lack.

Buy and Hold – But For How Long?

Yet another strategic issue has to do with the time horizon of your investments – that is, how long you will hold a share after you've bought it. Conventional wisdom used to say, 'Buy a good investment and let it run.' That is, simply hold on to the stock, bond, unit trust or OEIC as long as the investment outlook remains positive or until you need the money, for example, when your child is ready for university or you reach retirement age.

The Dangers of Over-Trading

The traditional wisdom wasn't far wrong. For the typical retail investor like you and me, buy and hold has been historically and remains a far better strategy than trade trade trade. The overall trend of the stock market over the long term has always been upward; naturally so, since the national and world economies, in general, continue to grow. Therefore, if you buy shares in a variety of good solid companies (either directly or through a unit trust or OEIC) and hold on to them for a period of years, the chances are pretty good that many (but not all) of the companies you invested in will increase in value – probably faster than inflation.

By contrast, day traders – that is, those who buy and sell investments frequently – tend to hurt themselves. Why is this so? There are several reasons:

- The trader is trying to 'outsmart' the market. That is, he is trying to anticipate price movements in the shares he owns so that he can buy them at or near the lowest possible price and sell them at the highest possible price. But outsmarting the market is a lot tougher than it looks. After all, share prices represent the consensus judgement of thousands of large and small investors concerning the value of a company. It's not so easy to out-think such a large number of investors. No wonder it's hard for any individual, no matter how clever, to remain ahead of the market curve for long.
- The day trader is also apt to make errors in judgement due to emotions. When you watch stock price movements throughout the day, every day, it's easy to get caught up in the excitement of the market roller coaster. But emotions aren't a sound guide to actions.

Many traders lose money by selling shares when feeling despondent over a downturn or by buying more when exhilarated by an upswing – moods that may *not* reflect the true long-term value of the shares.

- Every time you buy or sell a share you incur costs, especially the dealing costs and commission payable to the broker or brokerage firm that handles the transaction. When these costs are factored into the equation, they can seriously erode the profits you make on such short-term investing, even when using a discount broker.

So the old buy-and-hold philosophy of investment is a fundamentally sound one and far better for most people than active trading.

Have an Exit Strategy
Interestingly, many of us have slightly shifted our thinking about investments in light of what we saw happen to share prices during the recession. The drop in share prices made it clear that many investors would have been better off if they'd taken some money off the table – that is, if they'd sold some of their share holdings to realise some of the profits. If they'd done so, they would have turned some of the enormous gains they had made into hard cash that could have been deposited into a money market or bank account. Relatively few investors did this. Instead, they held on to stocks, believing – and hoping – that the price rises would continue, after perhaps only a modest and brief pullback. When the tide turned they lost a lot of their profits, at least on paper. And then they were left, in the words of Burt Bacharach, wishing and hoping and thinking and praying and planning and dreaming that the market would at least recover

to their break-even point or to the level it had been. The wait was quite long for many.

It is therefore prudent for you to make a plan for how and when you will consider selling your shares. At the time you buy them, I recommend that you set two parameters:

- How far the investment has to drop before you sell.
- How far it has to rise before you consider selling.

For example, suppose you buy shares of Company M at a price of £15 per share. Based on your analysis of the firm's fundamentals, you believe that Company M is poised to double its sales and profits over the next three to five years and you hope that the share price will grow at a similar rate. Of course, there's always a chance that your analysis may prove wrong, that some change in the economy or in Company M's industry may hurt the firm's prospects. So a downturn is possible as well. Under these circumstances, you might decide to:

- Sell your shares of Company M if they drop by 20 per cent or more below your purchase price or the share's current market price if they have gone up. Thus, if the price per share falls to £12, you will sell (thereby *cutting your losses*, in investment lingo).
- Sell your shares of Company M if they rise by 100 per cent. Thus, if the price per share doubles to £30, you will sell (thereby *taking your profits*). You could sell all or part of Company M's shares. One widely used strategy is to sell enough shares to recoup your cost, leaving only your gain invested.

Is either of these tactics foolproof? No. In the former case, it's possible that Company M might fall 20 per cent then suddenly rebound. If you sell your shares when they are down, you'll be upset over missing the rebound. On the other hand, millions of investors can tell stories about losing wads of money by trying to wait out downturns they hoped were temporary ('It's *sure* to come back, isn't it? Let's hold on just another week or two . . . or a few months . . . maybe next year . . .'). Setting a target price for selling, and sticking to it, will help you avoid that trap.

In the latter case, it's possible that Company M might double in value then go on rising for months or years longer. If you sell when the shares are only halfway up their climb, you'll feel a bit frustrated over missing some of the upside ('If only I'd held on to those shares!'). But you'll avoid another all-too-common trap: the danger of trying to squeeze out the last pound of profit from a success story, only to lose most of your gains when the shares finally stop rising and take a tumble.

⧓ *Alvin says* . . .

There's an old saying that contains much wisdom: *you never lose money by taking profits*. Don't become greedy. When shares have performed well for you, take your winnings off the table, and then look for another good company or product in which to invest.

Periodic Investing

If you've accumulated a sum of money you want to invest (or have received a lump sum from some windfall, such as an inheritance), don't put all your money into the market at once. Instead, 'feather' it in at regular intervals over a period of time. Experience shows that investing gradually can be less risky than taking a single big gamble. This strategy is particularly effective when investing in unit trusts and OEICs.

When you invest over a period of months, you'll be buying shares at several different price levels, sometimes during periods of euphoria when prices are riding high, sometimes during periods of gloom when prices are low. Your overall potential return can be better if you spread out your investing over such a range of price moves.

Pound-Cost Averaging

The concept of pound-cost averaging illustrates one of the benefits of periodic investing. This investment technique can actually *reduce* the average purchase price of your investments, thereby improving your potential return over time. Here's how it works.

The investor who wants the benefit of pound-cost averaging invests the same amount of money in a unit trust or OEIC at regular intervals. One easy way of doing this is to arrange for automatic investments of a fixed monthly sum – £50, £100, £200 or whatever amount you feel comfortable with. Since the price of a unit trust or OEIC fluctuates from time to time, this fixed monthly sum will sometimes buy more units or shares, sometimes fewer.

Now here's the beauty of pound-cost averaging: because you buy more units when the price is lower than when the price is higher, the average amount you spend per unit or share over the time you're making the investment is actually *less* than the average price of the investment during the same time period. Thus, your overall gains on the investment will be greater as a result.

The chart on page 270 illustrates how pound-cost averaging works. If you find the maths a little tricky, don't worry. The point is that you will benefit from regularly investing the same sum of money. And since this strategy also fits into the good habits of saving and investing that I've stressed throughout this book, the benefits of pound-cost averaging are simply another good reason to do something you ought to do anyway.

HOW POUND-COST AVERAGING WORKS

Suppose you invest the fixed sum of £100 every month in a unit trust. The price of the unit trust will vary from month to month, as shown in the third column below. (In this case, we'll assume that it varies between a low of £8.50 per unit and a high of £14.75 per unit.) Therefore, the number of units you can buy with £100 will vary, as shown in the fourth column.

Month	Sum invested (£)	Price per unit (£)	Units bought
1	100	8.50	11.76
2	100	9.50	10.53
3	100	10.00	10.00
4	100	11.25	8.89
5	100	13.50	7.41
6	100	14.75	6.78
7	100	11.00	9.09
8	100	10.50	9.52
9	100	10.25	9.76
10	100	9.50	10.53
11	100	10.50	9.52
12	100	11.00	9.09
TOTALS	1,200		112.88

The average **cost** (i.e. price you paid) of the units bought is £10.63 [£1,200 ÷ 112.88 = £10.63].

The average **price** of the units over the twelve-month period was actually £10.85. (This is the sum of all the prices in the third column divided by twelve.) Thus, the amount you *paid* per unit is £0.22 less than the average price over the same period. Your gain on your investment is calculated from the lower amount (£10.63), therefore your return on your investment is higher.

Tending Your Growing Portfolio

As your investment portfolio grows in value (and complexity) you'll need to consider one more important investment strategy. *Asset allocation* is the art of deciding how to divide your portfolio among various kinds of investment instruments (called asset classes) so as to produce a risk-reward scenario that is suitable for you.

First, let's recall a couple of basic facts about risk:

- Risk and potential reward tend to vary together. The greater the risk you undertake, the greater the potential for profit. The lower the risk, the lower your potential return.
- The amount of risk you should assume depends partly on your own psychology – how comfortable you are with the possibility of loss.
- It should also depend partly on your financial goals and especially on their time horizon. Money for short-term goals should be invested in less risky vehicles; money for long-term goals may be invested in more risky vehicles.

Based on these principles, investment experts have developed a number of models for asset allocation. These models are designed to combine different kinds of investments into a single portfolio that matches a particular investment style and objective to a person's risk tolerance. In general, these formulas involve blends of two or three asset classes:

- Shares, including unit trusts and OEICs whose portfolios consist of shares.

271

- Bonds, including unit trusts and OEICs whose portfolios are invested in bonds.
- Cash, including savings accounts with banks or building societies, money market accounts and cash ISAs.

The charts on pages 273–275 illustrate four classic asset allocation models. Which model is best for you? That depends. Consider a combination of factors that include your personal risk tolerance, your age, how far you are from your main financial goals and the overall size of your portfolio. Generally speaking, if you are younger, with a longer time horizon to reach your financial goals, or have a relatively large portfolio, you can probably afford to assume greater risk. If you are older, closer to your goals or have a small portfolio, you will probably want to be more conservative.

Naturally, you may want to develop your own customised asset allocation model that is slightly different from any of the four classics shown in our charts. Asset allocation is *not* a one-size-fits-all exercise.

Furthermore, you may want to change models when economic conditions change. If you sense that the stock market is about to suffer a serious downturn, consider shifting some of your money from shares into bonds or cash. When the market is about to rally, load up on shares. Naturally, no one can hope to time such shifts perfectly so don't buy and sell constantly in hopes of catching every wave. But you can't afford to ignore the business climate altogether. Over time, you'll develop a style of responding to shifts in the securities markets and the economy that fits your personality and your overall investment philosophy.

ASSET ALLOCATION: FOUR CLASSIC MODELS

MODEL 1: LOW RISK: THE BALANCED MIX

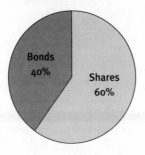

By allocating a full 40 per cent to bonds, this model greatly reduces exposure to the risk involved in share investing. Of course, the types of shares held will have a large impact on the overall degree of risk. If only blue chips are included, the overall portfolio will be low risk. If some of the stocks are small caps or foreign stocks, for example, the portfolio will have a greater level of risk.

MODEL 2: MODERATE RISK BUT STILL CONSERVATIVE: THE ROBOT MIX

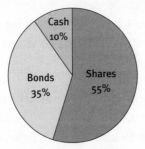

Like the balanced mix, the robot mix includes a sizeable proportion of bonds. However, the suggested 10 per cent allocation to cash is intended to create opportunities to buy shares or bonds when either is attractive. Thus, the actual proportion of shares in this mix may vary between 55 per cent and 65 per cent, depending on how optimistic you feel about share prices.

273

MODEL 3: FLEXIBLE: THE AGE-ADJUSTED MIX

At age 30:

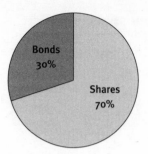

At age 50:

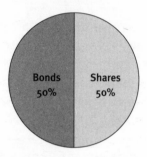

The age-adjusted mix is not a fixed model but rather a formula designed to move from relatively risky to fairly conservative over time. The formula is:

100% – your age = Percentage in stocks

The remainder would be allocated to bonds (or to a combination of bonds and cash). Thus, when you are thirty years old, this model would allocate 70 per cent of your portfolio to stocks (30 per cent to bonds). When you are fifty, this model would allocate 50 per cent of your portfolio to stocks (50 per cent to bonds). The first pie chart above illustrates the proportions for a thirty-year-old investor; the second shows how the proportions would change for a fifty-year-old.

MODEL 4: HIGH RISK: THE SO-CALLED OPTIMUM MIX

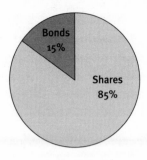

This is an aggressive portfolio model. If you have high psychological risk tolerance and believe strongly in the price potential of shares, consider this mix. However, be careful about the types of shares you choose. If most or all of your share holdings are in risky share types (such as small caps or foreign shares), you will run the risk of severe losses in the event of a market downturn.

Rebalancing Your Portfolio

Once a year, reconsider your asset allocation strategy. This is important for four reasons:

- Increases and decreases in the value of the holdings in your portfolio may have changed the allocation percentages from those recommended in the model.
- You may have reached one or more of your financial goals, which makes it useful to reconsider the blend of short-term and long-term money in your portfolio.
- There may have been a significant change in your life such as a marriage, the purchase of a house or flat, the birth of a child or a period of financial difficulty

that may cause you to reconsider your investment strategy.

- Changes in the economic and business climate may make you want to reconsider your approach.

The first point above demands a bit of explanation. Let's say your preferred asset allocation model is the balanced mix: 60 per cent stocks, 40 per cent bonds. At the start of Year A, the value of your portfolio is as follows:

Shares and unit trusts investing in shares: £ 9,000 (60 per cent)
Bonds and OEICs investing in bonds: £ 6,000 (40 per cent)

This means that your portfolio matches the balanced mix formula perfectly. However, suppose that during Year A the stock market performs famously. Consequently, the shares you own rise in value by a full £2,000. Meanwhile, your bond holdings remain stagnant and barely change in value. Now your portfolio looks like this:

Shares and unit trusts owning shares: £11,000 (65 per cent)
Bonds and unit trusts owning bonds: £ 6,000 (35 per cent)

Suddenly your holdings no longer match the model you prefer. The solution lies in *rebalancing your portfolio*. This means buying and selling investments in order to reset the percentages to the desired blend of shares and bonds in the model. In this case, you would sell £800 worth of shares and use the proceeds to buy bonds. Your rebalanced portfolio would look like this:

| Shares and unit trusts investing in shares: | £10,200 (60 per cent) |
| Bonds and OEICs investing in bonds: | £ 6,800 (40 per cent) |

One advantage of rebalancing is that it creates an automatic mechanism for taking profits, somewhat protecting the overall value of your portfolio and benefiting from the usual ups and downs of markets. If share prices have grown significantly, rebalancing forces you to capture some of the gains produced by your big winners and invest the money in bonds. Thus, you'll have taken some of your more risky money and put it into something safer. Conversely, if shares have plummeted, you'll sell some of your bonds and put the money into shares, taking advantage of the relatively bargain prices.

There's no need to obsess about rebalancing. If your portfolio varies from the ideal mix by a few per cent, you may decide to leave it alone till next year. (After all, it does cost money to buy or sell an investment.) That's fine. But *do* examine your holdings at least twice a year, so you'll recognise when your portfolio has got seriously out of balance.

Investing Can Be Fun

You can probably tell I'm enthusiastic about share investing. Why not? Thanks to the steady growth of the world economy, I've been able to build a nice nest egg through share ownership. So have millions of other people. I hope this chapter has convinced you to consider joining them.

If you are bitten by the investment bug you may find, as I did, that learning about businesses, trying to choose tomorrow's winning companies and developing an individual portfolio strategy is genuinely interesting and fun

277

– at least as challenging as crossword puzzles and far more rewarding! Approach share investing in a spirit of curiosity and adventure and, in time, you're likely to find that your personal balance sheet is reflecting a steadily growing share of the national wealth. Doesn't that sound appealing?

8

INSURANCE OPTIONS

*The Coverage You Need,
the Coverage You Can Skip*

Insurance is *Not* Fun

I admit it: there's nothing glamorous about insurance.
By comparison to some other money topics, life insurance is drab, humdrum, b-o-r-i-n-g. What's worse, it deals
with topics most of us would rather not think about:
illness, accidents, tragedies, unemployment and death.
Especially when we're young, most of us would prefer
to pretend we'll never get sick, get hurt, be made redundant or die. And surely we can think of more enjoyable
things to spend money on than insurance premiums.

I understand. So, I plan on keeping this chapter short
and sweet. I'll tell you only what you absolutely need
to know about insurance and I'll try to quickly zero in
on the issues of greatest concern: what kinds of insurance you really ought to have, what kinds you can skip,
and how to spend the least possible money on the
coverage you absolutely need. I know that the sooner
you can get back to planning your next holiday, the
happier you'll be.

A Price on Your Head: Basics of Life Insurance

As you probably know, life insurance is a financial product that provides a payment (known as a *benefit*) when you die. The association with death makes many people feel there's something ghoulish about life insurance. 'Let's not discuss insurance. It gives me the creeps to talk about dying,' they say. And some people refuse to buy life insurance because, 'I don't want to be worth more dead than alive.'

The truth is, not everyone needs life insurance. The whole point, as with any form of insurance, is *to protect you or those you care about from financial loss*. If there is no one who would be financially harmed by your death, then life insurance is probably unnecessary. Therefore, if you are single and have no children or other dependants, you can skip to the next section.

However, if you are married or in a committed relationship, have a child, or a mortgage or other significant obligations then you probably need life insurance. The questions then become: how much? and what kind?

Let's start with the first question. How much life insurance do you need? Some people – especially insurance salespeople – will suggest one-size-fits-all answers. For example, they offer the rule of thumb that everyone ought to have insurance coverage equal to fifteen times their annual salary. That would amount to a whopping £450,000 if you earn £30,000 per year. But I suggest a slightly more analytical approach.

Here are my guidelines:

- If you are responsible for paying a mortgage, begin by assuming that you need life insurance coverage equal to the outstanding amount of your mortgage debt. This way, if you die, your spouse or loved one will be able to pay off the mortgage in full, despite the fact that you'll no longer be around to contribute to the payments. Without this coverage, it might be impossible for your surviving spouse or partner to make the payments and the home might have to be sold.

- If you have a loved one whose life is intertwined with yours financially, figure out what his or her needs would be in the event of your death. This amount may vary greatly. If you have a partner with a job and a good income, then the needs your life insurance will have to cover might be few. If you have a stay-at-home partner who might need training or retraining before getting into the workforce and becoming self-supporting, then up to five years' income might be needed. And if you have a partner who, for whatever reason, is completely unable to be self-supporting, then lifetime maintenance may be appropriate.

- If you have children, consider the financial needs that would arise should you die. Depending on the ages of the children and the resources of your spouse or other caregivers, these needs might include day care, partial support throughout childhood, primary and secondary schooling and university education.

As you can see, life insurance needs are likely to vary widely from one person to another. Nigel, who is married to a successful solicitor and childless, may want some £100,000 of life insurance coverage – just enough to pay off the mortgage that he and Fiona are carrying. Bryony, with two small children (and no mortgage), may need £300,000 of coverage – one-third to help her spouse pay for day care and other costs while the kids are little, one-third to help with expenses during their school years and one-third to cover university tuition. And Craig, a prominent physician with a stay-at-home spouse and three teenage kids, may want £750,000 to £1,000,000 of insurance so that his wife and children can continue to live well – boarding schools, several holidays abroad each year, fine clothes – even in his absence.

Naturally, the larger the death benefits you want, the more costly the insurance coverage will be. Life insurance payments, or *premiums*, are based on several factors, including your age, your occupation and your health status. [NOTE: Since an EU ruling in December 2012, insurance premiums are no longer affected by your gender.] The insurers rely on statistical models that help them predict the likelihood that you'll die in a given time frame. Based on these models, they charge premiums that should cover the death benefits they must pay out, the expenses of running the insurance business and the profit they expect the business to produce. So think carefully about what your family's real requirements are and only buy the amount of life insurance coverage you need.

One way to save is by selecting the right *type* of life insurance policy. Broadly speaking, there are two kinds of policies: *term* policies and *whole of life* policies. For reasons that will become obvious, I strongly suggest you buy the former.

Term Life Insurance

As the name suggests, term insurance pays a death benefit only during a specified term of coverage, which usually ranges between ten and forty years although it can be longer. Term life is the cheapest and most financially efficient form of life insurance. For most young and middle-aged people, the premiums on term policies are relatively low, since the likelihood that they will die during the term of the policy is small.

Furthermore, term insurance is appropriate for most people because they can select a term that will cover them during their time of greatest financial need. Imagine a young parent with small children and a home mortgage (a typical life insurance customer). Depending on the term of the mortgage and the exact ages of the children, a fifteen-year, twenty-year or twenty-five-year term life policy will probably carry the family right through to the time when the home is paid up and the kids are finished with university. After that, the parents' need for insurance will be much, much less; they can replace their large term policy with a small policy or none at all.

Within the general category of term life insurance there are several variations you may hear about:

- *Level term insurance* involves premiums that don't change during the term of the policy. By contrast, *escalating term insurance* charges lower premiums when you are younger and higher premiums as you get older. If you can afford it, choose a level term policy. The premium hurts a bit at first but gets easier to manage as your income rises.
- *Decreasing term insurance* involves level premium amounts but gradually decreasing coverage. It is sometimes sold along with a repayment mortgage so as to provide coverage for the gradually decreasing amount of debt owed on the mortgage.

- *Convertible term insurance* gives you the option to convert the policy into a whole of life policy, which I'll explain below. I don't particularly recommend this.
- *Family income benefit insurance* enables your heirs to get a tax-free monthly payout up to the term of the policy instead of a single lump sum at your death. (See more information below.)

When you buy term life insurance, make certain that your policy gives you the option of increasing your coverage when you choose (for example, if you have a second or third child). Naturally, your premiums will rise accordingly. This option will save you money, since you'll be charged premiums based on your age at the time you first bought the policy rather than at the time you expanded your coverage and, of course, the premiums charged to younger people are lower.

The family income benefit life insurance is thought to be the cheapest way to buy life insurance. With this term life policy you specify the amount of tax-free monthly income that you want your beneficiary to receive for the remaining term of the policy upon your death. Importantly, the amount of the total payout decreases over the term of the policy. If, for example, you take out a policy with a 25-year term and you die 10 years later, then the policy has to make the fixed, tax-free monthly payments you specified to your beneficiaries for the next 15 years. However if you take out the same policy and die 20 years later, then the policy provider only has to make the fixed monthly payments for the remaining 5 years of the policy's term. Because of the declining total payout feature, this term policy costs less. It can be used, for example, to cover the costs of your child's care and education if you die unexpectedly.

Whole of Life Insurance

Unlike term insurance, a whole of life policy pays a death benefit no matter when you die. Of course, you usually have to pay premiums for a lifetime as well. For most people, whole of life insurance provides coverage that's actually unnecessary. If you die at age eighty-five, will your widowed spouse or children really need an extra £200,000 to keep going?

Insurance salespeople will try to persuade you to buy whole of life insurance because of its investment component. A portion of your premiums go into an investment fund which grows at a varying rate, depending on the performance of the stock market. This produces a couple of supposed benefits. For one thing, the premiums you pay may be reduced in the future if the investment fund performs well, generating dividend or interest that can be used to pay the premium. For another, the policy gradually develops a *surrender value* – an amount you can borrow against or cash in without having to die. However, the surrender value is generally less than the amount you've paid in the form of premiums.

You can tell that I'm not enthusiastic about whole of life insurance as an investment. As a life insurance policy, it can be useful in some circumstances as long as you can afford to continue paying the premiums throughout your life. The investment component complicates the insurance component without producing sufficient value to be worthwhile. My philosophy about this is similar to what I said about endowment mortgages: I'm all for investing, but I suggest you invest on your own and keep the insurance company out of it.

Who Owns the Policy?

When you buy a life insurance policy, in addition to choosing one or more beneficiaries to receive the proceeds when you die, you will also designate an owner for the policy. As we'll discuss in Chapter 10, your estate tax situation may be complicated if you are the owner of the policy. Consider simplifying the problem by naming the beneficiary of the policy as its owner.

Whatever type of life insurance you decide to buy, shop around. Premiums for the same coverage vary surprisingly widely. Figure out how much coverage you want and get quotes from several companies. Today some basic research can be done using one of the price comparison websites that aggregates information from different life insurance policy issuers. These sites also include links to the policy provider. You may be surprised to know that this does not necessarily make choosing the best policy for yourself easier. Getting advice from an experienced life insurance broker is the wise strategy. He or she will be able to point out and explain some of the often subtle but important differences – and there are many – among the policies. With the broker's help, you'll be able to track down the most appropriate policy for yourself and perhaps save a pretty penny at the same time.

When the Flesh is Weak: Understanding Health Insurance

In my American homeland, health insurance remains an expensive, complicated and politically contentious mess despite the passing of the Affordable Care Act (widely referred to as 'Obamacare') in 2010. The vitriolic opposition to having national health insurance in the US has always perplexed me since I've seen and experienced the benefits of such coverage in both Britain and France. Except in basic form for the elderly and the very poor, many Americans pay for medical care through a crazy quilt of employer-paid benefit plans, private insurance schemes and the traditional fee-for-service system. Because I'm essentially self-employed, I have to buy my own health insurance in the US. Even under Obamacare, I still pay a substantial monthly amount but less than before. Costs are expected to keep rising, employers and private insurers keep trying to reduce coverage and no one really understands how our non-system works. Obamacare's aim is to simplify the current system and provide lower-cost coverage to all Americans.

For British citizens, the situation is much better. Most people get their medical care through the National Health Service (NHS). However, there are still three kinds of health-related insurance that you ought to know about. As you'll see, I strongly suggest that you take advantage of the last of the three, as described below.

The three types of health insurance to consider are:

- *Private medical insurance.* This pays for private medical treatment above and beyond what the NHS provides. If you're satisfied with your care under the

NHS, there's no need to purchase private medical insurance. If you're worried about the stories of long queues for operations, you may want private insurance.

- *Critical illness insurance.* This pays a benefit to help with expenses and loss of income when you are diagnosed with a specific serious illness. Most critical illness policies cover cancer, heart disease, kidney failure, stroke and a handful of other conditions, and you won't be paid anything if you suffer from an illness that is not on the list. Premiums will vary depending on your age, medical history, occupation, and health-related lifestyle practices such as smoking. In practice, critical illness insurance provides coverage that overlaps with the third type of insurance, described below.
- *Income protection insurance.* Also known as *long-term disability* or *permanent health insurance*, this provides income when you're too sick to work. I consider this an essential form of insurance, especially since statistics show that *most* people will in fact suffer a disability at some point in their lives. Even single people who may not need life insurance ought to consider income protection insurance.

If you're self-employed like me, income protection insurance is especially necessary. (Those with regular jobs may already have some form of disability insurance. Check at work before buying additional coverage.) An income protection policy won't make up for your entire lost income. There's usually a coverage limit of 50 to 70 per cent of your normal pay. The limit depends on whether you buy the policy directly from the insurer yourself or whether your coverage is provided for you by your employer. Therefore, if you want to maintain your family lifestyle despite a disabling illness, having an emergency nest egg (as I've discussed throughout this book) is important.

Unfortunately, income protection insurance is pretty costly. As with any kind of insurance, you should shop around before buying. Different companies charge widely varying premiums. One way to trim the cost is by agreeing to wait sixty to ninety days before the disability payments begin. The insurance company saves a lot of money when such a waiting period is in effect and much of the savings are passed on to you.

Finally, make sure you understand the *definition* of disability that your policy includes. Some policies will pay you if you are unable to do your regular work. Some will pay you if you are unable to do your regular work or a similar job for which you are qualified. And some will pay you only if you are unable to do any kind of work at all. The first type of policy is the most costly; the third type is cheapest. You'll need to decide how willing you might be to take up a new line of work if (heaven forbid) you suffer an injury that makes your usual job impossible and how ill you would have to be so that you are totally unable to work at all.

In the Driver's Seat: How to Save on Car Insurance

As most drivers discover, operating a car is a risky proposition. What's worse, careless (or unlucky) drivers can easily cause harm and financial loss to other people too. That's why the law in Britain requires car insurance.

There are three levels of car insurance you ought to

know about. Here they are, together with my recommendations as to what you need and don't need:

- *Third-party-only* is the minimum car insurance coverage required by law in the UK. As the name implies, it provides reimbursement for the financial losses suffered by other people as a result of your driving. So, if you crush another driver's bumper or run over someone's cat, the injured party can recover money from your third-party-only coverage. This type of bare-bones car policy does *not* cover any damage to your car caused by your own poor driving or by such unpredictable occurrences as fire or theft.
- *Third-party, fire and theft* is the next step up from third-party-only insurance. I recommend that every driver buy at least this kind of policy. In addition to covering damage suffered by third parties whom you may harm, it covers fire and theft damage to your vehicle.
- *Fully comprehensive insurance* is the most thorough (and of course the most expensive) form of car insurance. In addition to the coverage provided by third-party, fire and theft, fully comprehensive insurance helps pay for the cost of repairs to your car after an accident, even if you are partly or wholly to blame. If you own a new car or a valuable used car, fully comprehensive insurance is worth considering. However, understand that if you do damage to the car that is not worth the cost of repairs you can't expect to be reimbursed for what you paid for it. Because of the process known as *depreciation*, the value of your car begins to decline the moment you drive it away from the showroom and every month you own the vehicle slices away another chunk of its value for insurance purposes.

Keeping Car Insurance Costs under Control

Just as life and health insurers base their charges on your age and medical status. Car insurers have developed elaborate protocols by which they judge the likelihood of costly benefit claims from specific types of drivers. These rules will determine the size of the premiums you'll have to pay. They include some points you have no control over. For example, drivers under the age of twenty-five pay more than those over twenty-five because statistics show they are more likely to experience serious accidents. In addition, drivers who operate their cars mainly in the suburbs or the country usually pay less than city drivers – but it's probably not worthwhile to pick up and move just to save a few pounds on car insurance premiums.

On the other hand, there are some risk factors you *do* control and you can influence these so as to reduce your insurance premiums. Consider the following options:

- *Drive a cheaper car with a smaller engine.* A 'souped-up', sexy sports car is usually more expensive to buy and repair than a modest saloon.
- *Protect your car against break-ins.* If you lock your car in a secure garage at night and equip it with an alarm or anti-theft device, you may be able to negotiate lower insurance premiums.
- *Buy a policy with a higher excess.* The *excess* is the initial portion of an expense that you pay for before insurance coverage kicks in. Thus, if you have a policy with an excess of £100 and you incur repair charges of £350, your insurer will cover only the last £250 worth. The higher your excess, the lower your premiums. To minimise your costs, consider an excess of £500 if you can afford it.

- *Drive safely*. Higher premiums are paid by drivers who have over three points for traffic violations on their licences and by those who've been found liable for accidents in the past. Keep a clean driving history and your premiums may go down.

The best drivers are eligible for a *no-claims discount* (also called a *no-claims bonus*). After five years of driving without a single insurance claim, you may be able to save up to 70 per cent on your premiums – obviously a substantial saving. As soon as you file a claim, whether the accident was your fault or not, your no-claims discount becomes less (e.g., from 75 per cent to 50 per cent) and your number of no-claim years is also reduced. Each subsequent claim filed would reduce both even more, until you are back to paying the full insurance premium. So keep track of your claims history and think carefully before filing a claim, especially if you're in a minor accident. You may be better off paying for repairs yourself rather than seeing your insurance premiums suddenly skyrocket.

You can also insure against losing your no-claims discount. This means if you have an accident and make a claim, you will still receive the substantial discount you have earned for making no claims for more than five years. Getting this insurance is best when you have qualified for maximum discounts offered by your insurer. This insurance can be helpful if, for example, an anonymous driver bashes your car while it's parked on the street and you have to make a claim after you're already qualified for the highest discount. If the premium for this type of insurance is modest then protecting your discount makes good sense. Make sure that the cost of the insurance premium that protects your no-claim discount does not negate the savings you've earned for your good driving record.

Finally, as with all types of insurance, shop around using the price comparison websites or talking to a broker before settling on a particular company and policy. Today most insurers assume you're comparison-shopping using the Internet. So don't be shy about asking them to best another insurer's offer. These tactics can save you quite a lot.

Where the Heart is: the Ins and Outs of Home Insurance

Most people have more of their total net worth wrapped up in their homes than in anything else they own. Thus, it's natural that the vast majority of homeowners have insurance policies to protect them from the financial losses they might suffer if anything happens to their homes. Furthermore, if you have a mortgage, you'll probably be required to have at least basic home insurance coverage (since the mortgage lender has a financial stake in protecting the value of your home).

There are two main types of home insurance, each with a number of variations to consider. I'll explain both and offer some suggestions about the kind of coverage you ought to have.

- *Home insurance* covers your house or flat against such dangers as fire, flood, explosions, storms, falling trees and other forms of disaster. It also covers damage incurred if your home is broken into or attacked by vandals. Most policies will protect both the property itself (walls, roof, floors etc.) as well as attached fixtures such as baths, toilets, kitchen cupboards and wallpaper. The typical policy is written to cover the cost of repairing or replacing what's damaged. Most policies also include some liability cover that pays for injuries suffered by other people in and around your home – if they trip on your front step, for example, or if a tree on your property falls on their car. Check to make sure your standard liability coverage and others are sufficient. Additional coverage can be added at an extra cost. Basic home insurance is worth buying for virtually every homeowner.

- *Contents insurance* covers the contents of your home against the same kinds of dangers as home insurance – fire, flood, theft and so on. Some types of liability are also usually covered so that, for example, if your overflowing dishwasher floods and damages the flat below yours, the costs of repairs to the flat will be covered but not the cost of fixing the dishwasher. Coverage against accidental damage – your TV falls from the cabinet and breaks – can be purchased for an extra charge.

Before deciding on whether or not to buy contents insurance, make a room-by-room survey of your home. List the things you own and estimate the replacement cost of each. Pay special attention to valuable items such as jewellery, electronic equipment, art and antiques. If the total value of what you own would represent a significant loss you'd have trouble bearing, then consider contents insurance.

If you do buy contents insurance, take steps to make

certain that everything you own is properly covered. The room-by-room survey suggested above is a good first step. Consider taking photographs of your nicest items and if you own anything of special value (a fine work of art, for example, or a really expensive diamond ring) have a written appraisal by an expert in your files. And keep a copy of these records in a safe place, whether at home or some other location *away* from your home; otherwise they won't do you much good in the event your place burns to the ground. I keep such information as computer files that I back up regularly in the 'cloud'. There is another interesting, free option available: Immobilise: The National Property Register (www.immobilise.co.uk). This is a service where you can maintain records of your possessions (including photos) and their serial numbers. You can also buy marking materials from Immobilise (this is the company's source of revenue) that enable you to put unique registration numbers on your items. This is not only helpful for making insurance claims in the case of a fire, for example, but the site also links to a national police database, called the National Mobile Property Register (NMPR). Using this, police officers can search for registration information and serial numbers of goods that have been reported lost or stolen. This means that your property may be returned to you if it's found. This service is growing in popularity in the UK.

As with car insurance, you can save on home insurance premiums by accepting a higher excess. You may also be eligible for a discount if you install high-quality locks on the doors and windows along with a burglar alarm or other security system.

Other Kinds of Insurance

In our risk-averse era, there are many other kinds of financial products touted as 'insurance'. Most of these are not worth buying. I'll conclude this chapter by briefly discussing some of the other forms of insurance you may hear about and explaining what you need to know about each.

Travel Insurance

This heading includes all forms of insurance that are intended to protect you while you're abroad on work or holiday. It takes many forms, covering a wide range of potential risks. If you are travelling internationally, especially to an exotic location, you should consider travel insurance. Before you even leave, you may be forced to cancel your plans due to a personal emergency. While you are on your trip, a natural disaster or an accident may turn what was supposed to be an idyllic vacation into a financial nightmare with substantial additional costs for lodging, food, transportation, medical care and more. Travel insurance would reimburse you for all or part of the cost. Make sure you check your other insurance policies to see if they cover some of the same risks though. For example:

- *Theft of your property while you are travelling* may be covered by your home contents insurance if you have 'all risks' cover or 'cover away from home'.
- *Health care emergencies* may be covered by your private medical insurance. In addition, countries of the European Union have reciprocal health service arrangements with the UK's National Health Service, which will provide at least a basic level of care for travellers in Europe.

- *Car accidents when driving abroad* may be covered by your comprehensive policy; however, most only provide third-party, fire and theft cover. For car rentals, you may have to take out the additional coverage provided by the rental car company, unless you have other options available.

In each case, you'll need to consult your existing policy (and talk with a representative of your insurer if necessary) to determine exactly what is and isn't covered. If you do a lot of travelling, you may want to consider buying insurance to cover any gaps.

Extended Warranties

These are offered by manufacturers of cars, appliances, cellphones and electronic gadgets as a form of insurance against repair costs after the initial guarantee has expired. When you buy one of these items, you'll probably find that the salesperson is very eager to sell you one of these policies. That's because they're highly profitable to the retailers; the warranties cost a lot and are rarely used. I recommend skipping them.

Legal Expenses Insurance

These relatively new insurance policies will cover the cost of hiring a solicitor if you're sued or need to take action against someone else. Sometimes additional services, such as access to a free legal information hotline, are included. Most people don't need this coverage. If you are doing things that you feel are likely to provoke someone else to haul you into court, my suggestion is – stop!

Take Advantage of Internet Resources

Insurance products and the terms on offer change frequently. Also, regulatory changes can affect the options that are available to you. Websites like www.savvywoman. co.uk, www.moneysupermarket.com, www.moneysaving expert.com and others, including those set up by the UK government, are updated continually. Some sites consolidate products from across the industry to make comparing easier, while others offer user-friendly and expert explanations that can help you make the right decision for yourself. In this fast-paced, constantly changing world of information and new products, find the site that works best for you and whose information you can trust and then use it when you need to make a decision or reassess a former choice. Remember, being knowledgeable can help you get the coverage you need and want at a price that saves you money.

9

Yes, You *Can* Retire

Planning for a Comfortable and Happy Old Age

Beating the Retirement Crisis: the Importance of Starting Young

One change I've noticed among people and the government in the UK in recent years is a growing awareness of the need to plan for retirement. That's all to the good because more and more of us are living longer, more active lives.

Like most of the rest of the developed world, Britain faces a future crisis in caring for its elderly citizens. As the ratio of younger workers to older pensioners is gradually declining, it's becoming harder and harder for government payments to stretch sufficiently to support our retirees. This is only set to become worse in the years and decades to come.

At the same time, thanks to improved medical care, most of us can look forward to longer lives in retirement than our parents or grandparents enjoyed. Not so long ago, relatively few people lived much past the retirement age of sixty-five. Today, it is not unusual to see quite fit and active individuals in their eighties and beyond.

Also, our standards and expectations have increased as well. You and I would probably define a 'comfortable retirement' in far grander terms than our counterparts a generation or two ago. We take for granted opportunities for travel, entertainment and other leisure activities that our grandparents considered rare luxuries. Factor in the higher standards of food, clothing, housing and medical care that we enjoy and you can see that supporting tomorrow's retirees in the style to which they've become accustomed will be no simple task.

So, retirement is now both a personal and a social responsibility. For you as an individual, the key is to start thinking about retirement as soon as possible. The earlier you start saving and investing for retirement, the less it will cost and the easier it will be.

Sadly, there are many reasons young people (as well as those who are somewhat older) tend to brush aside thoughts of retirement planning. There's the age-old truth that the young simply find it hard to imagine being old. In response to that, all I can say is: if you're lucky, getting old will happen – and it will happen sooner than you think. As Stephen Sondheim wrote succinctly in the lyrics to his musical *A Little Night Music*: 'It's a very short road from the pinch and the punch, to the paunch and the pouch and the pension.'

Then there's the siren song of what I call 'fake fatalism': 'What if I die early? Then all my scrimping and saving will have been for nothing.' This sounds tough-minded and realistic but actually it's silly. In the first place, most people today are living longer than their parents, not dying early. And anyway, so *what* if you die young? Do you really think that, in the afterlife, you'll be fretting over how you managed your personal finances? The chances are good that you'll have more important things to think about – no matter which set of gates you pass through! The dead don't have regrets but many of the living do.

A dose of reality may help you to focus on the benefits of beginning a retirement savings programme *now* rather than later. Let's start with a simple rule of thumb . . .

Alvin says . . .

Here's a handy rule for quickly estimating the amount you should be saving for your retirement. Take the age at which you plan to start saving and divide it by two. The result is the percentage of your income that you ought to be saving. Today the majority of retirement programmes allow you to contribute money to a retirement or pension plan from pre-tax income. So, if you're currently thirty years old and plan to launch a retirement savings plan this year, you ought to invest 15 per cent (30 ÷ 2) of your income towards retirement. If you're already forty-five and haven't begun saving for retirement until now, you have to set aside 22.5 per cent (45 ÷ 2) of your income each year. Obviously, the younger you start, the smaller the percentage; the longer you wait, the tougher the task becomes.

Start Sooner If You Can . . . But Start in Any Case

There is sound reasoning behind the government's automatic enrolment workplace savings plan requirement that employers began implementing in October 2012. All eligible employees must be enrolled no later than 2018. The scheme recognises that people should really start saving for retirement as soon as they begin working. Statistics have shown again and again that young people tend to make this type of saving or investment a low priority, especially in light of other things they may need or want to do with their money. Automatic enrolment is a proactive approach. It makes retirement planning an integral part of a person's employment, from the time he or she is age 22 until the age at which he or she is eligible to receive a State Pension.

For those like me, who did not have automatic enrolment and who, for one reason or another, have been unable to start a retirement savings programme until their thirties, forties or later, we need to act quickly and decisively to save a larger percentage of our take-home pay. You can still achieve your pension goal. I didn't start saving for my retirement until I was in my thirties. Today, after nearly three decades of diligent, continuous effort, I'm reasonably close to my goal.

Every young person fresh from university, in the process of launching a career, saving for a home and/ or starting a family ought to devote part of his or her attention to retirement planning – distant though that goal may seem. Automatic enrolment ensures that this occurs for all eligible employees and every employer must participate. So, if you're a 22-year-old, that's wonderful! Seize the opportunity to think about and become a proactive participant in your retirement programme *now*.

If you're older, automatic enrolment is still a benefit but a more aggressive savings plan will be necessary. I'll shortly walk you through a process to develop a plan tailored to your specific circumstances.

▶ *Alvin says . . .*

The government's automatic enrolment scheme has three clear benefits. First, eligible young adults begin contributing to their pension when they first start working. Because their retirement is many, many years away, this offers an opportunity for even small contributions to grow significantly over the time period. The second benefit is that the automatic enrolment programme makes long-term retirement more than something people merely think about; the scheme makes it a basic activity (albeit a largely passive one initially) of each person's working life. This is fundamental and essential to building a secure retirement. Importantly, without thinking much about it, each individual is working on his or her short-term and long-term financial goals at the same time. And the third benefit puts more money in your pension plan. Your employer must pay into the scheme too and the government gives you tax relief on your contribution. Effectively, this doubles each payment you make into your pension, which means more money is being allocated towards your financially secure retirement.

Retirement Planning: the Three-Legged Stool

Think of retirement planning as a three-legged stool. Each of the three legs plays a role in making a comfortable retirement possible.

The First Leg: Your State Pension

As everyone knows, there is currently a government pension to which every working British citizen is entitled. It begins to pay out when you reach State Pension age, which depends on the year you were born. Importantly, the government is gradually raising the state pension age to coincide with increases in life expectancy. To determine your State Pension age under the current government regulations, use the website:

www.nidirect.gov.uk/
calculating-your-state-pension-age

The State Pension is composed of two parts. The first is known as the *Basic State Pension*. You're entitled to this if you've made National Insurance contributions during your working life. To accurately determine the amount of your Basic State Pension, use the website:

www.gov.uk/calculate-state-pension

The amount of the Basic State Pension, which differs for an individual and a couple, increases every year in line with *the greater of* either 1) the average percentage by which wages increase in the UK or 2) the percentage of change in the Consumer Price Index (CPI).

If you haven't worked – for example, if you were a stay-at-home parent – or you worked irregularly and therefore did not make enough National Insurance contributions to receive your full Basic State Pension, you will receive a lower amount but no less than the minimum, which is 25% of the basic pension amount. [NOTE: If you have little or no income and are therefore eligible for a very small Basic State Pension, you may be eligible for a Stakeholder Pension. It allows low-earners to invest money for retirement up to a maximum set by the government. You must take the initiative to set yourself up in this scheme. Importantly, anyone can pay into the pension for you – your spouse, partner, grandparents, other relatives, anyone. I will discuss the Stakeholder Pension in more detail when I explain the third leg of building an effective pension: your personal retirement plan.

The second part is the Additional State Pension. It is made up of two schemes: *State Earnings Related Pension Scheme* (SERPS) that was in effect from 1978–2002 and the *State Second Pension* (SSP) that has operated since 2002. If you're an employee (*not* self-employed) during the years cited above and you did not contract out of these schemes, then you have been contributing to one or both of them. Additionally with SSP, you will have made contributions if you claimed certain benefits, such as Child Benefit or Carer's Credit.

In both cases, you will automatically receive your Additional State Pension when you begin receiving your Basic State Pension. No separate application or qualification process is needed.

The amount of Additional State Pension you get is determined by your earnings while you worked, as well as how many years you contributed to National Insurance (NI). Thus, the amount will vary from person to person. SERPS payments are partially means-tested, so they're reduced if you've managed to save a lot on your own.

For many retired people, Leg One, the State Pension, is all they have to live on. Unfortunately, it's very hard to live comfortably in old age on what the State Pension pays. And the cost-of-living adjustments that are made each year may not fully keep up with inflation. The result can be a gradual erosion of your quality of life as time passes – a sad prospect to look forward to.

The Second Leg: Your Workplace Pension

Under the Pension Act 2008, virtually all employers must provide their employees with access to a pension plan and each qualified person working there must be automatically enrolled. There are two basic types of employer plans: a *defined-benefit plan* or a *defined-contribution plan*.

In a *defined-benefit (DB)* plan, also known as a *final salary scheme*, your employer undertakes to guarantee that you will receive a regular monthly pension income when you retire based on the number of years you worked and your average salary, typically during your final three years of employment at the organisation. The way the 'final salary' amount is calculated varies among organisations so it is important to know what formula is used. In the past, some defined-benefit plans were funded totally by the employer. These are rare now. Instead, most are funded by contributions from both the employer and the employee. The employer decides how the money is invested (typically via a pension fund manager or investment adviser) and bears all of the investment risk. Defined-benefit plans may permit employees to make additional voluntary contributions (AVCs) to increase their final pension benefit.

Upon retirement, the employee receives a lump sum, payable tax-free, and monthly income payments that last as long as the person lives. If the person dies before retirement age, a pension is usually paid to the surviving spouse or dependants.

There are fewer and fewer defined-benefit plans being offered these days. Many employers who did offer them are phasing them out and offering a different pension scheme (usually a version of the defined-contribution plan) to new employees. Many employers say this is a cost-saving change that was necessary because of the large amount of money that had to be set aside to provide the monthly retirement income and other pension obligations to so many people in a defined-benefit plan. (There have been news reports about many large defined-benefit plans being underfunded.) Historically, this scheme has provided generous pensions. If you work for an organisation (such as the government, local council, health or educational services or a big corporation) that still offers this retirement plan, it is wise to stay in it if you can.

A *defined-contribution* plan is also known as a *money purchase plan*. Employees make pre-tax contributions to the plan that may or may not be matched by the employer. Matching all, part or none of employees' contributions is solely at the employer's discretion. The regular contributions, made by payroll deduction, are a percentage of the individual's salary up to a maximum set by the government. Unlike a defined-benefit plan, the employee is responsible for choosing the funds (typically unit trusts and OEICs) into which the contributions are invested. The employer arranges with several financial services companies to offer a menu of funds for the employees to choose from as part of the plan. Since all pensions are now required to automatically enrol all qualified employees, all pensions have a conservative 'default fund' into which money is automatically invested if the employee does not or cannot make a choice.

The value of each qualified employee's money will fluctuate with the performance securities in the selected funds. The employee can change the funds in which his or her money is invested depending on his or her outlook for the performances of different types of assets (that is, shares, bonds, commodities and cash), as well as any changes in the individual's financial situation and investment objectives. At retirement, the value of your pension depends solely on how the investments you've chosen have performed. Therefore, unlike a defined-benefit plan, the employee bears the investment risk. This is the most common type of workplace pension today.

While many corporations and other organisations set up their own defined-contribution plans through agreements with banks and financial services companies, many do not have the resources – human or financial – to do so. The same is true of self-employed people. These entities can now set up their own defined-contribution pension plan using the National Employment Savings Trust, commonly referred to as NEST. Under the general oversight of the Department of Work and Pensions, this non-departmental public body (NDPB) offers low-risk, but not particularly low-cost pension schemes that employers and self-employed people can sign up for. The government sets the maximum amount that can be contributed each tax year. Each participant in a workplace pension set up through NEST has an individual account (called a *pot*). The specific investments in the account can be managed by the employee, by NEST or by an outside financial adviser. Importantly, NEST offers a great deal of flexibility. Like a regular defined-contribution plan, the employees can:

- Adjust the amount or percentage of their income they contribute to the plan.

- Change the funds in which their contributions are invested.

They also have two other key advantages. In a plan set up through NEST, the individuals can:

- Carry on paying into their accounts if they change jobs, become self-employed or stop working.
- Continue to receive employer contributions into the same account if the new employer uses NEST for its pension plan.

It's important to note that currently it is not possible to move a NEST pot to any other pension scheme.

NEST represents the government's recognition that the workplace is not the same as it used to be and that individuals build careers in different ways compared to the past, typically involving several employers over their working lives. This means that if people are going to accumulate the money they need for retirement through their workplace pension, they need more options with greater flexibility and control. More information can be found at:

www.nestpensions.org.uk

The specific details of privately arranged company pensions can vary. As you set about developing your overall retirement plan, you need to get detailed information about the features (especially the expenses) and provisions of your pension from your employer as well as about the kinds of payments you can expect to receive on retirement.

🎀 *Alvin says* . . .

From April 2015, individuals, age 55 years or older in defined contribution or money-purchase pension plans, will no longer be required to use part of the pension to buy an annuity. Instead you will be able to access and use your pension in any way you wish. You are still permitted to withdraw up to 25% of the total value of the pension as a tax-free lump sum. What you do with the remainder is up to you, but bear in mind the reminder is treated as taxable income. Choice and added flexibility come with risk—the risk that you may not know what is suitable and appropriate for you in retirement. So when the rules go fully into effect in 2015, the Government will ensure that everyone in a defined contribution scheme will be "offered free and impartial face-to-face guidance" on their choices at the point of retirement.

Suppose, like many people today, you change jobs several times during your working life. At each job you prudently sign up for your employer's workplace pension. When you change jobs your private pension at your former employer can either be *frozen* or *transferred*. If frozen, your pension is held in your name by the company and continues to grow on your behalf as your invested funds earn income (although no additional contributions will be made either by the employer or by you). If transferred, then the funds in the plan are turned over to you to invest as you see fit.

These days few people remain with the same employer for more than a few years. Many end up owning a bunch of small, varied pensions investments from several companies. These investments don't necessarily add up to a coherent plan though. It's up to you to keep track of them and to make sure that the combination of investments makes sense. (This is one of the pension problems that NEST aims to solve.)

If you do have pensions at several different places that cannot be transferred, I recommend that you maintain a file or spreadsheet in which you track all of your pension plans, including frozen ones. In most cases today, pensions can be transferred; so most people can consolidate their various pensions.

> ### ⌘ *Alvin says . . .*
>
> If you do lose track of a company pension, or think you have forgotten about one or two over the course of your working life, contact The Pension Tracking Service at the website: www.gov.uk/find-lost-pension. You can also call 0845-600-2537.

If you are in a defined-contribution plan when you retire, up to 25% of the money that has accumulated in your account can be withdrawn as a tax-free lump sum. The remainder (75% or more depending on the amount withdrawn) will be the source from which your pension payments are made, or it can be used to buy an *annuity*. In 2014 this choice became optional, not mandatory. An annuity is an investment that pays out a specific fixed income for as long as you live. The amount you'll be paid from your annuity varies, of course, depending on several factors, including the amount of money in your lump sum and the prevailing interest rates at the time you retire. Annuities come in several varieties and are offered by many kinds of financial firms, including banks, building societies and insurance companies. Shop around

311

to find the annuity whose provisions you feel most comfortable with and suit your circumstances.

The Third Leg: Your Personal Retirement Plan

The third leg of your retirement programme – and the portion over which you have traditionally had the greatest control – is your personal retirement investment plan.

Many people use *personal pension plans* as part of their retirement planning. If you are like me, essentially a freelancer, this pension will be the primary part of your plan. These are investment schemes specifically designed for retirement saving. The two most common types are a *Stakeholder Pension Plan* and the *Self-Invested Personal Pension* (SIPP). They are offered by insurance companies, banks, building societies, unit trust managers and other financial services companies.

With a Stakeholder Pension, your money is managed by the pension provider (e.g., a bank, an insurance company or a building society) at which you open the account. Typically your money will be invested in unit trusts, OEICs or other pooled investments. The providers of Stakeholder Pensions must meet certain standards and qualifications set by the government. For example, the annual management fees are capped at 1.5% for the first 10 years and then drop to 1%. These limits mean that more of the money you deposit into the plan is working towards your retirement.

Importantly, Stakeholder Pensions were designed to be an easy-to-understand and flexible scheme. The minimum contribution is small (£20). You can stop and restart contributions or move your pension to another provider at any time without penalty. Anyone – a spouse, relative or close friend – can contribute to the pension for you, making it appropriate for many who only qualify for the minimum Basic State Pension. Since automatic enrolment began, stakeholder pensions offer a default low-risk fund into which your money will be invested if you do not or cannot make a choice.

A SIPP gives the individual (or someone he or she designates) the ability to manage his or her own investments. Therefore, it is appropriate for someone who has good investment experience or who has a well-trained, properly licensed independent financial adviser, investment manager or stockbroker. The investment products available via a SIPP vary among investment professionals but the overall range is still quite large. Determining what are suitable investments for an individuals risk profile is important.

▷◁ *Alvin says . . .*

It is not widely known that a parent, grandparent, other relative, godparent or generous family friend can invest money in a SIPP for a child as soon as he or she is born and receive the basic rate tax back from the government, even though the child is not paying tax. Unlike a JISA, the child cannot touch the money until aged 55 at the earliest. At that time, the person cannot access more than 25% of the value of the SIPP as a tax-free lump sum. The balance has to remain in the pension. If the money in the SIPP were invested prudently and wisely in the stock market, it could provide the individual with a nice retirement nest egg because the funds have over five decades to benefit from dividend reinvestment, pound-cost averaging and, most importantly, compounding through bull and bear markets.

You're eligible to make pre-tax payments into any personal pension plan if you are self-employed or if you're an employee who is not covered by an employer's pension scheme. You get tax relief on the money you contribute into the plan, up to fairly generous limits set by Her Majesty's Revenue and Customs (HMRC). And, like all pensions, all capital gains, interest and dividends made on money in the plan accumulate tax-free. However, any money put into a personal pension is locked away until you retire. (The earliest age at which you can usually access these funds is 55.) The timing and amount of your payments and the eventual size of your pension benefits will vary from one plan to another and may be difficult to predict, since they'll depend in part on how your invested funds grow.

You can also save for retirement using any of the saving

and investment methods I've discussed in this book, from ISAs to unit trusts to bonds and shares. But these do not come with all of the tax advantages of pension plans.

The art of retirement planning involves fitting together the retirement savings you can expect to have from all sources – including all three legs of the stool – so that they'll cover your needs in old age. Learning how to do this is so important that I'll devote the rest of the chapter to it.

Setting Your Retirement Goal

Of course, it's impossible to make a sensible investment plan for your retirement unless you know what you're trying to achieve – that is, how much money you'll need to live the 'good life' you dream of after retirement.

Making a financial plan for retirement is one of the trickiest money calculations you'll ever make. This is true for several reasons. For one thing, it's difficult to anticipate the lifestyle choices you'll make when you retire, especially if that time is many years in the future. If you have trouble guessing where you'll want to eat dinner this coming Saturday, how can you guess where you'll want to live when you turn 65 or older?

Another difficulty arises from the effects of inflation. As you know, inflation forces the prices of most goods and services upwards over time. It therefore gradually reduces the value or buying power of your savings and income. Inflation rates vary from year to year. But even in times when price inflation is low, its effects mount up over the decades. When making estimates related to something that will happen many years from now, inflation will have a real impact – and it is one of the biggest risks that people often overlook or ignore. Therefore, if your retirement is a decade or further in the future, you'll need to take the effects of inflation seriously.

Finally, the problem is made still trickier by the need to determine how much money you'll need on hand in order to produce a given amount of annual income during your retirement. To do this, some assumptions must be made about the investment income you can expect – assumptions that are sure to be slightly inaccurate and that will most certainly need to be changed over your lifetime.

So you can see that the challenge of setting a retirement goal is a tricky one. The result should also be checked and recalculated periodically (perhaps every two or three years) as your earnings change, as the domestic circumstances of your life evolve, as the demands of your money ebb and flow and as your savings and investment plans are gradually carried out.

Nonetheless, it's very important to perform the calculations and set the goal! Otherwise you'll never know what you need to do to have a hope of enjoying a comfortable old age. And for most people, the process of goal-setting proves to be a wake-up call.

To set your retirement goal, follow the instructions in the form on pages 318–324, entitled Your Retirement Planning Worksheet.

▶◀ *Alvin says* . . .

Frankly, most people are somewhat stunned when they learn how much *more* they need to do if they want to feel comfortable and secure in retirement. Seeing the number written down is an important wake-up call – one they are unlikely to forget. Thus, they know that taking some appropriate action must start soon because now, perhaps for the first time, they understand what's needed.

YOUR RETIREMENT PLANNING WORKSHEET

STEP ONE: *Your retirement budget*

DETAILED METHOD: To set your retirement budget, estimate your monthly living expenses after retirement in each of the expense categories listed on the next page. (These are the same categories we used in creating your current budget in Chapter 1.) In making these estimates, consider the following points:

- **Home**: Will your current mortgage be paid off? Will you remain in your current home or move to a different one? If you move, will you rent or buy? And if you buy, will it be with a mortgage or without?

- **Transport**: You probably will no longer have to commute to work. But this doesn't mean you will sit at home! While you will get free or reduced-fare transport once you reach a certain age, don't assume that transport costs will necessarily drop.

- **Less-than-Monthly Expenses**: Expect the cost of medical care to increase as you age, especially if you go into care.

- **Discretionary Spending**: As your family constellation changes (with the birth of grandchildren, for example), your spending patterns may change – for gift-giving or helping a grandchild who is taking a gap year or going to university, for example. How much travel will you want to do after retirement? For some retirees, travel becomes a major budget item.

A. Fixed costs   Amount (£)

HOME
_____

TRANSPORT
_____

OTHER MONTHLY BILLS
_____

LESS-THAN-MONTHLY EXPENSES
_____

OTHER EXPENSES
_____

TOTAL FIXED COSTS:
_____

B. Discretionary spending

FOOD AND DRINK
_____

ENTERTAINMENT
_____

AROUND THE HOME
_____

LESS-THAN-MONTHLY EXPENSES
_____

OTHER EXPENSES
_____

TOTAL DISCRETIONARY SPENDING:
_____

TOTAL SPENDING
_____

QUICK-AND-DIRTY ALTERNATIVE METHOD: If you feel daunted by the Detailed Method, you can set your retirement budget more quickly (though less accurately) by assuming that you will spend about 80 per cent of your pre-retirement income.

STEP TWO: *Adjusting your retirement budget for inflation*

First, make an assumption about the average annual rate of inflation during the years between now and your planned retirement date. Then locate the place in the table below where your assumed annual inflation rate intersects with the number of years until you retire. The number there is your 'inflation multiplier'. Multiply your monthly retirement budget by the inflation multiplier to obtain the inflation-adjusted amount of money you'll need each month to live as you hope.

For example, suppose you plan to retire in twenty-two years. If you assume that inflation over the next twenty-two years is likely to be around 5 per cent per year, then find the place in the table where 5 per cent intersects with twenty-two years. The number in that place, 2.93, is your inflation multiplier. If you decided, in Step One, that your monthly retirement budget should be £2,600, then multiply 2,600 by 2.93 to obtain your inflation-adjusted budget:

2,600 × 2.93 = 7,618

Therefore, you'll probably need about £7,618 per month to live as you hope to in retirement twenty-two years from today.

Your Inflation Multiplier

Years to Retirement	Assumed Inflation Rate						
	2%	3%	4%	5%	6%	8%	10%
1	1.02	1.03	1.04	1.05	1.06	1.08	1.10
2	1.04	1.06	1.08	1.10	1.12	1.17	1.21
3	1.06	1.09	1.12	1.16	1.19	1.26	1.33
4	1.08	1.13	1.17	1.22	1.26	1.36	1.46
5	1.10	1.16	1.22	1.28	1.34	1.47	1.61
6	1.13	1.19	1.27	1.34	1.42	1.59	1.77
7	1.15	1.23	1.32	1.41	1.50	1.71	1.95
8	1.17	1.27	1.37	1.48	1.59	1.85	2.14

Years to Retirement	Assumed Inflation Rate						
	2%	3%	4%	5%	6%	8%	10%
9	1.20	1.30	1.42	1.55	1.69	2.00	2.36
10	1.22	1.34	1.48	1.63	1.79	2.16	2.59
11	1.24	1.38	1.54	1.71	1.90	2.33	2.85
12	1.27	1.43	1.60	1.80	2.01	2.52	3.14
13	1.29	1.47	1.67	1.89	2.13	2.72	3.45
14	1.32	1.51	1.73	1.98	2.26	2.94	3.80
15	1.35	1.56	1.80	2.08	2.40	3.17	4.18
16	1.37	1.60	1.87	2.18	2.54	3.43	4.59
17	1.40	1.65	1.95	2.29	2.69	3.70	5.05
18	1.43	1.70	2.03	2.41	2.85	4.00	5.56
19	1.46	1.75	2.11	2.53	3.03	4.32	6.12
20	1.49	1.81	2.19	2.65	3.21	4.66	6.73
21	1.52	1.86	2.28	2.79	3.40	5.03	7.40
22	1.55	1.92	2.37	2.93	3.60	5.44	8.14
23	1.58	1.97	2.46	3.07	3.82	5.87	8.95
24	1.61	2.03	2.56	3.23	4.05	6.34	9.85
25	1.64	2.09	2.67	3.39	4.29	6.85	10.83
26	1.67	2.16	2.77	3.56	4.55	7.40	11.92
27	1.71	2.22	2.88	3.73	4.82	7.99	13.11
28	1.74	2.29	3.00	3.92	5.11	8.63	14.42
29	1.78	2.36	3.12	4.12	5.42	9.32	15.86
30	1.81	2.43	3.24	4.32	5.74	10.06	17.45
31	1.85	2.50	3.37	4.54	6.09	10.87	19.19
32	1.88	2.58	3.51	4.76	6.45	11.74	21.11
33	1.92	2.65	3.65	5.00	6.84	12.68	23.23
34	1.96	2.73	3.79	5.25	7.25	13.69	25.55
35	2.00	2.81	3.95	5.52	7.69	14.79	28.10
36	2.04	2.90	4.10	5.79	8.15	15.97	30.91
37	2.08	2.99	4.27	6.08	8.64	17.25	34.00
38	2.12	3.07	4.44	6.39	9.15	18.63	37.40
39	2.16	3.17	4.62	6.70	9.70	20.12	41.14
40	2.21	3.26	4.80	7.04	10.29	21.72	45.26

STEP THREE: *The nest egg you'll need*

Once you've determined your inflation-adjusted monthly retirement budget, you're ready to calculate how big a nest egg you'll need to produce that much income. Here's how to do it.

A. Insert here your estimated monthly retirement spending, as calculated in Steps One and Two of this worksheet: _____

B. Now estimate how much you can expect to receive from the first two legs of your retirement plan.

As explained on page 305, you can obtain a forecast of your State Pension payments at the following website:

https://www.gov.uk/calculate-state-pension

Insert the monthly forecast amount on the next line.

Leg 1: Your State Pension: _____

If you are covered by one or more employer pensions, check with the pension administrator(s) to learn the estimated payments you'll receive on retirement. Insert the monthly amount of these payments below.

Leg 2: Your Company Pension: _____

Now add up the payments from Leg 1 and Leg 2, and enter that figure below.

Total of Leg 1 and Leg 2: _____

C. To determine the shortfall, subtract the Total of Leg 1 and Leg 2 (above) from your estimated monthly spending (Step A). This amount must be made up from your personal retirement plan. Enter that figure below.

Your Personal Retirement Plan: _____

D. Now you need to calculate how much savings it will take to generate the monthly shortfall amount. You'll do this using the table on page 324, titled.

First, you must estimate how long your retirement will last. Figures are provided on the table for periods ranging from fifteen to thirty years. (Uncertain how to guess how long you'll live after retirement? Consider family longevity patterns and your own health history; and, to be safe, add a few more years to your best estimate.)

Second, you must estimate the growth rate your savings and investments will earn during your retirement. It's impossible to predict this with certainty, but the table provides figures for growth rates ranging from 5.5 per cent to 10 per cent. Use a rate from the middle of this range if you like, or stick closer to the bottom of the range for a more conservative approach.

Third, find the pound figure in the table where your retirement time span and estimated interest rate meet. Then multiply this figure by how many thousands of pounds your monthly shortfall amounts to. Thus, if your monthly shortfall is £1,300, multiply the figure from the table by 1.3.

The result of this calculation will be the approximate size of the nest egg you need to accumulate in your personal retirement plan in order to generate the kind of retirement income you'd like to have.

For example, to supply a monthly shortfall of £1,300 for a time span of twenty years (covering age sixty-five to eighty-five) at an assumed growth rate of 8 per cent, multiply £119,550 x 1.3. The nest egg or personal pension needed is £155, 415.

The amount of savings required to generate £1,000 of monthly income for different time periods.

Assumed Growth Rate

Years	No. of Payments	4% (£)	4.50% (£)	5% (£)	5.50% (£)	6% (£)
15 yrs	180	176,432	175,989	175,547	175,107	174,683
20 yrs	240	235,235	234,644	234,084	233,480	232,914
25 yrs	300	294,075	293,329	292,585	291,888	291,149
30 yrs	360	352,883	351,999	351,117	350,239	349,364

NOTE: The table assumes that you will spend both interest and principal during retirement, so that when you die your total nest egg will have been spent. It does *not* provide for an inheritance for your children or other heirs. If necessary, you'll need to plan for that separately. Taxes and fees vary according to each person's circumstances. Furthermore the value of fixed monthly income may diminish over time due to inflation.

Retirement Investment Choices

Now that you have an idea of your retirement savings goal, you face the next major question: where should you put your savings for retirement?

The prevailing wisdom favours equity securities – that is, shares or unit trusts that invest in shares – for retirement purposes. There's a certain logic to that. History shows that, over a long time period, shares generally grow in value faster than any other investment. (In the short run, the picture is less clear since shares go up and down unpredictably on a day-to-day basis.) Thus, any long-term investment plan will probably enjoy the greatest success if most of the money is invested in shares, especially those that pay regular dividends.

But, as with any investment decision, your personal risk tolerance must be considered. You need to assess whether you can stand to watch the value of your retirement money go up and down from time to time. If you can, then equity investments are probably the best choice. If you can't, err towards conservatism: keep at least a significant portion of your investment money in short-to-intermediate-term bonds, a cash NISA or a building society savings account where growth will be much slower but more predictable than in shares.

In any case, as you get older, consider reducing the percentage of your money that is invested in shares. One popular rule of thumb: the percentage of your investment money put into shares should equal 100 per cent minus your age. (This is the same as the Flexible Asset Allocation Model, which I discussed on page 274 in Chapter 7.) Thus, if you are forty years old, your retirement investments should be 60 per cent in shares (since 100% – 40 (your age) = 60). By the time you are

---

⌖ *Alvin says . . .*

One option for very conservative people 65 years of age and older looking for a reliable income stream, while also preserving their capital, is the NS&I's Pensioners Bonds, which will be issued in January 2015. These are bonds will have a fixed rate of interest and a relatively short maturities, e.g., 1-year to 4 years. The shorter-term maturities will help lessen (not eliminate) the decline in the value or purchasing power of the pensioners' money if inflation increases, but rates will not be linked to inflation.

sixty-five, the share percentage would be reduced to 35 per cent (since 100 – 65 = 35). This conservative guideline works well for the average person. As your share investment percentage declines, move the money into safe investments that preserve your capital: a savings account, a cash NISA or bonds.

Many older people are enticed by investment schemes that are supposedly designed to generate high income. Some of the people who hawk these schemes say they 'guarantee' 15 per cent annual growth. If it were real, growth at that level would be quite attractive. It would make your retirement nest egg throw off a lot more money to live on while lasting longer. Unfortunately, these schemes are based on risky premises, usually involving complicated 'hybrid' securities whose real performance is unpredictable or Ponzi schemes, like the one perpetrated by Bernie Madoff. Many people who buy into the 'guaranteed' schemes end up losing everything.

⫷ Alvin says . . .

In Chapter 11, I'll offer guidance – and some warnings – about how to recognise reliable investment advisers from those who are unscrupulous. Meanwhile, heed the old adage: If it sounds too good to be true, then it probably is.

Tracking Your Retirement Funds

Many people also make the mistake of putting money away for retirement – and then ignoring it. Your retirement investments need to be monitored at least twice a year. Always remember that building your retirement nest egg is a dynamic process because your life and career are always changing. To track your holdings, use the form entitled 'Tracking Your Retirement Funds' provided on page 328 as a template. You can also create a spread-sheet. Set this up in whatever way works best for you. On the page that follows, you can see a sample of how this form might be filled out by someone who has been investing for retirement for only a few years. As you can see, she still has quite a way to go to reach her retire-ment goal.

TRACKING YOUR RETIREMENT FUNDS

Investment	Date	Amount (£)	Current Value (£)	Growth (%)

TOTALS:

RETIREMENT GOAL:

HOW FAR TO GO?

TRACKING YOUR RETIREMENT FUNDS

Investment	Date Purchased	Amount (£)	Current Value (£)	Growth (%)
SHARES				
DEF Inc. shares	10/2013	1,800.00	2,345.67	30
JKL Co. shares	9/2013	2,400.00	4,678.20	95
NOP Co. shares	2/2014	2,000.00	1,115.08	(44)
UNIT TRUSTS				
ABC Tracker Fund	5/2009	1,500.00	2,989.90	99
TUV Intl. Fund	10/2013	1,750.00	2,110.00	21
XYZ Growth Fund	1/2009	1,000.00	2,130.45	113
VC Bond Fund	4/2010	2,500.00	3,610.60	44
XYZ Growth Fund	2/2014	1,600.00	1,720.50	7
TOTALS:		14,550.00	20,700.40	68
RETIREMENT GOAL:			350,000.00	
HOW FAR TO GO?			329,300.00	

After a few years, if your retirement portfolio becomes more complex, you will want to create a spreadsheet that captures more detail about your investments and updates automatically via a financial website or secure link with the firm that handles your account. On page 333 you can see the form a friend of mine uses to track his retirement portfolio. Although it may look complicated, it only took my friend about an hour to set up originally and now it takes him around 30 minutes or so to update and review the figures each quarter.

On the form, my friend has listed all his retirement investments, coding each one according to type. For example, his investments in unit trusts with capital growth as their investment objective are all coded 'CG', while those unit trusts that are tracker funds are coded 'T'. The coding system makes it easy for the spreadsheet to calculate automatically what percentage of his holdings are in each type of asset or segment of the market, thereby keeping track of his asset allocation. (Refer to Chapter 7 for an explanation of asset allocation.) The totals in each area are itemised at the bottom of the table. As you can see, he currently has about 47 per cent of his investments in capital growth unit trusts.

At the bottom of my friend's form, he has projected the future growth of his portfolio based on the assumptions that his investments will grow until he is aged sixty-five at an average annual rate of 6 per cent (some years it may be less; other years it may be more) and that he will invest an additional £5,000 each year. If these projections hold true, by the time my friend is sixty-five he will have accumulated a little under £700,000 in his portfolio – a pretty attractive nest egg, I must say.

The one weakness I see in my friend's system is that he hasn't indicated a retirement goal, a nest-egg amount he hopes to accumulate. Without this, it's hard to see how he can tell whether or not his investment plan is on track. When I asked him about this, his explanation was revealing: 'It makes me nervous to think about a goal. I'm afraid I might be too far away from reaching it! I'm a little like a poker player who doesn't want to count his chips, thinking it might bring bad luck.'

The psychology is understandable but it's mistaken. Being *aware* of what you need for your future won't bring you bad luck. Only being *ignorant* can do that.

As for me, I review my retirement investments twice a year. The first is usually on or around my birthday. (Around the same time, I have a medical check-up each year. It seems fitting somehow to combine the two activities.) I do a second review about six months later. I still vividly remember the year when I did my financial check-up and I was within 15 per cent of my retirement goal. One year later, the stock market dropped and, when I updated my finances, I was fully 40 per cent shy of my goal. Since then I have remained very conscious of the need to prioritise my spending, save and invest more money, but also to trust my instincts. I've taught about and watched the financial markets for over three decades. I've learned to pay more attention to the warning signs I see or sense and then adjust my asset allocation appropriately. I've managed to close that 40 per cent gap quite nicely and put myself back on target to accumulate the amount of money I want for my retirement.

What if I'd hit my goal early? Would I have retired? No, I would have gone on working. I enjoy teaching and writing about money, the economy, art, culture and social issues. I still have lots of ideas and projects (books, TV shows, radio series) that I want to realise. But knowing that I have my retirement money 'in the bank', so to speak, would give me greater mental freedom, knowing that I could slow down, take time to develop a project I am passionate about or take a break from work any time I wanted (or needed) to do so.

It's always important to have a retirement goal in mind. After all, you never know when you may hit it!

A FRIEND'S CURRENT RETIREMENT ASSETS

Pension – Company L			(£)	
	Equity Growth Fund A	G	26,518	
	Equity Tracker Fund C	T	28,065	
	Equity International Fund N	I	32,515	
Pension – Company R				
	Gilts	B	22,092	
	Equity Growth Fund O	CG	19,016	
	Bank account	C	35,000	
Pension – Company J				
	Equity Dividend Growth Fund X	DG	6,485	
	Equity Tracker Fund V	T	2,787	
	Equity Growth Fund M	G	25,194	
	Equity International Fund U	I	7,219	
	Equity Growth Fund Q	G	44,722	
TOTALS				
	Growth unit trusts	G	121,935	47%
	International unit trusts	I	39,734	15%
	Tracker funds	T	33,735	13%
	Bonds (Gilts)	B	21,074	8%
	Cash	C	42,470	16%
	Grand Total		**258,948**	

PROJECTED GROWTH
TO AGE 65
WITH 6% GROWTH
PLUS £5K/YEAR

2015	279,485
2016	301,254
2017	324,329
2018	348,789
2019	374,716
2020	402,199
2021	431,331
2022	462,211
2023	494,944
2024	529,640
2025	566,419
2026	605,404
2027	646,728
2028	690,532

▶️ *Alvin says . . .*

The likelihood that you could live so long that you use up all of the money you have saved for retirement is known as *longevity risk*. People who are not part of a defined benefit retirement plan or who don't own an annuity must consider this risk when they are planning how to manage the assets and cash they have accumulated for retirement. A rule of thumb used by many financial planners to lessen this risk is known as the "4% Rule." If each year you withdraw only 4% of the money in your self-managed retirement pot, then with periodic rebalancing of your asset allocation, your money should at last at least 25 to 30 years.

Accessing Your Home's Value: Trade Down or Equity Release

A common flaw in some people's retirement plans is an over-reliance on the growth in their home equity.

It's an understandable misconception. At some times and in some places, home values have risen explosively for a number of years. Hearing about such run-ups (and perhaps experiencing one yourself), you might be tempted to say, 'Maybe I don't need to invest in shares or bonds. I'll be able to retire on the value of my home!'

There are two big problems with this assumption. First, as you saw in the chapter on buying property, home values don't always rise rapidly. Sometimes they increase slowly or even fall.

Second, you have to live somewhere. So there's a practical limit to your ability to take advantage of any increase in the value of your home. Even if you sell the home, you'll need to use at least part of the proceeds to buy or rent another home and the chances are great that the cost of *that* home will also have risen. So, for the vast majority of people, it doesn't make sense to think of the home as the primary vehicle for retirement investment.

Of course, it is possible to take advantage of a portion of your home's built-up equity when you retire. The most natural way of doing this is by downsizing – that is, by selling the large house you needed while raising kids (and perhaps housing parents or other relatives as well) and buying a smaller, less expensive home that's adequate for your scaled-down lifestyle after the children or not-quite-so-young adults have moved away. The difference between the amount you clear when you sell the big home and the smaller amount needed to buy the more modest home can be added to your retirement nest egg.

Sensible as this approach may be, many people are reluctant to or cannot trade down in their housing choices when they retire. There are obvious psychological reasons for this reluctance. Most people develop an emotional attachment to their homes and it can be difficult to move away from a neighbourhood and a circle of friends who have become familiar.

Some people insist on staying in their large (often too large) houses, that are costly to maintain thus wasting the opportunity to realise and use the equity they've built up. For people in this situation, there are definite advantages to trading down. A smaller home is easier to care for. If you move from a house into a flat, exterior repairs and garden chores are no longer your responsibility. Many older people feel relieved when they have fewer stairs to climb, shorter hallways to navigate and simpler kitchens to clean. And it's certainly much easier and less costly to decorate and refurbish a four-room flat than a ten-room house. Trading down isn't for everyone but it may be appropriate for you. Many retirees find it gives them a new lease of life. I urge you to consider it.

Other people who are about to retire or who have retired may already live in modest homes or flats that they bought many years ago at what seem like low prices today. For this group, downsizing just is not a reasonable option. Yet they too may need additional cash to help make retirement more comfortable. An option available to them as well as to people who don't want to downsize is *equity release*. For people fifty-five years of age or older (depending on the type of equity release), this is a way of funding retirement that should be evaluated carefully, with clear knowledge of the advantages and disadvantages to the homeowner.

There are two types of equity release. The first is a Lifetime Mortgage. In this case, the homeowner takes out a loan against the value of the house. No repayments are ever made. The loan is repaid when the homeowner dies or the house is sold. During the time the loan remains unpaid, the interest charged is added to the amount of the loan. Therefore, the amount of the loan increases. (This is known as *negative amortization*.) So when the property is finally sold, the loan repaid will be higher than the original amount borrowed. Depending on the interest rate, the amount repaid can be significantly higher.

The second type of equity release is a Home Reversion plan. Here, the homeowner sells part or all of their house to an insurance company. The homeowner can continue to live there until death and is responsible for the upkeep and maintenance of the property. No repayments are made until the homeowner dies and the property is sold. The insurance company is repaid its percentage of the value of the property at that time.

Companies offering equity release products must be

members of the Equity Release Council. As part of its Code of Conduct that each member must sign and comply with, all providers must guarantee that the homeowner can remain in the property until death or it is sold and that the amount of the loan will never be more than the property is worth. In both cases, the loan can be taken as a lump sum or as a series of small payments as you need them.

While the above features are common to all equity release programmes, other details must be considered such as the amount you can borrow, arrangement and legal fees, the effects equity release might have on any benefits the homeowner is already receiving, early repayment penalties, option to repay interest and more. While there are only two types of equity release plans, there are a variety of products with different combinations of features. It is advisable to have an independent financial adviser or solicitor help you understand all of the details and risks so that you can make an informed decision and so you have no surprises in the future.

Alvin says . . .

Equity release providers are continually developing new products with different features to appeal to needs of the different retired people who want to access the equity in their homes to help fund their retirement. Use an independent financial adviser who has access to the product offerings of several providers. Thus, you will know the full menu of choices available to you and can make a more suitable decision. Each provider must be a member of the Equity Release Council, which seeks to make sure the offerings are safe. More up-to-date information about the organisation and equity release can be obtained at the website:

www.equityreleasecouncil.com

A Final Word about Retirement Savings

For most people, saving for retirement is a long trek; a marathon race rather than a sprint. It calls for patience and steady determination. As you've seen, it's much easier to build up a handsome retirement nest egg if you start young. But, of course, the younger you are, the less real the prospect of retirement appears and the weaker your motivation is likely to feel. It's a psychological paradox, a little like the one involved in a successful weight-loss programme. You need somehow to find the strength to say, 'No' to a small satisfaction today (that is, the pleasure felt by spending an extra pound or two right now) so that you can enjoy a much greater satisfaction some years in the future (that is, the pleasure of being able to say 'Farewell forever' to the drudgery of work and the anxiety of wondering how next month's bills will be paid).

I hope you'll resist the urge to cut back on your retirement savings plan when you're tempted by an attractive spending option – a new outfit, a weekend getaway, a hot date or some needless spending on your children. And also resist the temptation to borrow against your retirement money or withdraw a slice of it for other purposes. Keep it sacrosanct and, if you can, forget that it exists – except when you sit down periodically to review how well it's been growing.

And finally, parents, please remember that the best gift you can give your children is *your own* financially secure retirement. This way they are free to pursue their lives and careers without having to worry about you or your money.

Alvin says . . .

Be careful and diligent when accumulating money for your retirement. For every person who manages to retire early to Spain or southern France, there are many others – just as hard-working, just as deserving – who never got to enjoy the fruits of a lifetime of labour because they didn't plan, save and invest for the long term. Don't be one of them.

10

PASSING ON YOUR WEALTH

Estate Planning for the Not-So-Filthy Rich

You Can't Take It With You, So Write a Will

Two adages come to mind when I think about inheritance. The first is, 'Where there's a will, there're relatives.' The second is, 'Where there's no will, there're angry relatives.' Making a will is something that too many people ignore, avoid, are indifferent to or simply neglect to do – sometimes quite wilfully – although they would never admit it. In fact, according to some estimates, as many as two-thirds of people in the UK die *intestate*, meaning without a valid will. The percentage is much higher among people who are under 35 years old.

When I think of wills, I invariably think of a friend who is married with children. He also has a child from a relationship before his marriage. My friend, who is much older, and his wife assume that his entire estate will go to her if he dies first and then she will be able to pass along the estate to their children. Needless to say, this would make the child from the previous relationship quite unhappy. The couple's refusal to write a will because of their uninformed assumptions will result in a conflict among the children that may not end well. This is unfair to all of the family members.

The only way to be certain that your possessions end

up in the hands you want to have them after you've died is to draw up a will. Unfortunately, many people ignore this truth. Some neglect will-making because they prefer not to think about death, almost as if pretending it doesn't exist will protect them from it. Of course, that's not how life (or death) works.

If You Die Without a Will

One way to appreciate fully the importance of having a will is to consider the alternative. If you die intestate, your *estate* – your savings, your investments, your home and your personal possessions – will be divvied up among your closest relatives according to the Rules of Intestacy established by the government. (England and Wales have the same rules but Scotland's are different.) Though thoughtfully designed by well-meaning people, these rules are inevitably somewhat arbitrary and capricious.

Perhaps you assume that, if you're married or in a civil partnership, your estate will automatically go to your spouse when you die – just as my friends do. Not so. In most cases, if you are a married person or civil partner with children under eighteen, your spouse will inherit the first £250,000 of your estate, plus half the balance. The remainder will be held in trust and split equally among your kids when they turn eighteen. Does this make sense? Does it fit the needs of your family? Maybe, maybe not. It doesn't matter. When you make no will, the government's one-size-fits-all rules kick in.

In other circumstances, the mismatch between the rules and your actual needs and wishes may be even worse. For example, if you are unmarried but living with a partner (not in a civil partnership), that person is practically invisible under the Rules of Intestacy. If you die without a will, any blood relatives you might have will receive your estate, while your life partner has no automatic right to inherit anything. [NOTE: The surviving partner would have the right to joint saving and investment accounts and *may* have the right to property if it is owned as joint tenant. The partner can also make a claim through the courts, but there is no guarantee of what he or she will get.] And if you die with *no* next of kin, your entire estate will go into the government's coffers. You may like the idea of turning over everything you've worked for to Her Majesty's Revenue and Customs (HMRC) . . . but maybe you can think of a better alternative.

So, making a will is important no matter what your circumstances. It helps ensure that those who are financially dependent on you will be cared for properly after you die. It also allows you to leave your assets and your personal belongings to family, friends and charities in ways that will make you and the recipients happy.

Your Will is Not a DIY Project

It's smart to engage a solicitor in creating your will. Even simple estates are more complex than people realise and a lawyer is well-versed in the inheritance laws. He or she can walk you through 'if-then' scenarios you might never consider and make certain that you and your loved ones are protected even in unusual circumstances that just might happen. For example, you may want to make your spouse your heir. Fine. But supposing you and your spouse die simultaneously – on holiday, for example? What if one of you dies while the other is hospitalised and incapacitated? Will your money go into legal limbo, where it can't be used to provide needed care? Perhaps it seems morbid to raise such possibilities but a lawyer can help you make certain you're prepared to handle them appropriately.

In drawing up a will, many people overlook some of the assets they own that ought to be accounted for in the document. The personal balance sheet that you drew up in Chapter 3 will be a good start in creating your will. Bring it with you when you visit your solicitor. Other steps to follow when planning your will can be found in the checklist on pages 344–346.

As you'll see, I suggest that at the same time you write your will you also make plans for the care of your children, the disposition of any business interests and any other final arrangements. Thoughtful planning of such things can be a real blessing to those you leave behind. When my beloved grandmother was dying at age eighty-five, she not only accepted her fate but embraced it. She planned her own funeral right down to the cars in which we would ride to the service (which she rented in advance). For her friends and family, saying farewell to Grandma was like attending a party – all we had to do was show up.

YOUR WILL CHECKLIST

☐ What are your assets?

Draw up a list of everything you own in whole or in part. (The personal balance sheet you drew up in Chapter 3 will be a helpful place to start.) Include bank accounts, investment accounts and property, as well as personal possessions, business(es) you own and other assets.

☐ Who should carry out your wishes?

Select a trusted family member or friend to serve as the executor of your estate. This person will be responsible for carrying out the wishes expressed in your will. He or she will gather together your assets, pay any outstanding bills (including funeral expenses) and distribute the remainder of your estate to your heirs as specified in the will.

Your executor must be over eighteen years of age and should have the right personality and temperament to handle the job. He or she should be trustworthy, diligent, logical and reasonably knowledgeable about finances and the law. The executor need not be a lawyer or accountant, although some people do select a trusted professional adviser to fill this role. There's no reason why an executor may not also be one of the heirs to your estate.

It's also wise to list a back-up executor, in case your first choice is unavailable for any reason. Before listing an executor, ask to make certain the person you've selected is willing to handle the job.

☐ Make plans for any children

If you have children under eighteen years of age, your will should spell out how they would be cared for in the event both parents die. You'll need to choose a personal guardian, who will be entrusted with raising the children, as well as a financial guardian, who will be in charge of handling any assets and income you provide for them. (This may or may not be the same person.) It's wise to provide for a secondary guardian in the event the first guardian is dead or incapacitated at the time your will goes into effect. As with the executor, ask beforehand to make certain that the people you name are willing to undertake the task.

☐ Decide how to distribute your property

List in general how you want your assets to be distributed (your bequests). While you can list specific amounts, you can also indicate percentage amounts. Describe the distribution of personal possessions in general terms (e.g., 'My jewellery to my sister Elaine'). If there is a long list of specific bequests to particular people ('My diamond and ruby brooch to cousin Agnes'), consider writing up a separate list rather than incorporating this detail into the will itself. Keep this list with the will.

☐ Write up any special wishes you may have

You may want to specify your preferences concerning your funeral, the disposition of your remains and the kind of memorial service to be held in your honour. You may also want to express your wishes about the upbringing of your children, the wrapping-up of any business interests you leave behind and the charitable purposes towards which some of your assets may have been left.

As with any detailed list of inheritance items, these wishes should probably be spelled out in a separate document kept with the will rather than in the will itself. The requests you make here will not be legally binding but they will probably carry considerable weight with those you leave behind.

☐ **Review your will periodically**.

At least once a year, review the terms of your will and make certain they continue to reflect your wishes and your current financial status. Also update your will whenever your circumstances change. Any time there's a change in the status of a person mentioned in the will (an heir, for example) or a major change in any asset you own, you should consider whether a change in your will is required. Among the events that should trigger a review of your will:

- You get married or divorced.
- You have a child.
- One of your heirs dies.
- Your children grow up and become financially independent.
- You buy a home.
- You buy, found, or sell a business.
- You inherit a piece of property or any significant wealth.
- You retire.

☐ **Keep the will and related documents in a safe, accessible place.**

Keep your will somewhere that your spouse, partner, next-of-kin, or other concerned party will be easily able to get it when you die. A safety deposit box at your bank is *not* a good location, since such boxes are often legally sealed after the death of the owner. Instead, consider keeping one copy in a file cabinet or desk at home and a second copy at your lawyer's office. You may want to give a third copy to the executor named in the will.

Basic Estate Planning

In drawing up a will, you've taken the first big step towards getting your estate in order. Now it's time to consider whether some other steps might be worth considering. The answer will depend in part on how large and complicated your estate is. First, you need to understand what will happen after you die.

The Probate Process

When the bell tolls for you, someone will have to deal with your estate by paying debts, compiling all the assets and distributing the estate according to the will. *Probate* refers specifically to the issuing of a legal document, generally called a *grant of representation*, to one or more people that authorises them to handle these matters. It also refers, more generally, to the financial winding-up of your estate under the watchful eye of the government, which seeks to make certain that your wishes are obeyed, that no laws are broken and that the government receives any tax payments that may be due.

Normally, the executor named in your will receives the grant of representation. If you have no will or name no executor, a relative will usually be given the grant, with spouses, civil partners and children getting first priority. The grant is given by the nearest Probate Registry (a government office), which will ask to see the original will, a death certificate and a list of the assets included in the estate. In turn, they'll ask the executor to fill out a set of forms and to submit to an interview at the Probate Registry to confirm the information provided. No grant of representation is needed if the estate is held in joint names (such as a joint current or savings account) and if the estate does not include property, land or securities (such as unit trusts, bonds and OEICs).

Inheritance Tax (IHT)

It is necessary to get an inheritance tax reference number at least three weeks before you can pay inheritance tax. Before a grant of representation is issued, any inheritance tax (IHT) due must be paid by the executor (or other grantee). But will IHT be due on your estate? That depends. The most important factor is the *size* of your estate.

You can estimate the size of your estate right now. Just calculate the total value of your assets. Your estate includes everything owned in your name and your portion of everything you own jointly. (Thus, if you own a house in partnership with a spouse or civil partner, your estate would include half of the value of the house.)

Your estate also includes your share of any gift you've given to others from which you still receive some benefit. For example, if you've turned over ownership of a home to one of your children with the stipulation that you will continue to live there as long as you want, then a portion of the home remains a part of your estate. In the same way, any assets held in trust from which you receive some benefit (such as interest or dividend income) remain part of your estate. Finally, the proceeds on any life insurance policy you own will be counted as part of your estate. (Thus, if you own a £250,000 term life insurance policy of which your spouse is the beneficiary, you should add £250,000 to the total value of your estate.)

Note, however, that business property and agricultural property are subject to 100 per cent relief from IHT. If you own buildings or property used for business or farming purposes, consult a tax lawyer for more detailed information; the rules defining such property are fairly complicated and will be applied precisely.

For IHT purposes, your estate will be valued as of the day you die. For most assets, this is a simple matter. Savings accounts have a clearly stated value. Bonds, shares and other securities are valued as of their closing price on the day you die. Property, however, is valued at the opinion of an expert appraiser and valuing the assets of a private company may be quite complex.

Once all the assets have been valued, any bills you owe at the time of your death will be subtracted from your estate. So will funeral expenses, outstanding care costs or medical bills and any other payments due related to your passing. What remains is the final value of your estate.

Now a bit of maths is necessary. In the UK, the first £325,000 of your estate is completely exempt from IHT. This amount is known as the *inheritance tax threshold* and it is a substantial amount of money. Over 96 per cent of all estates in the UK have a value below this amount and therefore pay no inheritance tax at all. [NOTE: The government periodically raises the inheritance tax threshold. The current amount and other information about how the government applies it to an estate can be found at the website: www.gov.uk/inheritance-tax.]

If, however, you've accumulated sizeable assets over the years, you may find your net worth creeping over the £325,000 threshold. For example, if the value of your home has increased substantially, it may raise your estate over the inheritance tax threshold even if your savings and investments are quite modest. And, once you pass the threshold, the taxes can be substantial. IHT is levied at a rate of 40 per cent on the value of your estate *over* the threshold amount. Thus, if your estate has a total value of £600,000, IHT in the amount of £110,000 will be due. [£600,000 − £325,000 = £275,000, and then 40 per cent of £275,000 = £110,000]. Typically the inheritance tax must be paid within six months after the end of the month in which the individual died. Interest usually begins accruing on the amount of the taxes due after this six-month limit.

If you have a significant estate (or hope to have one someday), you may now be waxing indignant: 'What? Those vultures from HMRC won't even leave my corpse alone! After I worked hard to make all that money, I can't simply leave it to whomever I please without the tax man grabbing a share?'

If you feel this way, it's time to give some serious thought to estate planning. There are a number of simple steps you can take to reduce your exposure to IHT.

Shift Insurance Ownership
As I've mentioned, insurance proceeds are counted as part of your estate if *you* are listed as the owner of the policy. This can complicate your tax problems by increasing the overall size of the estate, perhaps pushing it up over the threshold.

You can avoid this problem by making the beneficiary of the policy – your spouse or your child, for example – the owner of the policy. This step does have disadvantages. For example, you can't change the beneficiary once you've done this and, if you own a whole of life policy, you will forfeit your right to any cash value the policy accumulates. Check with your insurance company or insurance agent to decide whether or not you want to make this change.

Give Your Wealth Away

A very popular way of reducing IHT is by giving away a portion of your assets while you're alive. The idea, of course, is that by reducing the size of the estate you leave behind, you can reduce or eliminate the amount that is exposed to IHT.

Perhaps it occurs to you that a person suffering from a terminal illness could escape IHT altogether by simply signing papers that transfer everything to a child or other heir – one big 'gift' in place of inheritance. Well the same thought has occurred to HM Revenue and Customs. They've developed rules about gift-giving that are designed to prevent this. The rules are fairly complicated so if you want to adopt gift-giving as a way of reducing IHT you should consult a financial adviser or solicitor who can walk you through the regulations so that you can come up with a detailed plan. However, there are two basic rules that you should keep in mind. First, if you give a gift, such as an investment account, to your children, for example, but you continue to benefit from it, then it is not exempt from the inheritance tax. So, giving your house to your children and then continuing to live in the property means it remains part of your taxable estate when you die.

The second basic rule is that any gifts you give prior to seven years before your death are excluded from your estate. Gifts given within the seven-year window before you die are subject to IHT at a gradually increasing rate: 20 per cent of the usual tax during the sixth year prior to death, 40 per cent during the fifth year and so on.

In addition, some other kinds of gifts are excluded from IHT even within the seven-year window:

- Gifts or bequests to a spouse or civil partner.
- Annual gifts of up to £3,000 per year.
- Small gifts of up to £250 per year to any one person (which are counted outside the £3,000 window and cannot be made to the same person to whom you gave the £3,000 exemption amount).
- A wedding gift of up to £5,000 to your child or to the person your child is marrying or entering into a civil partnership (grandparents can give up to £2,500).
- Gifts or bequests to UK registered charities, the National Trust, museums, universities and others.

⊱⊰ *Alvin says* . . .

If you have a large estate, consider starting an annual gift-giving plan so as to reduce the amount of IHT your heirs will ultimately have to pay. Of course, any assets you give away during your lifetime will be out of your control – otherwise they are not real gifts. Thus, your desire to trim your tax liability will have to be balanced with the need to make certain that you keep hold of enough assets to support you comfortably for as long as you live.

Plan Your Will

You can also reduce IHT by planning your will provisions intelligently. As I noted above, anything you give to your spouse or civil partner during your lifetime or leave to him or her on your death is excluded from IHT.

This so-called spousal exemption offers a significant savings opportunity to married couples and those in civil partnerships. You can take advantage of the exemption by drafting a will that does *not* leave your entire estate to your spouse or civil partner. Instead, leave a certain amount or percentage to others, such as your children, with the balance to your spouse. The potential benefit of this strategy kicks in when your spouse or civil partner in turn dies.

A bit confused? Here's an example to illustrate how the strategy works. [NOTE: Remember that the amount of the inheritance tax threshold, currently £325,000, changes periodically. However, the basic mathematics in the following example are still valid.]

Suppose Philip and Gillian are married with two children and they have an estate with a total value of £800,000. For simplicity's sake, we'll assume that half of this value is owned by each spouse. If Philip dies with a will leaving everything to Gillian, she will inherit his £400,000 part of the estate tax-free (thanks to the spousal exemption). But now suppose Gillian dies ten years later. She leaves an £800,000 estate, whose value in excess of £325,000 will be subject to tax. The total IHT due will be £190,000 (£800,000 – £325,000 = £475,000; and then 40 per cent of £475,000 = £190,000).

Instead, suppose Philip's will specified that £325,000 of his £400,000 estate would be left to the two children, with the balance going to Gillian. As his spouse, she will therefore inherit £75,000 tax-free and the children's inheritance, since it falls within the £325,000 tax exemption, will also be tax-free.

Gillian's net worth is now £475,000 [£75,000 (inherited) + £400,000 (her part of the estate)]. Now, when Gillian dies ten years later, she leaves a £475,000 estate to her children. Tax will be payable on the amount of her estate that exceeds £325,000. The total tax due will be £60,000 [£475,000 – £325,000 = £150,000; and then 40 per cent of £150,000 = £60,000].

Do you see what has happened? Almost £130,000

[£190,000 in the first example *minus* £60,000 in the second example] in IHT has been saved through the redrafting of Philip's will more than ten years earlier! Of course, this strategy only works if your spouse or civil partner has enough to live on even when the estate is split between her and other heirs. The advice of a lawyer is essential, as it always is when you are drafting a will. Nonetheless, this is a basic tax savings technique that many couples can take advantage of – and that too many people know nothing about.

[NOTE: In the example above, we specified that Gillian died ten years after her spouse. We specified this time in order to avoid dealing with one specific complication of the IHT law. If you leave your estate to someone who then dies within five years, Quick Succession Relief reduces the IHT payable on the second death according to a declining scale, depending on how many years have passed since your death. But I'm going to stop here. Consult a tax lawyer if you really need to know more about this.]

Getting Fancy

There are other more complicated estate-planning techniques. Some people use specially designed life insurance policies for the purpose of paying off IHT that may be due after their death, thereby leaving the full value of the estate available to their heirs. The maths of making this work properly are complicated. If you're curious, get advice from a tax lawyer or life insurance specialist.

Another popular estate-planning option among people with large estates is the use of trusts. A *trust* is a legal entity specifically created to administer assets and income on behalf of a beneficiary. By creating a carefully crafted trust to handle wealth on your behalf, or on behalf of your children or other dependants, you may be able to shift some of your estate outside the probate process and thereby save time and taxes.

If you are interested in considering a trust strategy, consult a financial adviser or solicitor who specialises in tax issues . . . which leads nicely into my next topic: how to choose and work with a financial adviser.

11

WHO TO BELIEVE?

Choosing and Using Financial Advisers

Many people in the UK think that the proper role of a financial adviser is to enable the individual investor to take a back seat in managing the growth of their money, with no responsibilities other than to enjoy their money and do whatever makes them happy. They believe they should give control of their money over to a financial adviser whose authority and decision is not to be questioned, just as the average patient wouldn't question the advice he or she gets from their doctor or GP.

I believe this is the wrong approach. Working with a financial adviser should be a partnership, one in which the two of you are working towards two goals: the preservation of the value of your money (i.e., protecting it against the effects of inflation) and increasing the amount of money you have through capital growth. A key part of your role as the investor or client is to listen carefully, ask tough questions and insist on clear answers that you can understand. A key role of the investment adviser is to 'know the customer' – i.e., understand your financial objectives and your risk tolerance and capacity for loss, help you understand the markets and investment products, suggest investments that are suitable for you and to always make you aware of the potential rewards and risks of each investment decision. You are on the financial journey together but *your* best interests must always be the first consideration. Never lose sight of the fact that the money is *yours* and that only you can determine how it should best be saved, invested and spent. Ongoing reviews of your financial situation and any changes are essential.

Who Needs a Financial Adviser?

If you've really absorbed the contents of this book, you already have a leg-up on most other people. You know more about the basics of prudently managing, saving and investing money than the average person, and you're pretty well-equipped to handle many financial issues on your own. And, of course, I've scattered guidance throughout the book concerning where to turn for specific additional information you may need on matters such as saving tax-free, recovering from too much debt, preparing a proper will, choosing the right investment vehicles and more.

You're also lucky to be living in a time when sound, easy-to-understand money advice is more widely available than ever before. You can increase your knowledge about basic financial matters, current trends, new savings and investment products, and smart money strategies by using such information sources as:

- Websites – some independent, some company sponsored – devoted to virtually all aspects of personal finance, basic money management and investing.
- Government or agency websites offering objective, unbiased information and explanatory examples.

- The money pages or personal finance sections in newspapers and their accompanying websites.
- Magazines that focus on financial and investment topics.
- TV and radio programmes and news coverage.
- Books on personal finance.
- Financial seminars, workshops and courses.
- Trade associations and financial services firms.

Of course, not all of these sources are equally reliable. Consider the Internet, for example. Information spreads faster and easier on the Internet than anywhere else and everyone with access is free to contribute thoughts and ideas. Because little of the content is edited or controlled, the reliability and timeliness of the information can vary wildly. Search on the web for information on a topic such as 'mortgages', 'high interest savings accounts', 'best credit cards' or 'share investing' and you'll find thousands of websites offering information. Unfortunately, many of these will not be helpful. Some will contain scanty information, while others offer material that is dated, incomplete, grossly biased, plain wrong or just a sales platform.

When you're trying to sort the reliable from the treacherous in today's flood of financial information, start by using the same sort of common sense and scepticism you'd apply to a television advert, a door-to-door salesman or a phone solicitation. Always consider who will benefit from any advice you read or hear. A person or company with an interest in selling a particular financial product or service has a huge incentive to slant the information they present, not necessarily by lying but by playing down or ignoring

certain risks and over-emphasising the potential benefits. (And there *are* firms and individuals who don't bat
an eyelid at committing out-and-out fraud.)

Part of evaluating any financial information source is
considering its reputation, background and history. Also,
weigh the ideas you get from different sources against
one another. An investment strategy touted only by one
or two obscure firms ought to be examined with extreme
scepticism, while a strategy that's been widely reported,
tested by independent journalists and industry experts,
and used with success for years by many individuals may
be worth considering for your own portfolio.

So, there's a lot you can do to advance your own money
knowledge, enabling you to make many money decisions
on your own. But for many people there comes a point
when soliciting professional advice is important. You
may need professional financial advice if:

- You need help in developing a savings and investment
  programme for goals such as retirement or paying your
  children's school and university fees.
- You're in the market for life insurance, a private
  pension plan, a savings plan or an annuity and are
  unsure which product will best suit your needs.
- You want to begin investing in collective investments
  (i.e., unit trusts, OEICs, etc.), shares, bonds or other
  securities and feel uncertain about how to get started.
- You want to invest your money – the money you've
  diligently saved – so that it may grow faster than it
  would in a traditional bank or building society savings
  account.
- You already own a number of pension plans, shares,
  unit trusts, OEICs or other investments and don't

know whether they add up to a coherent and appropriate investment strategy.

- You're facing a major change in your life situation (marriage, divorce, retirement, selling a business) and aren't sure how to adjust your finances accordingly.
- You're deep in debt or facing other financial problems that you don't know how to solve on your own.
- You've built a large estate and are concerned about reducing the inheritance tax liability your heirs will face.

If one or more of these circumstances fits you, then the time may have come when your personal finances are a bit too complicated for you to handle on your own.

Types of Financial Advisers and Financial Advice

However, it's not enough to recognise that you may need financial help. It's equally important to decide what *kind* of help you need and what sort of professional is best equipped to provide it. Here's a brief rundown of the main types of financial advisers, with some guidelines as to what to expect from each.

Independent Financial Advisers (IFAs)
The job of an IFA is to provide financial advice on investments and other money matters based on your personal status, current assets and long-term goals. Regulatory changes called the Retail Distribution Review (widely referred to using the initials RDR) that went into effect at the end of 2012 were designed to make it easier for you to:

1. Understand the type of advice you are receiving.
2. Know how much the advice is costing you. (Recent regulations on commission will be explained shortly.)
3. Give you greater confidence in the qualifications (both current and ongoing) and professionalism of the financial adviser.
4. Know that the IFA is treating the customer fairly and placing the customer's interests first.

An IFA can offer one of two types of advice – independent or restricted – and he or she must make clear which type is being provided.

- *Independent advice* means the IFA can recommend all types of retail investment products from almost any provider or company offering them in the marketplace. The products would include all types of pooled investments (e.g., unit trusts, investment trusts, open-ended investment companies (OEICs), exchange-traded funds (ETFs), etc., certain types of pensions and life assurance that has an investment feature.
- *Restricted advice* means the financial adviser is limited to working with a certain type of product (annuities, for example) and/or a limited number of providers. There are some providers who only offer their products direct to the consumer or via their own distribution team. (Note: The old term, *tied agent*, was used to describe an adviser who represented one provider and its products. The term is no longer used.)

Under the new RDR regulations, financial advisers can no longer earn commissions, either directly or indirectly, on the pension, investment and annuity products they recommend. [NOTE: They can still earn commissions on life assurance and insurance products.] They can charge fees in one of four ways:

1. A menu of fees based on the amount or kind of work involved.
2. A fixed percentage of the total value of the investment.
3. A fixed monthly retainer.
4. An hourly fee.

Whatever method the financial adviser uses, the charges must be clearly stated and explained up front to the customer. Additionally, the adviser must disclose how the fees or charges will be paid. This could be a debit from the client's investment account or a cheque from the customer. This regulation is designed to make the costs associated with getting investment advice totally transparent.

The concept behind eliminating commission payments is the belief that an adviser whose payment is fee-based should generally be counted on to provide unbiased investment suggestions (which is not to say that his or her suggestions will always be right). By contrast, an adviser who was paid in part or in whole from commissions might be tempted (and some indeed were) to offer advice that favours investment products on which greater commissions are paid to him or her. It also meant that it was difficult for advisers to recommend products that didn't pay a commission, because they would not get paid. RDR removes this commission-based bias in which the customer's best interests may not have always been the primary consideration.

Investment advisers vary widely in their knowledge,

experience and interests. Not all are equally knowledge-able about every financial field. Be sure to select an IFA with experience working with clients like you, as well as knowledge of the specific financial topics you are keenly interested in. For example, if you are interested in getting started investing, seek out an IFA with in-depth knowledge of unit trusts, exchange-traded funds and other securities. Most IFAs would recommend a portfolio of collective or pooled investments (unit trusts, OEICs). Very few are authorised to recommend shares. This would be the role of a stockbroker.

Solicitors and Accountants

Some lawyers and accountants offer financial planning as part of their professional services work. Their professional training can equip them to understand specific aspects of the financial world. For example, there are solicitors who specialise in tax-saving strategies, estate-planning techniques, small business finance and other legal matters related to your money. The more specific you can be in describing the kind of legal or accounting guidance you need, the easier it will be for you to find just the right professional to help you. However, investment advice and financial planning should always come from someone with the proper training in that area.

Stockbrokers

At some point in your financial life, you will probably want to work with a stockbroker. A broker acts as a middleman between an individual and the investment market. A broker handles the purchase and sale of securities (shares, bonds, unit trusts, OEICs, ETFs and others), keeps track of the investment income (dividend and interest payments) and capital gains or losses in your account, sends out trade confirmations and statements, maintains financial records for you and otherwise helps you navigate – and hopefully profit from – the investment markets. There are three main kinds of brokers:

- *Execution-only brokers* simply buy and sell shares or other securities at your direction, for which they are paid a relatively small commission. They offer no financial or investment advice. The cheapest execution-only brokers offer their services over the Internet. They're also called *online brokers*.
- *Advisory brokers* handle your trades but they also offer investment ideas and advice. Since your broker handles most or all of your investment transactions and maintains your financial records, he or she knows your portfolio well and is in a good position to suggest ways of helping it grow, as well as ways of avoiding or reducing potential losses. Remember that the broker is required to 'know their customer' and do an in-depth and accurate assessment of your objective, risks and needs before opening the account. However, after working with you for a while, he or she should develop a more refined sense of your money personality and become more skilful at making the kinds of investments that are most suitable and interesting for you.

  Advisory brokers also have access to a wealth of useful investment information. Through the brokerage houses that employ them, they have access to company reports, analysts' assessments of a firm's financial prospects and the quality of its management, and strategic reports prepared by experts (often in-house) on all manner of financial topics: interest rates, foreign developments, new business sectors, economic cycles and so on. Thus, an advisory broker can help accelerate your financial education. It's a bit more expensive to work with an advisory broker than with an execution-only broker, since the fees you pay on trades must also cover the costs of maintaining the brokerage company's research department and its operations areas (also called the *back office*).

If you employ an advisory broker, take full advantage of the research and advice he or she can offer. When you're curious about a particular business sector or a company's shares or other securities, ask your broker for information. He or she will probably have some research to send you: an analyst's report, an email showing the company's financial data or the like. He or she may also be able to suggest other similar investments that are worth examining for comparison's sake. And he or she may have advice to offer based on the experience of other clients with these investments.

- The *portfolio manager* is the third type of broker and is generally employed only by the wealthy. In addition to executing trades requested by clients, this individual or team of professionals actually makes investment decisions on their clients' behalf and has discretionary authority over the account. The portfolio manager and the client may agree together on a general set of goals and investment strategies, but the details involved in the execution of those strategies (i.e., the selecting, buying and selling of securities) are left up to the manager who simply reports results to the client according to strict regulatory requirements. Hence the alternative name for this type of portfolio manager is a *discretionary broker* since you (the client) give this person the written discretionary authority (called a *power of attorney*) to act on your behalf. He or she is generally paid a significant fee, typically based on a percentage of the total amount of money invested.

Naturally, it's not possible for a broker to act in this capacity unless the client has given him or her legal authorisation to invest money on his or her behalf. This kind of arrangement is *not* recommended for the average investor, nor indeed for anyone working with a broker in whom he or she has less than absolute, implicit trust.

It's great when your broker provides research ideas but always remember that you must make or participate in the final investment decisions. Sometimes investors feel intimidated by their brokers or feel obligated to them because of the time and effort they've expended in generating investment ideas. Don't! Remember: providing you with investment information is part of your broker's job, for which he or she gets well paid. You must not worry about hurting the person's feelings if you decide not to invest at all or to invest in something different.

⌖Alvin says . . .

If your beloved Uncle Nigel has been successfully managing the family fortune for the past forty years, then *maybe* you should give him the power of attorney to trade on your behalf. Even with a relative, however, you must exercise diligence and pay attention to what's happening in your account. If someone less trustworthy asks for that power, just say 'no' strongly or run in the opposite direction. It's like you're being invited, not to make your net worth grow, but to make yourself a victim.

Choosing a Financial Adviser

When you're considering working with a financial adviser – whether an IFA, a broker or any other type of professional – be prepared for your initial meeting with a list of questions. (Your list should *not* include, 'Can you make me rich?' or 'Are you rich?' which is either naïve or cynical.) See the list on pages 369–372 for a good starting point. The questions presented there can be used with any kind of financial adviser – an IFA, an insurance agent or a stockbroker. Also, go armed with a statement of your personal financial goals, which must be much more specific than 'to make money'. The more information you can give the adviser about your current financial situation, your goals, your short-term and long-term objectives as well as your worries, the better. Your conversation needs to be specific and detailed, enabling you to get a very clear sense as to whether or not this adviser has the right investment philosophy, communication style and trustworthiness for you.

Be Sceptical but Not Cynical

When considering a particular adviser, don't ignore any sense of disbelief, doubt or discomfort you may feel. Listen to your intuition! Don't let yourself be swayed by an adviser's flashy accoutrements, nice office, posh accent or shiny car. You want someone to whom you can talk straight and from whom you can receive clear, definitive answers, not necessarily someone with an impressive appearance or a silver tongue. Don't be shy about asking friends for recommendations or an introduction to their IFA.

Take notes during your initial meeting. Then have

meetings with a couple of other advisers and compare their answers. You do not have to pay anything to have these meetings with financial advisers. Look for one who offers advice that is clearly tailored to you and your circumstances rather than generic advice that applies to everyone.

Some people feel shy about asking a question when they don't understand what the adviser says. They worry about being thought to be stupid or about wasting the adviser's time. Just open your mouth and ask the question! Remember, the adviser should want to work for you, not vice versa. He or she owes you thoughtful, respectful service, just as any employee owes his or her employer.

TEN QUESTIONS TO ASK A FINANCIAL ADVISER

☐ **What are your charges likely to be in the first two years that we work together?**

He or she should enumerate all fees and other expenses and show how much his or her services will cost in real numbers, using concrete examples, not just percentages. Two years is a realistic time frame to ask the adviser to predict: the first year will include any initial costs, and the second year will reflect ongoing expenses. All charges must be clear and totally transparent. Unexpected fees or charges are never a good sign.

☐ **How long have you been active in your field?**

The longer the adviser's experience, the better. It's most crucial that he or she has been active through both bull and bear stock markets and through financial recessions and periods of inflation. Without such longevity, an adviser may lack certain crucial insights into market behaviour and psychology. On the other hand, if the individual has had the proper training and is working with a reputable team or company, he or she may have other insights and knowledge about specific sectors that fit with your investment objectives.

☐ **How successful have your clients been in following your advice?**

He or she should be able to show some records or reports that indicate the kind of financial results his or her clients have enjoyed in the past (without names, of course). It's even better if these records are *audited* — that is, bearing a mark of authenticity and accuracy from a recognised accountancy firm that has reviewed them independently.

☐ **Have you had any clients with backgrounds and goals similar to mine? How did you work with them?**

The adviser's answer will help you gain a sense as to whether or not he or she really understands your position and what you hope to accomplish. It will also help you gain a feeling for how fully he or she customises his advice for each client (as opposed to offering 'canned' advice that scarcely varies from one client to another).

☐ How do you differ from other financial advisers? What makes you unique?

Listen here as much for what the adviser *doesn't* say as for what he or she does say. Avoid an adviser who makes inflated claims, promises 'risk-free' results or claims an 'inside track' on 'secret opportunities'. Instead, look for someone who works hard to stay on top of news and developments in the financial sphere and will take the time to work with you and for you. Be realistic about the adviser's results, even when the markets are having a good year. And if the results produced and the answers to your questions sound too good to be true, leave quickly but graciously!

☐ Have there been any complaints from clients about you?

If you feel the least bit doubtful on this point, check the records maintained by the Financial Conduct Authority (FCA) concerning public complaints against financial advisers and the firms they work for. Of course, one or two complaints aren't necessarily fatal but a pattern of many complaints, or a history of charges that involve deception or incompetence, spell bad news. Information about such complaints can be found at the FCA's website:

http://www.fca.org.uk/firms/systems-reporting/register/search/individuals

☐ What licences do you have? What professional organisations do you belong to?

Financial advisers may belong to any of several reputable professional organisations. The first two listed below are the organisations to which the majority of IFAs belong. If in doubt, you can call or visit the organisation's website to check the claimed credentials:

- **Personal Finance Society**
    - website: www.thepfs.org or www.findanadviser.org
    - Email: customer.serv@cii.co.uk
    - Tel: 020 8530 0852

- **Institute of Financial Planning**, which lists fee-based financial
planners
    - Website: www.financialplanning.org.uk
    - Email: enquiries@financialplanning.org.uk
    - Tel: 0117 945 2470

- **The Wealth Management Association (WMA)**. [NOTE: Until October
2013, this organisation was known as the Association of Private
Client Investment Managers & Stockbrokers (APCIMS).]
    - Website: www.thewma.co.uk
    - Email: enquiries@thewma.co.uk
    - Tel: 020 7448 7100

- **The Association of Solicitor Investment Managers (ASIM)**, lists
solicitors' firms that provide legal and financial advice.
    - Website: www.asim.org.uk
    - Email: contact@asim.org.uk
    - Tel: 01892 870 065

- **The Ethical Investment Research Services (EIRIS)**, which lists firms
that specialise in ethical investments.
    - Website: www.eiris.org
    - Email: info@eiris.org
    - Tel: 020 7840 5700

Call the Financial Conduct Authority (FCA) Register (0800 111 6768) if
you're in any doubt as to the authenticity of an adviser's professional
credentials. You can also visit The Financial Services Register's website
(www.fca.org.uk/register/) to check all public information about
individuals, firms and other financial services industry participants

regulated by the FCA. An unauthorised financial adviser may be committing fraud and violating the law. And if you lose money when doing business with an unauthorised adviser, you may find that you will be unable to recover your losses — a risk that is much less with a properly regulated and registered adviser.

☐ **How will my assets be held – by me, or by some other party? If the latter, how are they authorised to hold client money? What form of insurance do they have?**

You want to be certain that your shares, bonds, and other assets will be held by a responsible organisation (for securities, a registered depository) and that their value is fully insured against loss due to the failure of the organisation.

☐ **Are you the person I will deal with on a day-to-day basis? Can I call you on the phone with questions or concerns? How often?**

Surprisingly, some advisers are reluctant to provide this kind of personal service. They seem to feel that talking with clients is a nuisance. This is a bad sign. Remember, it's your money. And if you don't know what's being done with it, or why, trouble is apt to follow.

☐ **How frequently do you provide written reports to your clients? May I see a sample?**

You should receive written reports about the performance of your investments every six months, although a larger account would receive reports quarterly. Today most clients have 24-hour online access to their account and information about its performance. The sample report should be clear and easily understandable, and the adviser should be willing to explain anything on the report that is less than obvious. If the adviser shares a real client report with you, notice whether the name and identity of the client are shielded. They should be, for privacy's sake.

Ask a Hypothetical Question

Here's an approach I like to follow when screening a new investment adviser. I first think about how much I might like to invest with the new adviser, based on the amount of assets I currently have in reserve. Then I give the adviser two scenarios: 'If I gave you X pounds per year to invest on my behalf, what might you do with it? And if I gave you Y pounds per year (citing a significantly larger portion of my portfolio), what might you do with it?' And I ask for the answers in writing. If the potential adviser is reluctant to provide *written* responses then that would make me uncomfortable.

What's the point of asking this hypothetical, two-part question? First, I want to see if there's a difference between the two plans, depending on the amount of the money to be invested. Or does the broker use a formulaic approach that applies willy-nilly to everyone? And secondly, I want to see how it fits into my overall financial goals.

The Questions You Should Expect to Answer

Of course, the adviser must get to know you in order to provide truly customised advice. A reputable adviser will want to spend time during an initial meeting learning about your background, financial knowledge, investment experience, objectives, interests, preferences, risk tolerance (your ability to tolerate a decline in the investment markets) and risk capacity (your ability to withstand a financial loss in your portfolio before the loss affects your lifestyle). On page 374 we've provided a list of the questions an adviser ought to ask you. If these topics are never broached in your first conversation with an adviser, it may be a warning sign.

SEVEN QUESTIONS A FINANCIAL ADVISER SHOULD ASK you

1. What are your short-term and long-term financial goals? [You should come prepared to give clear answers to the question.]

2. What is your risk tolerance or how risk averse are you? Is your focus more on capital growth or preservation of the capital you have accumulated?

3. Do you understand inflationary risk and the negative impact it can have causing a reduction in the value or purchasing power of the money you've saved?

4. What are your personal assets and liabilities?

5. Have you bought securities (e.g., shares, bonds, unit trusts) before? If you have, what did you buy? How long did you hold them? How well did your investments do?

6. What is your investment time horizon? Or what are you various investment time horizons for your money? [People usually have several goals they are working towards.]

7. How closely do you want to be involved in making your investment decisions? [The right answer is always.] Even if you are busy or have total confidence in your IFA, you should know what is happening in your account, although you may not be actively involved in every investment decision.

You should feel that the adviser has asked you for enough information to truly understand your financial circumstances. Only in this way can the adviser offer guidance that is personalised and appropriate for your needs and goals.

Maintaining a Good Relationship with Your Adviser

Once you've chosen a financial adviser, expect to invest some time and effort in making the relationship productive. Remember, you're in the front seat, helping to steer the car, not snoozing in the back. Your chance of maintaining a successful and happy relationship with your adviser will be much greater if you:

- Keep complete, accurate records of your transactions. Start a file or a folder on your computer in which you store all your financial paperwork and keep it up-to-date. Be prepared to review the decisions you've made and to evaluate their success or failure. This is crucial if you hope to learn from your successes and failures and gradually sharpen your financial acumen.
- Make notes of your conversations with your adviser. Be sure you capture your adviser's suggestions, advice and warnings accurately. Otherwise, you can never be certain whether your investment gains (or losses) are occurring because of your adviser's help or in spite of it.
- Keep your adviser fully informed about your financial status, goals, needs and wishes. Let him or her know how you're feeling about your finances as well as your outlook for the economy and the markets. And speak up when your objectives, your risk tolerance, your need for money, your employment status, your lifestyle or your interests change.
- Keep yourself generally informed about financial and economic trends. Read the business news and discuss with your adviser how the latest developments may affect your personal investments and financial plans.
- Ask questions. Make sure you understand the risks

and costs before you agree to any investment or other financial plan. If your adviser insists on using technical jargon and can't or won't translate it into plain, understandable English, consider changing advisers.

- Be willing to listen and learn. The investment markets are constantly changing and new products introduced, such as the different types of exchange-traded products (ETPs). Some of these can offer new investment opportunities that may be quite appropriate for your objectives and needs. When your adviser talks to you about such a product, take the time to learn about it. And proceed when you are comfortable with your understanding of the risks and rewards.

For his or her part, your adviser should always:

- Explain both the risks and the potential benefits from any financial strategy he or she is proposing. Remember, no investment is risk-free. Run away from any adviser who claims to offer one that is.
- Be able and willing to explain the fees and other expenses associated with a proposed investment. Insist on clear answers, not vague ones.
- Explain how and why a proposed investment or other strategy is suitable for *your* financial goals, risk tolerance and other personal characteristics. A one-size-fits-all approach is *never* the best.
- Explain the firm's investment philosophy which will include, for example, how it is likely to act in response to certain market events, how frequently it is likely to rebalance a customer's portfolio and other key approaches and responses to the investment markets.
- Tell you how long you have to change your mind once

you've signed up for an investment. Many financial products – but not all! – are required to provide a cooling-off period during which a new investor may cancel and receive a full refund, less any losses caused by market fluctuations.

- Provide regular written reports (e.g., statements) showing the current performance of your investments as well as any investment transactions from the most recent time period. If you have any difficulty understanding every detail on these reports, he or she should be willing and able to explain them to you in plain English.

However, for a happy financial relationship, you *shouldn't* expect a financial adviser to:

- Make investment decisions for you, unless you specifically authorise the person to do so with a proper written power of attorney. (And as I've suggested earlier, this is generally *not* a good idea unless you completely trust the individual as well as the firm he or she works for.)
- Assume investment risk on your behalf. If the adviser informs you appropriately about the risks involved in any investment decision, then any losses you suffer as a result of those risks are simply part of the price of being an investor, not something you can blame on the adviser or expect him or her to repay.
- Be responsible for your making decisions that are ill-advised or inappropriate. If you insist on choosing a particular investment or strategy despite receiving reasonable notice about its disadvantages from your adviser, then you alone are to blame for the consequences.

- Remember and consider every aspect of your personal financial situation when making a financial recommendation. Be prepared, if necessary, to remind your adviser of any relevant data about yourself: 'Are you sure I ought to be moving a lot of money out of cash right now? Remember, my daughter is starting university next autumn and there will be big tuition bills to pay.'
- Hold your hand or play psychiatrist during every market swing. Managing money can be emotionally trying. Part of your adviser's role is to give you the information and perspective you need to decide whether you want to stay with your current investment strategy or make changes. If you find yourself becoming unduly anxious, fearful, confused or angry when your investments shift, don't take out your moods on your financial adviser. Instead, tell him or her about your feelings and consider moving your money into less risky vehicles where you are more comfortable. However, once you've made such a change, don't look back with regret if you miss out on an unexpected gain if you had stayed with your old strategy.
- Make money on every investment in securities. However, your adviser should be right more often than wrong. Always picking winners is simply not possible. When an investment starts to lose money, the adviser should have a clear strategy for cutting your losses.
- Time the market – i.e., buy securities before a price rise and sell them before a price decline. It is difficult to know exactly when is the best time to buy or sell a security. A wise adviser will help keep your long-term investment goal in focus instead of concentrating on the short-term ups and downs of individual securities and the overall market.

What If a Dispute Arises?

Knowing the most effective way to complain and what organisation to complain to about matters related to personal finance is something everyone should know. My key advice: put your complaint in writing to the Compliance Officer. Details of who to write to will be in the firm's Client Agreement or Terms of Business letter given to you at the start of your relationship or on the most recently revised version. Yes, I know it takes more time. However, writing it forces you to organise and present your complaint in a clear logical way that can be understood by others without the emphasis that comes from your tone of voice when you complain over the phone. Importantly, this starts your 'paper trail', a record of your accusation and what happens subsequently. Also, regulated firms must respond to all complaints, which are defined as 'an expression of dissatisfaction, either written or verbal'.

If you feel that your financial adviser has been giving you poor advice, neglecting you, misleading you, cheating you or even lying to you, start by bringing your complaint directly to the person and his firm in writing. Be prepared to explain exactly what is troubling you and to suggest an appropriate remedy. If the problem arose from a simple misunderstanding or a minor error, a letter should suffice to correct it.

If not, you can move up the chain of command within the company that employs your adviser. All financial services companies must have a well-established procedure for handling client complaints and you are entitled to request a copy of their complaint procedures if you wish. At the website below, the Financial Conduct Authority (FCA) lists the four steps you must follow in order to make a complaint and the time frame in which the company must acknowledge receipt of your complaint and respond to it:

www.fca.org.uk/consumers/complaints-and-compensation/how-to-complain

If your complaint or charge is valid, the firm will try to resolve it in an appropriate way. Of course, you may have to find another financial adviser with whom to work.

If you're still not satisfied with how your complaint is resolved, take it to the Financial Ombudsman Service (FOS). It is a free, independent organisation that helps to settle complaints between financial services companies and their customers. If the FOS cannot negotiate a settlement that is satisfactory, your final option is to take the dispute to the courts.

If your complaint is about credit cards, any type of consumer credit, loan or hire-purchase agreements, contact the Financial Conduct Authority's Consumer Helpline, 0800 111 6768. [NOTE: At the beginning of April 2014, the FCA took over the regulation of all consumer credit that had been the responsibility of the Office of Fair Trading (OFT).] If you are owed money by a registered financial services company that has gone bust, then contact the Financial Services Compensation Scheme: www.fscs.org.uk. Other organisations like Citizens Advice (www.citizensadvice.org.uk) and the Pensions Advisory Service (www.pensionsadvisoryservice.org.uk) also provide free services in helping to settle complaints related to financial services companies and their products. Impartial information and guidance in the other areas can also be obtained from the FCA.

DIY Investing: Online Brokerage Firms

Given the amount of up-to-the-minute investment information that is available for free online or that one can subscribe to via a wide variety of data providers, some people prefer making all their own investment decisions. For these individuals, trading their own account usually starts as an avocation but it can quickly become their primary job as their trades become more profitable, their assets grow and their investing acumen improves.

One of the primary incentives for trading yourself is that you are totally in control. You research and select the companies or products (e.g., gold) in which to invest and then you decide when to sell them to realise your gain or cut your losses. And you can do this at any time of the day or night from your home or office computer. (Of course, if you submit a trade during hours when the Stock Exchange is closed, the transaction will actually take place when the market opens the next morning.) Another incentive is the relatively low commissions charged by online brokerage firms. This makes DIY investing quite economical compared to using a full-service stockbroker.

However, there are other costs to keep in mind, such as subscriptions to newsletters, periodicals, emails (like The Motley Fool), charting services and third-party analysis that give you the details you need to make an informed investment decision. And there are seminars many people attend to get new ideas, understand new products or learn new strategies. It is important to decide what additional tools you will need to help you be a successful trader.

A significant challenge is the need to continually update your knowledge of the dynamic financial markets.

A strategy that produced profits six months ago may not work today. So, keeping your knowledge and investment ideas up-to-date is vital. Take advantage of the learning tools (e.g., tutorials, simulations, videos, quizzes etc.) that are available at the websites of many third-party data providers like Morningstar:

www.morningstar.co.uk/uk/funds/learningcenter.aspx

Being a DIY investor can be exciting, satisfying and lucrative. But it can also be highly risky. The pitfalls are well-documented and numerous: over-trading, letting emotions cloud your decision, becoming overly concentrated in one security or business sector, failing to have a clear exit strategy, trying to compensate up for a past mistake and more. The key assets needed for success are reliable knowledge and self-discipline.

▰▰ *Alvin says . . .*

I don't think online brokers are appropriate for most novice investors. It is virtually impossible to become an investment expert overnight or after only a few courses or seminars. At a traditional, full-service brokerage firm, you'll have a real, live person who makes an effort to know you and to guide your investment choices. This is a valuable service for anyone who is new to investing. But if the time comes when you feel emboldened to manage your investments without the benefit of a broker's advice, then the online brokerage firms offer the best value.

Investment Clubs

An investment club is an attractive option for individuals who want to share their investment ideas and pool a portion of their financial resources with others who have the same interests. It is also a great opportunity to learn from other people who may have in-depth information about how different business sectors work and make money.

An investment club usually has between ten and twenty members. They may be friends, family members, neighbours, business colleagues or simply people with a mutual interest in profitable investing. The club members meet regularly – usually once a month – to make decisions about a shared portfolio of investments. Generally the members take turns researching companies whose shares are being considered. At each meeting, one or more members will present findings about a company and a recommendation as to whether or not to invest. The final decision is based on a vote from members of the club. Other members may be assigned to track and report on economic or business trends, to read and present insights from classic books on investing or to arrange for expert guests to speak before the club. These varied activities help make the investment club a social and educational enterprise as well as a financial one.

Each member of the club is expected to pay in a fixed amount each month to help build the investment kitty. This amount may range from as little as £20 to £100 or more. The ownership of the investment portfolio is shared by the members, along with the profits (or losses) the portfolio yields. Of course, the club uses a broker to handle investment transactions and to manage record-keeping for the portfolio.

Many people love being part of an investment club. It's a fine way to learn more about share investing, since it 'forces' you to regularly read about shares and discuss their strengths and weaknesses with a bunch of like-minded friends. The investment club also helps broaden its members' financial perspective. As a club member, you may get to hear a report on retailing shares by a fellow member whose wife manages a department store or an analysis of a new technology or social networking company by a member who works in that industry.

Furthermore, a well-managed investment club can be a lot of fun. Clubs meet in members' homes or in pubs or restaurants and refreshments or a meal are a regular part of most meetings. Profitable investment clubs sometimes sponsor parties and outings to celebrate their successes.

The investment club movement remains a worldwide phenomenon. Today there are around 12,000 clubs in the UK and they are supported by an organisation called ProShare Investment Clubs. They provide many kinds of information and guidance about all aspects of investment clubs, from setting up a club to conducting meetings to dissolving a club. The site has a library of useful and interesting articles about various aspects of an investment club. It also has a message board on which club members, new and seasoned, can share ideas, insights and other information. If you're intrigued by the idea of joining or starting an investment club, visit ProShare Investment Clubs' website at:

www.proshareclubs.co.uk

12

STAYING THE COURSE

Creating, Maintaining and Adjusting Your Personal Money Plan

If you've followed all the recommendations in this book, you can now say that you are truly in charge of your money and the fundamental aspects of your financial world.

You know your income and especially your outgoings, in detail.

You are in control of how it is being spent, saved and invested.

You have financial goals, both short-term and long-term, and you have realistic plans for achieving them.

Congratulations! You are far ahead of most people of *any* age, class or background. In fact, there are plenty of 'trustifarians' and *nouveaux riches* who need to learn how their money works, just as you've done.

This final chapter focuses on what you need to do to remain in control of your finances and keep them flourishing for years to come. The hardest part is completed: the clearing, planning and planting of your money garden. Now it's a question of doing what it takes to maintain its healthy growth. For most people, this is a matter of one hour a week or less – no more than you probably spend on your hair, your car or your pet and certainly more important and more rewarding than all three.

Online banking and 24/7 Internet access to your credit card statements, your investment portfolio and other records of your financial life (including information about and applications for new financial products) have made it much easier and faster to keep track of your money and make changes when you find a better deal. However, there are still many people who do not use this access to help them keep up-to-date about their money and therefore in control.

For convenience, I've broken down the subject into four categories: what you need to do weekly, monthly, quarterly and annually. For each, I've provided a handy checklist of activities. Please add any items that are particular to your financial situation. You might want to copy these checklists and insert them in the proper pages in your personal activities diary or any other location where you'll be sure to see them at the right times. You can also create an alert on your computer or mobile device that will remind you to take the proper actions related to the items on your checklist.

Once a Week

Tracking Your Cash Flow

Have a single place at home where you put all your purchase receipts, charge slips and cash withdrawal tickets every evening. It could be any convenient place, just so long as it's *one* place rather than a collection of random nooks and crannies throughout your home. Some stores make the process easy by offering to email the receipt to you. Create a folder on your computer in which all of these electronic receipts are accumulated.

Once a week, grab the stack of slips (real and electronic) and add them up. Monitor the totals for each type of spending – food, entertainment and so on – against your budgeted figures.

It doesn't matter much when you do this chore as long as you do it consistently, at the same time every week. Otherwise you're apt to put it off and, as the pile of receipts grows, the task will become so daunting that you start to avoid it and eventually ignore it altogether. Pick a time that feels right to you. I like to handle this task on Friday night while sipping my end-of-the-week extra dry martini. I have only one and I have to nurse it through the entire task. My friend Karl (co-author on the first edition of this book) saves it for Saturday morning. He says that getting a grip on his finances before tackling the weekly shopping at the supermarket and the shopping centre helps him keep his cravings – and his wife's – in perspective, and in check.

This exercise forces you to relive the week from a financial point of view. The number of receipts you have is always an interesting indicator. Sometimes this is an unpleasant exercise, sometimes a delightful one – but it's always eye-opening. You see your own impulses at work and you'll recognise the things you bought that you didn't need and perhaps didn't even really want. (Maybe you can return those.) By matching your spending to the categories we used back in Chapter 1, you can see when you're saving in one area and when you're overspending in another.

Doing this exercise weekly gives you a chance to remedy any financial troubles before they get out of hand. If you overspent one week, you know you have to cut back the following week. This saves you from the sick, panicked feeling of receiving an out-of-control credit card bill or seeing your shockingly low bank balance due to excessive use of your debit card or bank overdraft.

The weekly budget exercise can also be a way of augmenting your regular savings plan. Every time you come in under budget for a particular category for the week, move that money into savings. For example, suppose you have budgeted £160 per month for entertainment. That amounts to about £40 per week. If one week you spend only £24 on entertainment (maybe there were no good shows at the cinema that week), deposit the difference in the bank. Then you get to say, 'Oh, I saved £16 this week!' and feel pleased with yourself . . . but not so pleased that you waste the money on something else!

Paying Your Bills

The other weekly exercise is bill-paying. Why weekly? Because, if you're like most people, you have a host of expenses, most often payable monthly, that are due at different times during the month: mortgage due the 1st, car loan due the 5th, phone bill due the 14th and so on.

Here's a simple way to make sure you never lose track of what's due when. Keep all your outstanding bills in the same place. It doesn't matter where – a basket in the kitchen, a cubbyhole in your desk, a corner of your dresser drawer. As they arrive in the mail, open them and stack them in the order of their due dates. Then simply pull out the stack once a week and pay the ones that are due during the next seven days. Of course, if you know you're going to be on holiday or otherwise unavailable beyond that date then pay the next week's bills as well. This easy system will ensure that you never suffer the embarrassment of a dunning notice in the mail or a phone call from an overdue bill collector.

Direct debits make paying one's bills much easier but they can also cause you to treat these payments as something you no longer have to attend to. If direct debit is how you pay the majority of your bills, use this time to reconcile your statements online if possible, making sure the right amounts have been paid. This is also a time when you can plan for and evaluate the necessity for some of the expected expenses during the upcoming week.

⊷ *Alvin says* . . .

If you find you have a lot of receipts and bills to manage every week, you may have let your finances become too complex. Look for ways to simplify the situation, whether by spending less frequently, reducing the number of bills you have or getting rid of some of your credit cards or bank accounts. When your finances are simple they are easier to control.

Once a Month

Balance Your Current Account

Electronic banking makes doing this much easier but for many people it is still a bore. I find it tedious too but it needs to be done. It only gets worse if you put it off. Done monthly (or periodically throughout the month using your online banking account), it takes just a few minutes. Wait six months (for example) and there will inevitably be a tangle of maths errors, unexpected fees and bank charges, forgotten withdrawals, cheques and direct debits, as well as other small mistakes to rectify, which can turn this into a two- or three-hour chore. Furthermore, you'll greatly increase the chances of miscalculating your balance and writing a cheque that goes into your overdraft, costing you more money in needless bank fees.

Balancing your statement is like brushing your teeth, exercising regularly or any other beneficial habit: once you've done it half a dozen times, you'll find it easy to do and you may even wonder, 'Why did I ever make a fuss about this?'

Other Monthly Chores

Also once a month, pay your council tax and any other monthly expenses. Check out the cash-back websites to see what savings are available on some of the purchases (including new utility contracts) that you regularly make or are planning for the future.

Deposit into your savings account the extra money you've accumulated through wise saving and spending during the month. Of course, this will be cash over and above the automatic savings deposits you've arranged through the bank.

Monitor your investments monthly (if curiosity doesn't drive you to do so more often). Check the latest prices of your unit trusts or shares and update the spreadsheet or other tool you use to track how much your individual investments and overall accounts are worth.

If any individual investment has grown a lot, consider realising some of those gains by selling a portion of your holdings and letting the rest of your profits run.

If you are self-employed, set aside money for taxes monthly. Keep these funds in a specially dedicated savings account. And yes, make the deposits monthly, even though you only have to pay the taxes twice a year. If you wait to find the money until the payments are due, the chances are good that you *won't* find it – or may end up working for months just for HM Revenue and Customs. And really, which is easier: to save regularly for taxes or to end up regretful and resentful over your own negligence?

Once a Quarter

Your Mortgage Check-Up

This is a financial exercise that's a little like the regularly scheduled maintenance that gets done on your car. If you have an interest only mortgage, check the value of the investment plan that will pay off the capital at the end of the mortgage. Remember, this is the investment portion of the mortgage which, in theory, is supposed to grow enough to pay off the balance due at the end of the mortgage term. If the endowment isn't growing fast enough, consider changing to a repayment mortgage (if possible) or making extra payments to reduce the amount that comes due at the end of the mortgage.

Mortgage-holders should also take a look at current interest rates. How much have they risen or fallen since you first signed on for your mortgage? If they've fallen significantly, consider refinancing your mortgage at the new, lower rates if that option is available to you.

Scrutinise Your Savings and Investments

Review how business or economic news during the past quarter has affected the value of your investments and consider whether upcoming events are likely to drive prices higher or lower. In particular, check the growth of your pensions and other retirement investments. Are they proceeding in line with your goals? Do you need to talk to your financial adviser about changing the mix of cash, stocks and bonds in your investment portfolio? Maybe you need to increase the amount you invest every month. Even an extra £10 or £20 can make a substantial difference when it's allowed to accumulate, earning interest and/or dividends over time.

Also check whether you are saving enough for your children's education – basic school fees and university fees – and whether these invested funds are growing appropriately. Again, if the answer is no, the remedy is the same: begin to put away a little more each month.

If you happen to receive quarterly bonus cheques from your employer (as some people do), consider putting these in to your savings rather than spending them. Because this 'found money' isn't part of your regular budget, you'll never miss it.

Look Over Your Wardrobe

Once a quarter is also a good time to plan your clothing purchases for the coming season. Survey your wardrobe and that of the kids and decide what you really need for the next few months, whether it's for school, for work or for play. *Planning* these purchases and budgeting for them will help you buy what you really need and want (and can afford) rather than simply snapping up what-ever's on sale.

Once a Year

Your Annual Financial Maintenance

For many people, it feels natural to perform their once-a-year financial check-up in late December or early January, right around the New Year holiday. With so many year-end retrospective shows on the telly and stories in the newspapers, it's easy to get into the spirit of 'new year, new you', looking back and looking forward in hopes of making next year even better than last year.

On the other hand, if you find the holidays too hectic or too festive, any other time of year can work equally well. As I've mentioned, I like to do a personal financial check-up around my birthday in June and I sometimes revisit my overall plan again six months later. Other people like to time their annual check-up to coincide with spring cleaning or with the autumnal beginning of the school year. The important thing is to pick a date when you have a bit of time to spare and will *not* be tempted to blow off the exercise.

In any case, here are the items to consider in your annual financial check-up.

Boost Your Saving

In a growing economy, many people get a pay rise annually. Remember that one excellent way to start or accelerate a savings programme is to dedicate this rise entirely to savings. If this is a bit tough for you (or if you're already doing reasonably well when it comes to saving), consider this half-measure: split your rise, putting half into savings and allowing yourself to spend the other half. Also consider the same sort of fifty-fifty arrangement with any annual bonus you may receive.

Plan Major Spending

Once a year is a good time to plan your major spending for the coming year. This includes appliance and furniture purchases, a new (or used) car, house improvements (repairs, major maintenance and renovations), large charitable donations and holiday travel. Sit down with your spouse or partner and make a plan that fits your shared priorities. Consider including your kids if they're old enough. Making such plans together provides a great opportunity to talk through your differing goals for the year ahead and to work out compromises that will leave you all reasonably satisfied: 'Well, if we *must* spend our summer holiday with your sister in Cornwall, then what about letting me trade in our nine-year-old car for a newer model?'

Rebalance Your Investments

Once a year, re-examine your investment portfolio and rebalance it as needed to maintain the proper asset allocation mix. (I described the process in Chapter 7.)

Look Back to Make a Better Future

Review the past year's statements from banks, credit cards, store cards, investment accounts and other places. As you do this, look for three things you did that clearly wasted your money and three things that helped increase your overall net worth. Reviewing your bad money decisions won't be easy, but it is important that you do. Ask yourself: What caused me to spend money so needlessly this way? How can I prevent this from happening in the future? Choose the action that was the worst, most undermining use of your money during the last year and make it the activity you work on controlling, mitigating or eliminating during the new year. At the same time, select from among the three actions that were financially beneficial and work on making one of them (or a variation on it) even more beneficial for your financial future.

Finally, look back over the *past* year and review what has changed in your life. Have you added a child (or children) via birth or adoption? Have you got married or divorced? Have you changed jobs, started a business or retired? These and other lifestyle changes may call for alterations in your spending budget, your insurance coverage, your will(s) and your estate plans. Update them as needed.

CHECKLISTS FOR KEEPING YOUR FINANCIAL
HOUSE IN ORDER

ONCE A WEEK

- ☐ Add up your expenses for the week by category. Compare them with your monthly budget. If you have overspent in any category, cut back during the following week. If you have saved in any category, consider banking the difference.

- ☐ Pay off all bills that come due in the week ahead.

ONCE A MONTH

- ☐ Balance your current account statement.

- ☐ Pay your council tax and other monthly expenses.

- ☐ Check if you can save on new purchases (including new utility contracts) using 'cash-back' websites. Deposit the extra money you've accumulated into your savings account.

- ☐ Monitor your investments.

- ☐ If you are self-employed, set aside money for taxes for your January and July payments to HM Revenue and Customs.

ONCE A QUARTER

- ☐ Do a 'mortgage check-up'. If you have an interest-only mortgage, check the value of your investment plan. Make sure it's growing quickly enough to pay off the capital due at the end of the mortgage term.

- ☐ Compare current interest rates to those you're paying on your mortgage. If they've fallen significantly, consider refinancing.

☐ Check the growth of your pensions and other retirement investments. Also check whether you are saving enough for your children's education — basic school fees and university fees — and whether these invested funds are growing quickly enough.

☐ Evaluate the outlook for the economy and the stock market's performance the next quarter to decide if you need to change your asset mix (e.g., the percentages of cash, shares and bonds) in your portfolio.

☐ Plan and budget your clothing purchases for the coming season.

☐ Use price comparison websites to check your insurance, electric and gas rates to see if there's a better deal available to you.

ONCE A YEAR

☐ Dedicate half or all of your annual pay rise to savings.

☐ Do the same with your annual bonus payment.

☐ Plan your major spending for the entire coming year: appliance and furniture purchases; a new (or used) car; house repairs, major maintenance and renovations; charitable donations and holidays.

☐ Re-examine your investment portfolio and rebalance it as needed to maintain the proper asset allocation mix.

☐ Review what's changed in your life and update your spending budget, your insurance coverage, your will(s) and your estate plans as needed.

Living Your New and Better Financial Life Each and Every Day

The real key to managing your money day in and day out is to keep your financial plan simple and comfortable. Your new life shouldn't feel constrained and restrictive. If you're earning a reasonable amount of money but find that you still feel financially trapped there are three possible explanations.

One is that you have not set the right priorities for what you need to do and what you can afford to do with the money you earn. Few of us earn enough to have every single thing we want. I certainly don't. And neither do nearly all of the people I know. However, we all know what expenses we must pay every month to meet our financial commitments and most of us know what we can do with the remainder to give us the most long-lasting satisfaction at the most reasonable price. This could be a night out at your favourite restaurant, saving for a classic item of clothing that you know you will enjoy every time you wear it, attending a play that interests you or buying a nice bottle of wine and inviting friends over to share it. Your treats don't have to be costly. They just need to make you happy and give you pleasure so that you feel you are living well and feeling satisfied.

Another explanation could be that you may have fallen prey to a subtle or not-so-subtle sense of entitlement. I meet many people who explain their excessive spending by saying, 'I work hard. Don't I *deserve* this kind of lifestyle?' If this sounds familiar, reconsider your attitude. The ability to buy things isn't a matter of what you 'deserve'. It's a matter of making choices that will benefit you in the long run. If you insist on having everything you think you deserve today, you're likely to find you lack even the basic things you *need* tomorrow.

A third possible explanation is that you may attach too much importance to money or to material things. If you find that you are unable to stop obsessing over having to own certain possessions, taking part in certain activities (especially shopping) or enjoying other rewards that you associate with happiness, love or 'the good life' then take steps to figure out *why* and to learn how to control these desires. For some people, a time of self-reflection, conversations with loved ones, writing a journal or meditation may go a long way towards helping you gain insight into the problem. For a few, counselling with a professional may be needed.

If money (or the lack of money) has become a huge obstacle to happiness for you, take whatever steps are necessary to overcome it. Remember that there are no quick, painless, magical solutions. And certainly, if you are at risk of ruining your life or the lives of people you love through overspending, debt addiction, a gambling habit, speculating on get-rich-quick schemes or other financial illnesses, find a way to stop before you go completely over the edge.

Finally, it's also possible that you've established a money regimen that is simply a little too strict, a little too joyless. No one should be expected to live without a few well-chosen indulgences. But notice the two adjectives I've used: 'few' and 'well-chosen'! Build into your money plan an occasional reward for perseverance. For every two or three months that you keep your spending within budget, treat yourself to a dinner out or something else that gives you real pleasure: a new pair of shoes, a round of golf, a couple of music downloads. For every six months that you save according to budget, give yourself an inexpensive weekend in the country or something comparable.

But remember, you get the rewards *only* if you stick to the plan (or do better)! If you bend the rules and reward yourself for 'coming close' or 'trying really hard', you are undermining your own effort to build a new set of good habits.

In addition, look for regular ways of treating yourself (and those you love) that *don't* involve spending money. There are dozens of life-enriching activities that cost little or nothing to enjoy. Why don't we think about them more often? That's easy: it's because such low-cost pleasures are rarely promoted on television, on radio or in advertising. After all, when something is free there's little profit to be made from it so no one has the incentive to push it.

So, in a world where 'growing the economy' is a mandate for every politician as well as every business leader, the incentives for spending more and more on every possible activity are enormous. And it's all too easy to follow the crowd rather than using a bit of imagination to find our own ways of enjoying life.

Aldous Huxley's classic novel *Brave New World* is a horrific vision of life in a mindless, ultra-consumer-led twenty-first century. In his imagined new world the government has imposed one simple rule for any new sport or amusement: it *must* require more and more costly equipment than the *most* complicated existing sport! Have we moved into Huxley's brave new world without realising it?

If you're ready to fight back against the trend of

spending for spending's sake, consider rewarding yourself and your loved ones, not by spending money, but by enjoying such free or low-cost activities as:

- Playing a sport with a group of mates in the park.
- Enjoying a picnic in a nature spot you've always wanted to visit.
- Taking a drive in the country.
- Touring your local art or history museum.
- Going bird-watching or nature-walking.
- Trying your hand at drawing, painting or photography.
- Reading poetry – and maybe writing your own.
- Attending free local talks, lectures or concerts.
- Joining (or forming) a local singing, acting or dancing group.
- Joining (or forming) a book club.
- Teaching yourself to cook a true gourmet dish.
- Flying a kite.
- Starting a collection.
- Tutoring local youngsters.
- Taking up a new sport.
- Learning a new language.
- Reading about a country you've dreamed of visiting.
- Volunteering to help at a service organisation or charity.
- Making love.

I've found that the key to financial happiness isn't how much money you have – it's using the money you have in ways that bring lasting enjoyment.

Finally, get into the habit of talking every day with your partner or your family, not only about money matters but about everything that is really important to you. If you do this during the usual ups and downs of life and of a relationship, there will be a solid foundation for communication and problem-solving when things are tough. This can be a relationship-saving practice – and sometimes even a life-saving one. Such talks can reward you handsomely in ways that extend well beyond your financial life.

Alvin says . . .

I find that two kinds of people tend to fall into the worst financial traps: those who refuse to think about money at all and those who think about nothing else. Give money its due. It has a major impact on your life and it deserves to be treated with respect, consideration and thought. But keep money in its place. The money you earn, spend, save and invest should serve you and your life, not the other way round. If you keep money squarely in the context of what matters most to you – the people, activities and places you most deeply love – then you'll never have to choose between your money or your life. Instead you'll be able to enjoy them both fully!

Appendix

Selected List of Informative Websites about Personal Finance

Newspapers and magazines regularly publish lists of the best websites and apps for everything, including those that will help save money. I enjoy discovering or being made aware of money-saving websites or apps and then exploring each one to see if it really does what it promises to do, thereby improving my financial life in a way that is meaningful to me. Some have little relevance to the way I live and handle my money, but they may be totally on-target and useful for you and your financial situation and lifestyle. The choice you make comes down to knowledge: knowing what your individual financial objectives and needs are, deciding how you want to handle your money, and determining what tools yield the most value for the time spent using them.

To make the best choice for your life, you need to begin by becoming an educated, financially literate consumer. I know the words 'educated' and 'literate' scare people a bit. But remember, like all things in life, you don't have to learn everything at one time. You build your knowledge over time, learning about a specific financial topic when it becomes important in your life.

Simply put, financial literacy is *dynamic*, an ongoing process. So, I've selected a list of websites that will help you improve your financial literacy, becoming a better-educated and knowledgeable consumer of those fundamental and essential personal finance concepts and products.

From my list, I want you to choose the sites that are most meaningful to your life, that provide the greatest value for the time spent educating yourself. Importantly, that value doesn't have to be monetary. It can be making something you do easier and therefore less stressful. It can be giving you the knowledge and comfort level you need to make a decision that is the most suitable for you. It can be supporting you as you work to sustain and increase your understanding of the options and choices available to you as the economy and regulations change. Know that your personally selected list will evolve as the things that are meaningful in your financial life change.

General

Bank of England: www.bankofengland.co.uk
Financial Conduct Authority: www.fca.org.uk/consumers
Financial Ombudsman Service (FOS): www.financial-ombudsman.org.uk
Financial Services Compensation Scheme (FSCS): www.fscs.org.uk
Financial Times: www.ft.com (You must be a subscriber to obtain much of the information.)
Money Advice Service: www.moneyadviceservice.org.uk

Money Box: www.bbc.co.uk/programmes/b006qjnv (Radio 4's long-running investigative, informative and instructional programme about all aspects of personal finance.)

MoneySavingExpert: www.moneysavingexpert.com

MoneySupermarket: www.moneysupermarket.com

National Savings and Investments (NS&I): www.nsandi.com

National Statistics: www.statistics.gov.uk (for current and past editions of the Family Spending Report)

SavvyWoman: www.savvywoman.co.uk

The Telegraph (Finance section): www.telegraph.co.uk/finance/

The Times (Money section): www.thetimes.co.uk/tto/money/

This is Money: www.thisismoney.co.uk (this is the *Daily Mail*'s popular, widely used, and highly informative personal finance website)

Subject-Specific

ADVFN: www.advfn.com (investment research information)

Affordable Home Ownership Scheme: www.gov.uk/affordable-home-ownership-schemes/overview

Association of Solicitor Investment Managers (ASIM): www.asim.com (lists solicitors' firms that provide legal and financial advice)

Benefits: www.gov.uk/browse/benefits

Bloomberg: www.bloomberg.com (financial information)

CallCredit: www.callcredit.co.uk (credit reference agency)

Child Poverty Action Group: www.cpag.org.uk

Citizens Advice: www.citizensadvice.org.uk

Company REFS: www.companyrefs.co (investment research reports)

Council of Mortgage Lenders: www.cml.org.uk (offers a range of useful publications on home buying)

Debt Advice Foundation: www.debtadvicefoundation.org

Department for Work & Pensions: www.gov.uk/government/organisations/department-for-work-pensions

Dr Ros Altmann: www.rosaltmann.com/ (solid advice on all aspects of pensions)

Equifax: www.equifax.co.uk (credit reference agency)

Equity Release Council: www.equityreleasecouncil.com

The Ethical Investment Research Services (EIRIS): www.eiris.org

Exchange-Traded Funds: uk.ishares.com/en/rc/about/about-etfs (while this website focuses on iShares, much of the information applies to all types of ETFs)

Exchange-Traded Products: www.morningstar.co.uk/uk/news/67711/what-is-the-difference-between-an-etf-and-an-etp.aspx

Experian: www.experian.co.uk (credit reference agency)

FactSet: www.factset.com (investment information)

Family Action: www.family-action.org.uk

Financial advisers: www.unbiased.co.uk (the most common site used to find an Independent Financial Adviser)

Financial Services Register: www.fca.org.uk/register (gives people the ability to check all public information about individuals, firms and other financial services participants regulated by the FCA)

Help to Buy: www.helptobuy.org.uk

Income Taxes: www.hmrc.gov.uk/income tax

Information Commissioner's Office (ICO): www.ico.org.uk/for_the_public/topic_specific_guides/credit (provides access to detailed information explaining credit, credit reference agencies, how to get and correct your credit reference files, and more)

Inheritance Tax (IHT): www.gov.uk/inheritance-tax

Institute of Financial Planning: www.financialplanning. org.uk (good information and a useful feature on finding a financial planner)

Investegate: www.investegate.co.uk (offers a free, reliable service used by both professionals and the public to research companies across the broad investment market.)

Junior Individual Savings Accounts (JISA): www.gov.uk/ junior-individual-savings-accounts/overview

London Stock Exchange: www.londonstockexchange.com

Morningstar: www.morningstar.co.uk (has a well-designed and useful learning centre)

National Debt Line: www.nationaldebtline.co.uk

National Savings and Investments (NS&I): www.nsandi. com/savings or www.nsandi.com/savings-direct-isa

NEST (National Employment Savings Trust): www. nestpensions.org.uk

NewBuy: www.newbuy.org.uk

New Individual Savings Accounts (NISAs): www.hmrc. gov.uk/isa/

Noddle: www.noddle.co.uk (an offshoot of CallCredit that gives you access to your credit report for free)

Pension (State): www.gov.uk/browse/working/state-pension

Personal Finance Society: www.thepfs.org or www. findanadviser.org

ProShare Investment Clubs: www.proshareclubs.co.uk

Self-invested personal pensions (SIPPs): www.money adviceservice.org.uk/en/articles/self-invested-personal-pensions

StepChange (formerly CCCS): www.stepchange.org

Stockopedia: www.stockopedia.com (charges retail investors a modest up front and monthly fee for access to key investment data.)

Student Finance: www.gov.uk/student-finance/overview

The Motley Fool: www.fool.co.uk

The Pensions Advisory Service (TPAS): www.pensions advisoryservice.org.uk

The Pension Service: www.gov.uk/contact-pension-service (government service administering state pension payments)

The Student Room: www.thestudentroom.co.uk (brings together millions of current and former students who share information via video, articles and forums about all aspects of their lives and experiences at university)

Wealth Management Association: www.thewma.co.uk

Yahoo! Finance UK & Ireland: uk.finance.yahoo.com

INDEX

An invitation from the publisher

Join us at www.hodder.co.uk, or follow us
on Twitter @hodderbooks to be a part of
our community of people who love the very
best in books and reading.

Whether you want to discover more about a book
or an author, watch trailers and interviews, have the
chance to win early limited editions, or simply browse
our expert readers' selection of the very best books,
we think you'll find what you're looking for.

And if you don't, that's the place to tell us what's missing.

We love what we do, and we'd love you to be a part of it.

www.hodder.co.uk

@hodderbooks

HodderBooks

HodderBooks